America's WATER AND WASTEWATER CRISIS

America's WATER AND WASTEWATER CRISIS

The Role of Private Enterprise

Lewis D. Solomon

Transaction Publishers
New Brunswick (U.S.A.) and London (U.K.)

Library of Congress Catalog Number: 2011003369
ISBN: 978-1-4128-1823-0
Printed in the United States of America

Library of Congress Cataloging-in-Publication Data
Solomon, Lewis D.
America's water and wastewater crisis : the role of private enterprise / Lewis D. Solomon.
    p. cm.
    ISBN 978-1-4128-1823-0
    1. Water resources development—United States—History. 2. Sewage disposal plants—United States. 3. Privatization—United States. I. Title.
    ✓ HD1694.A5S74 2011
    363.6'10973—dc22
                    2011003369

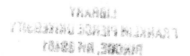

Contents

1

Introduction

The challenges of water quantity and quality represent a looming planetary crisis. Water will likely become the new petroleum in the twenty-first century.

Estimates indicate that water shortages in more than forty countries currently impact more than two billion people. One billion one hundred million people lack sufficient drinking water; two billion four hundred million have no provision of sanitation. Unless the world alters its water supply and consumption patterns, the amount of water need by a rapidly growing population will double by mid-century. At least one in four people in 2050 will likely live in nations affected by chronic or recurring freshwater shortages.[1]

Leaving aside the globe's current and future water problems, this book focuses on the looming water and wastewater crisis in the United States. America's water and wastewater sectors encompass the production of potable water, its transmission and distribution to end users, including households, agricultural, and industrial, the collection of wastewater, and the treatment and recycling of wastewater back to the surface or underground. The acquisition of water rights by private entities is, however, beyond the scope of this book.

In the United States, as is true worldwide, water serves multiple uses simultaneously. It is a vital human resource; one that is critical to life and health. We cannot live without it for more than a few days. There is no substitute for water. It is also an essential factor in agricultural and industrial production.

Water has traditionally been regarded as a public good with residents having a "right" to nearly free water supply and sewage services. Similar to public goods, water supply and wastewater systems provide benefits beyond the individuals who consume water and dispose of sewage, such as improved public health.

Because water is an essential resource, a non-substitutable good required for living—a necessary component in our lives, everyday—its ownership and management has tended to be entrusted, generally, but not entirely, to the public sector in the United States.

1

Public ownership and management of America's water supply has been based on a desire to provide sufficient quantities of safe water, where and when needed, for the benefit of people, not to turn a profit. However, water differs from pure public goods, from which nobody can be excluded, because it can be rationed and denied to specific users.

From the beginning, in the United States, the ownership and management of water and wastewater systems was decentralized. Today, America's water and wastewater industry remains relatively fragmented, run largely at the local or regional level, with the vast bulk of assets serving most of the population under public ownership.

Americans generally take water for granted. Apart from an occasional regional drought, for urban and suburbanites, it magically comes out of faucets and shower heads, fills swimming pools, and flushes through toilets. In most places, it's nearly free. Water bills do not amount to too much.

In the United States, water remains cheap relative to its value. Americans pay, on average, a quarter of a penny per gallon for clean drinking water or about $20 per month for the typical family.[2] Few, if any, products have a value so much in excess of its price or whose price is unrelated to its true costs. In this century, more Americans will need to deal with water scarcities and bear the costs of rebuilding our decaying water and wastewater infrastructure. Today's for water prices do not reflect these huge costs.

America faces increasing challenges in both its water supply as well as meeting the funding required for maintaining and improving its water and wastewater infrastructure. Parts of the United States are waking up to the realities of finite water supplies and the ensuing scarcities, which will be inadequate to meet economic and population growth needs at current usage rates. In the future, in many U.S. regions, water will become a more expensive resource, impacting economic growth and the quality of life.

During the twenty-first century, the challenges facing America's aging water supply and wastewater infrastructure will become one of the nation's more pressing problems. Many of America's water treatment plants, storage reservoirs, and distribution pipes were built fifty to one hundred years ago and are rapidly decaying, with significant leakage rates in older cities.

The growth of the U.S. population, inadequate past and current infrastructure investment, and need for future capital to update water supply and wastewater systems place the nation's public sector agencies in a difficult situation. The urgency of these infrastructure needs will become evermore apparent. However, water treatment components—mains and pipes—are big-ticket items. Water is cheap to store in reservoirs, but generally expensive to transport in relation to its value, on a per unit volume basis, thereby requiring large-scale capital investments in infrastructure. In the coming decades, hundreds of billions of dollars will be required to maintain and upgrade the U.S. water and wastewater infrastructure.

Despite the emerging scarcities and the capital needs quandaries, we deplete America's freshwater resources at an alarming rate. We turn away and refuse to face America's crumbling water and wastewater infrastructure. We seem unable to face the need to finance the necessary rehabilitation and expansion. In short, there is a head-in-the-sand mentality. The public sector typically upgrades its water treatment and distribution systems, as well as its wastewater infrastructure, only as these systems (or significant parts) begin to fail. Or, the public sector applies temporary fixes to problems that ought to be solved by more thoughtful planning and investment strategies.

The challenge of water scarcity and infrastructure renewal and expansion will likely become far more important, if not defining, political and economic issues during this century. We likely will see a revolution in how we think about water. We likely will see far-reaching changes in the way water is treated, distributed, used, and recycled.

The Role of the Private Sector in America's Water Supply and Wastewater Industry

It is helpful to get some idea of the magnitude of America's water and wastewater industry. Today, the U.S. water and wastewater industry generates revenues of more than $120 billion per year.[3] Primary water and sewage services comprise about two-thirds of the total annual spending on water in the United States. Most of these revenues initially pass through the public sector, not private companies. The goods and services that industry and municipalities, among other public sector entities, buy to provide water and wastewater comprise the other one third of the U.S. water and wastewater business.[4]

This book focuses on the involvement of private firms in the American water and wastewater industry. Private sector involvement includes its role as vendors and as privatizers of facilities. Private suppliers play a significant role across the water and wastewater industries, regardless of the mode of infrastructure ownership. Consultants provide design services, contractors build (or repair) facilities, vendors supply water treatment equipment, chemicals, instruments, and testing, among other goods and services, to the systems that provide water to the public and handle sewage.

Privatization of infrastructure involves the shift in control from the public sector to the private sector. Privatization of water supply and wastewater treatment services primarily take one of two basic forms. First, through transfer of ownership, full privatization, involves the sale of assets to the private sector. Post-privatization, a water utility, typically regulated by state public utility commission owns and operates the system as a for-profit enterprise. In a public-private partnership, the other form of privatization, a private company operates and manages a municipal or regional system under a contractual arrangement on behalf of the public sector asset owner.

The need for efficiency and capital place a key role in the water supply and wastewater industry and will increasingly do so in the future. A pressing need exists to manage facilities more efficiently and to invest more capital in water supply and wastewater infrastructure. The private sector, whether alone as asset owners and through public-private partnerships, offers both a proven management technique and a financial tool.

Despite the vehement objection of ideologies and special interest groups, during this century, slowly attitudes toward the benefits of water and wastewater system privatization will change. In addition to private ownership of systems, hybrid public-private agreements will more likely become a means to attract private firms to operate and manage existing facilities and hopefully, supply some of the enormous capital needs. Through public-private partnerships, the private sector will play a constructive role in fixing or replacing the nation's geriatric water pipes, among other aspects of water supply system. These public-private partnerships may provide a financial mechanism to allow for-profit sector firms to put their funds to work for the public benefit, yet earn a competitive rate of return on their capital in the process.

For the foreseeable future, all levels of the U.S. public sector, federal, state, and local, face fiscal constraints. The urgent infrastructure capital needs, limited public funds, and the difficulties involving in raising taxes or fees will likely make the various forms of privatization a greater reality in America's water and wastewater industry.

Overview of the Book

Chapter 2 provides an historical overview of America's water and wastewater industry. It surveys the role of the private and public sectors in meeting America's water supply and wastewater treatment needs over the centuries. Today, private involvement in the water supply industry increasingly involves the operation and maintenance of publicly-owned systems. Little private sector ownership exists in the wastewater industry.

The chapter also analyzes the role of the federal government as a key funder of water supply and wastewater treatment infrastructure. Its role as regulator of water quality is considered. Spanning nearly four decades, the federal government has sought to mandate environmental standards as part of its water policy framework. The chapter concludes with a discussion of the post 9/11 security concerns regarding the possible contamination of drinking water supplies by terrorists and limited funding provided by the 2009 economic stimulus package to meet the current and future capital needs of America's water and wastewater industry.

We are in the midst of a transition viewing water as an abundant resource to a scarce one. Chapter 3 examines the growing water scarcity in some regions of the United States. Today, the United States faces not only water quality issues but also water quantity dilemmas. Growing demand and decreasing freshwater supplies have put great stress on the nation's water resources. The chapter focuses on the dwindling supply of freshwater resources, particularly in the southwest. Groundwater depletion is also discussed.

Chapter 3 examines the growing water scarcity in some regions of the U.S. water is not always a renewable resource. Depletion results from groundwater extractions at a rate higher than recharge. Contamination of surface water and ground water sources has occurred as have diversions of surface waters in excess of flows from feeder sources. Consumption patterns sometimes exceed the capacity of a water basis or a region to accommodate them.

Using the latest scientific studies, the chapter considers the possible impact of climate change on water availability and quality in the United States. Without attempting to resolve the scientific debate, the chapter presents, the evidence by the proponents and opponents regarding the global warming hypothesis. Finally, demand management by the public sector designed to reduce water usage, specifically, voluntary conservation programs and mandatory restrictions, are analyzed.

Chapter 4 analyzes how the technology commercialized by for-profit firms can help increase water supplies, for example, through water reuse and desalination. Companies apply existing technologies to meet water scarcity needs and more generally, reduce consumption. Water loss management products and services locate and reduce vast water losses resulting from decaying infrastructure. Innovative irrigation systems and technologies help achieve more efficient and decrease consumption; by the for profit companies profiled in this chapter are active as suppliers to U.S. water supply and wastewater systems regardless of their ownership and management arrangements.

As background for the analysis of privatization as a financial tool and managerial technique, Chapter 5 examines various forms of privatization. Using the contrasting privatization models adopted by England and France, the chapter provides an overview of asset sales, contractual arrangements, and design-build-operate-transfer agreements. The impact of state utility regulation on privatization transactions and federal tax and non-tax incentives to facilitate privatization are reviewed.

In the United States, as is the case globally, the discussion of private sector involvement in the water supply and wastewater treatment industry is controversial. Chapter 6 begins with an examination of the dilapidated condition of America's water supply and wastewater treatment infrastructure. The chapter then analyzes the funding crisis facing America's water supply and wastewater industry. The gap between current infrastructure spending and the required funding is enormous and will continue growing. Chronic underinvestment in capital-intensive water and wastewater infrastructure represents an ongoing problem. Besides the aging infrastructure, meeting enhanced environmental standards comprises another capital expenditure driver in this sector. In the face of current and future funding shortfalls, the need for capital may lead the public sector to turn to some form of privatization.

The chapter then considers the arguments in favor of privatization, including cost savings, improved performance, and increased efficiency. The chapter also presents the potential disadvantages of privatization, all of which, except for transaction costs, can be met through carefully negotiated, drafted, and monitored contracts.

A demanding and critical public will judge private infrastructure owners or operators by their performance, not merely through theoretical arguments. Chapter 7 summarizes the empirical studies dealing with privatized water and wastewater systems. General empirical studies point to the benefits of privatization, including cost savings, increased compliance with environmental regulations, and improved customer and employee satisfaction. More specific empirical studies present a mixed picture of the impact of privatization. The chapter concludes that localities that have privatized are content with some type of privatization. The overwhelming percentage of municipalities renew their partnerships at contractual expiration.

Chapter 8 presents two case studies of privatization via public-private partnerships, Atlanta and Indianapolis. As shown by Atlanta, although there were extenuating circumstances, privatization did not achieve the proponents' goals. In contrast, despite some difficulties and substantial rate increases, both implemented and projected, Indianapolis offers a generally more hopeful scenario. The chapter offers some basic principles that the public sector can use in the bidding process and contractual negotiations to facilitate private involvement in the water supply and wastewater treatment industry, but satisfy the "public interest" and generate enhanced public acceptance. Public-private participation in partnerships can bring residents the clean water and sewage disposal they need and want.

Chapter 9 offers a brief conclusion. Privatization is neither the universal answer to meeting America's water and wastewater treatment crisis nor the number one enemy to providing affordable drinking water and sewage disposal. By entering into long-term contractual arrangements, private firms may provide substantial capital investments for infrastructure modernization and expansion.

The chapter also considers the need to treat users as customers buying a commodity, not citizens entitled to a service. Pricing water more realistically can both reduce America's water needs and help meet the industry's capital requirements, whatever the asset ownership or management arrangements. The equity aspects of full-cost pricing are reviewed.

Before examining America's water scarcities and the rationale for infrastructure privatization as a management technique and financial benefit too, Chapter 2 provides a historical overview of the development, ownership, federal funding, and regulation of water supply and wastewater treatment systems in the United States.

Notes

1.   The statistics in this paragraph are from United Nations World Water Development Report, Water for People Water for Life, 2003, 10. See also Celia W. Dugger, "Need for Water Could Double in 50 Years, U.N. Study Finds," New York Times, August 22, 2006, A12.

2.   Steve Marxwell, "Water is Cheap-Ridiculously Cheap!," *Journal of American Water World Association* 97:6 (June 20050: 38-41, at 38-39.

3.   TechKNOLEDGEy Strategic group, The State of the Water Industry: Blood of the Earth... *Store of Economic Value: A Concise Review of Challenges and Opportunities in the World Water Market*, 2009, 12.

4.   Ibid. See also Steve Maxwell, "Introductory Overview" in *The Business of Water: A Concise Overview of Challenges and Opportunities in the Water Market*, ed. Steve Maxwell (Denver: American Water Works Association, 2008), 4.

Part I
Historical Overview

2

The Development, Ownership, Federal Funding and Regulation of Water and Wastewater Systems in the United States: A Historical Overview

Few things are as vital to a nation's growth and development as the provision of water and wastewater services. This chapter surveys the role of the private and public sectors in meeting America's water supply and wastewater treatment needs, including contemporary corporate involvement in these systems, particularly through public-private partnerships.

During America's early years, private ownership of water supply infrastructure represented the initial approach taken. However, as private arrangements proved inadequate in the nineteenth century, cities increasingly turned to public control. After local governmental entities took the lead in the construction and maintenance of water works and sewage systems, the federal government increasingly stepped into the arena in the twentieth century, particularly the New Deal's role in funding water infrastructure. For nearly four decades, the federal government has actively sought to ensure clean water and safe drinking water by environmental regulation and various funding mechanisms, most recently grants to state revolving loan funds. Two twenty-first century developments, a focus on water security and increased federal funding, conclude the chapter.

Development and Ownership of Water Supply Systems
in the United States

Private water companies are not a new concept in the United States.[1] Private firms have supplied water to U.S. consumers since 1652 when the Water Works Company of Boston was chartered. Using primitive technology, that firm supplied water using wooden conduits. Although rotting and leaking were chronic problems with a wooden distribution system, in case of fire a hose could be connected to a conduit by simply drilling a hole in it. In 1755, Hans Christiansen opened America's first pumped waterworks in Bethlehem, Pennsylvania. In 1772, the state of Rhode Island chartered two private water supply enterprises.

Initially, private development and ownership of water systems represented the overwhelming approach taken. Early in the nineteenth century, lacking the financial ability to fund and provide water services, localities turned to private companies to supply water. The widely felt need for urban water supplies during the 1790s and early 1800s was everywhere met by private enterprise. Localities often investigated the possibilities of building municipal waterworks, but almost always drew back in view of the heavy expenses involved. Capital was, however, usually available for private water companies that could benefit the community and at the same time provide dividends to stockholders.

However, in 1801 Philadelphia completed a major municipal waterworks and water distribution system, a first in the nation.[2] At the time, the share of public waterworks in the United States was only 5.9 percent (1 out of 17) of total waterworks in 1800, 20 percent (9 out of 45) by 1830. Public provision of water services developed slowly. But as early as 1880, public ownership had achieved a relative parity with private ownership with 48.9 percent (293 out of 599) in public hands.[3]

By the end of the nineteenth century, about two hundred cities had taken over private water supply systems and the public sector owned more than fifty percent of all U.S. waterworks, a 52.9 percent share (1,690 out of 3,177) by 1896.[4] Two factors spurred the trend toward public ownership: financial-technological and a concern for public health. In the context of booming population growth, the private sector evidenced an inability (or unwillingness) to invest sufficient capital to implement the necessary improvements and expansions. Because of the need for reservoirs, steam-powered pumping plants, and complex distribution systems, the required capital outlays to build and maintain modern waterworks proved too large for many private enterprises. Some firms exhibited an unwillingness to provide services the public considered essential to the well-being of society. These companies could (or would) not deliver sufficient water for various public uses or build network extensions to meet population growth or serve more outlying areas, manifesting in two major problems in urban areas, fire and disease.

Fire represented a major problem in the nineteenth century America because of the construction of urban dwellings so close to one another, and the use of wood as the primary construction material. Fire fighting equipment was primitive, so even minor fires could become dangerous. A waterworks capable of putting out large fires required substantial investments over and above those needed to serve ordinary consumer needs. A water supply system had to provide larger distribution mains, higher pressures, more generous storage tanks and reservoirs, and enhanced capacity and more reliable pumping facilities to serve fire protection needs adequately.[5]

In addition to fire prevention, concerns over public hygiene and disease prevention spurred public sector involvement in water supply services.[6] In 1832, a cholera epidemic in New York City claimed 3,500 lives, and resulted in the flight of 100,000 New Yorkers. The outbreak was eventually traced to a single water pump, where the waste from nearby houses had contaminated the water. In response to this public health disaster, the Old Croton Aqueduct and Reservoir was completed in 1842, built by the public sector at a cost of about $13 million. This aqueduct provided the foundation for Manhattan's first viable municipal water system.[7]

In 1840, the Chicago Hydraulic Co. received a seventy-year charter from the city of Chicago to provide water to residents. But as the result of a severe cholera epidemic in 1852, the city assumed control of the private water company because the private effort proved inadequate.[8]

During the nineteenth century, the change to public ownership was especially noticeable in major cities, which grew in population. By 1860, all of America's sixteen largest cities owned their waterworks. As of 1897, forty-one of the 50 (or 82 percent) largest U.S. cities had public systems.[9]

In major cities, adequate supplies of water became necessary to meet the needs of residents as well as commercial and industrial users. A viable waterworks became key in the competition among cities for people, trade, and industry. A need to protect the public health led to centralized systems under municipal control; private owners were increasingly pressured to sell out. By 1896, water systems in two hundred municipalities had changed from private to public ownership, while only twenty public systems went to private ownership.[10]

Provision of a clean, abundant water supply served as the first municipal service demonstrating a public commitment to economic growth and development. Cities became responsible for providing infrastructure systems, including water, thereby creating the networked city. By the turn of the twentieth century, as one historian noted:

> A healthy community was an essential ingredient in the process of growth. Many city leaders concluded that control of the sanitary quality of its water service would be difficult if the supply remained in private hands. The push for municipal ownership, therefore, had as much to do with the desire to influence the growth of cities as to settle disputes with private companies over specific deficiencies.[11]

As city leaders began to recognize the desirability of public provision of water supply services, the need to find a funding source for these large-scale, capital-intensive projects became apparent. Seeing the inadequacy of real estate taxes and special assessments to fund major capital improvements, such as water infrastructure, cities turned to a new source: municipal debt obligations. Many cities went into debt in the mid- to late-nineteenth century to fund a variety of municipal improvements to attract new residents and businesses through efforts to improve local infrastructure.[12] In addition to the increased use of municipal debt to fund the public ownership of water utilities, the willingness of state legislatures to expand home rule and allow localities to meet problems themselves, fueled the trend. Greater home rule for municipalities provided more latitude for cities to respond to local needs.

The continued inability of private firms to deliver adequate services, comprehensively and fairly, including an inability to meet the increasing demand for water, poor performance, marked by lingering questions about water quality, and high rates also played a role in the trend to public ownership of water systems. Public ownership seemed to offer the means to satisfy the demand for water, allow municipalities to grow, economically and in terms of population, but questions continued about inefficiencies and service quality abounded regardless of ownership.[13]

Despite the increased prevalence of public water systems in most major cities, private waterworks often continued in America's then smaller cities, such as Denver, until the twentieth century. A few larger, western cities, such as San Francisco, bucked the trend of municipal ownership because of satisfaction with the performance of the local water company.[14] Because water was treated in western states as a resource for private ownership, municipal water systems directly confronted this tradition, thereby delaying the implementation of public responsibility for water provision. However, as a result of the failure of private irrigation projects in the west during the last quarter of the nineteenth century, beginning in the early twentieth century, public water systems developed primarily for agricultural irrigation, not for residential water use. Public provision of water for rural areas often preceded municipal responsibility for urban water supplies.[15]

By the first decades of the twentieth century, public ownership of waterworks had become the dominant mode by which Americans received their water. By 1924, 70 percent (6,900 out of 9,850) of all waterworks in the United States were in public hands.[16] By the middle of the twentieth century, regional, publicly-owned water systems increasingly replaced municipal ones.[17]

Over the last fifty years or so, the ownership of water systems has remained remarkably consistent. By the mid-1960s, in cities with more than 25,000 people, 83.4 percent of water supply facilities were publicly-owned, with only 16.6 percent in private hands. In the mid-1980s, about 82 percent of the water supply systems serving cities with 50,000 or more people were publicly-owned; while there were about 15,740 privately-owned water systems serving about 37.5 million people. The largest of the private systems were investor-owned; homeowner associations and developers ran the smaller ones. In addition, some 17,000 ancillary systems served mobile home parks, other smaller developments, and hospitals.[18]

Today, there are about 155,000 water systems in the United States. Of these, roughly, 53,000 are classified as Community Water Systems (CWSs), serving at least twenty-five people a day, all year round. These CWSs provide about 90 percent of Americans with their drinking water. A vast number of rather small water systems exist in the United States. Very small, small, and medium systems serving fewer than 10,000 people comprise about 92 percent of all CWSs. However, 82 percent of the population receives their drinking water from larger systems that each serve more than 10,000 people.[19] Although only about 43 percent of all CWSs are publicly-owned, almost 90 percent of the systems serving more than 10,000 people are under public ownership.[20] Of the remaining 57 percent of CWSs, 24 percent are ancillary systems, such as a mobile home parks that is, they deliver water but not as their primary business and 33 percent are privately-owned.[21] Of the 33 percent of CWSs that are privately-owned, some 22 percent of these (about 4,000 entities) are shareholder-owned, about 35 percent of these are owned by homeowner associations, and the remainder (43 percent) are owned by individuals or others. Thus, about 16 percent of all CWSs are privately-owned; 84 percent are publicly-owned.[22] Private companies provide water to about one in six U.S. homes,[23] figure that has remained relatively steady since World War II.

Development and Ownership of Wastewater Treatment Systems in the United States

Before the introduction of wastewater systems, in American cities, sewage was collected in privy vaults and cesspools, which employees of private excavator companies emptied every few weeks. A privy vault, a temporary storage facility, was a hole in the ground lined with brick or stone, in the backyard of a residence. Sometimes, homeowners joined forces to build a sewer for their street, which drained into a nearby body of water.

Beyond emptying waste, private individuals and firms played a role in the development of America's wastewater systems, building sewers, often for one street, with private capital. Because of limited private investment in wastewater systems, however, provision of sewers and drainage facilities mostly fell to the local public sector.[24]

Systematic sewer construction by local governments to remove human wastes in U.S. cities generally began in the middle of the nineteenth century. Even earlier, in 1823, Boston repealed a 1709 act and took public control over private sewers. By the mid-nineteenth century, the growth of U.S. cities and the development of large water supply systems led to a wastewater disposal crisis in many urban areas.

During the nineteenth century, wastewater systems were transformed into citywide systems under municipal ownership.[25] Public health concerns led to the implementation of centralized municipal sewage systems. The development and expansion of sewer systems represented a capital-intensive enterprise that could not be paid for by only fees, which necessitated public ownership and financing, through municipal debt.[26]

Beginning in mid-nineteenth century, systematic public sewage systems construction began. Although some publicly-owned underground sewer lines were laid in several American cities prior to the 1850s, the first planned systems appeared from the late 1850s through the 1870s. In 1857, Brooklyn, New York, at that time a separate city, used Hamburg, Germany, the world's first locality with a comprehensive sewer system, as its model for a planned, municipal sewage system to remove sanitary wastes and storm water. Then, in 1859, Chicago began the construction of a comprehensive, citywide sewer plan. The Chicago effort became America's premier system at that time.

Many citywide sewer systems were built towards the end of the nineteenth century and the beginning of the twentieth century. By the early twentieth century, American cities had adopted public water and sanitation standards to protect public health and promote economic development. Citywide wastewater treatment systems developed at this time when public health became a municipal responsibility. In a few instances, private developers built sewage systems to new, wealthy subdivisions; private firms also operated sewage systems in a limited number of company towns. Additionally, some municipal systems were privately expanded to residential areas, because private developers sought to increase the value of their land holdings. Generally speaking, however, wastewater treatment systems came under public ownership by the turn of the twentieth century. By 1902, no American city with a population of more than 30,000 people had a private sewer company.[27]

Similar to the development of water supply infrastructure, the rise of the publicly-owned sewer system resulted from the increased ability of cities to issue debt obligations. Cities floated bonds to expand their urban infrastructure; between 1860 and 1922, municipal debt in the U.S. increased from $200 million to more than $3 billion.[28] Localities could borrow at better rates than available to the private sector.

Lacking in-house expertise in system design and construction, many cities hired private consultants to design and supervise the building of municipal waterworks and wastewater systems. While some consultants helped design and supervise the construction of systems, in various parts of the United States others later became city engineers and heads of local public works. Likewise, cities hired private contractors to build water and wastewater systems.[29]

Over the decades, public ownership brought about the further development and expansion of wastewater treatment systems in the United States. The percentage of the urban population served by sewers increased from 50 percent in 1870 (4.5 million) to 87 percent in 1920 (47.5 million). During this fifty-year period, the number of communities with some type of sewer system rose from 100 to 3,000, with the highest percentages in the Northeast and the lowest in the South and West.[30] However, far fewer cities initiated wastewater systems than had water supply systems.

Only slowly did cities come to implement the modern treatment of sewage, beginning with sand filtration. Chlorination became an effective and relatively inexpensive water disinfectant around 1915. In 1900, for example, about 1,100 out of 1,500 cities and towns with populations of more than 3,000 had some type of sewage system, but in 1905 there were only 89 municipal wastewater treatment plants in operation. In 1920, some 860 cities, representing 20 percent of the U.S. population served by a wastewater system, treated sewage. By 1940, more than one half of the U.S. urban population with sewers had treated wastewater.[31]

Because of the funding provided to wastewater treatment infrastructure by the federal government in the twentieth century, as discussed later in this chapter, privately-owned wastewater systems serve an even smaller portion of the American public than do water supply systems. By 1945, for example, 8,154 out of 8,824 sewage systems were in public hands; with private systems comprising mostly small ventures that could more easily meet the capital costs.[32]

At the beginning of the first decade of the twenty-first century, 98 percent of all U.S. wastewater treatment works, totaling some 16,000, were publicly-owned; only two percent were privately-owned. Additionally, approximately 25 percent of the nation's households were not connected to any centralized treatment instead using on-site systems, such as septic tanks.[33]

Public-Private Partnerships for Water Supply and Wastewater Treatment in the United States

Public and private ownership statistics provide only part of the picture with respect to how Americans receive their water supplies and have their wastewater treated. As analyzed in Chapters 5 to 8, localities have formed public-private partnerships, by entering into contracts with corporations to manage their water supply and/or wastewater treatment systems. In this type of partnership, the public partner retains ownership and control of the assets. The private partner typically operates and maintains a system or a facility. In another trend, an American subsidiary of a multinational corporation, headquartered outside the United States, often serves as the private partner.

The nation's first public-private partnership was formed in 1972, between the city of Burlingame, California and Envirotech Operating Services (now Veolia Water North America, a subsidiary of the French-based firm Veolia Environnement), for the management of a wastewater treatment facility. After repeated contract renewals spanning nearly four decades, the Burlingame partnership represents America's longest running water services partnership between the public and private sectors.

Some statistics illustrate the growth of public-private partnerships in this sector. In 1980, private firms operated approximately 100 publicly-owned water and wastewater facilities. By 2007, private firms managed more than 2,000 publicly-owned water and wastewater facilities.[34] As a result of an Internal Revenue Service rule change in 1997 (discussed in Chapter 6) the number of public-private water partnerships in the United States rose markedly from about 400 in 1997 to 1,100 by 2003.[35]

Federal Involvement in Water Supply and Wastewater Systems: The Developmental Phase

Over the last century, beginning with the Reclamation Act of 1902, followed by New Deal efforts, the federal government has played an increasingly important role in the development of water and wastewater systems in the United States. After World War II, especially beginning in 1972, federal attention turned to improving water quality standards. This section provides an overview of federal developmental efforts, focusing on funding.[36]

With the enactment of the Reclamation Act of 1902,[37] the federal government became involved in water sector activities, especially irrigation.[38] If the nation's arid and semi-arid lands were to be settled and developed, the federal government needed to play an active role by helping provide the infrastructure requisite for the irrigation of family farms. As a result of the Reclamation Act of 1902, the U.S. Bureau of Reclamation developed mammoth water engineering works, giant federally-funded dams and reservoirs, including the Hoover Dam on the Colorado River and the Grand Coulee Dam on the Columbia River, that to this day sustain agriculture and urban areas across the west from the Great Plains to the Pacific Ocean.[39] The act created the Reclamation Fund with the proceeds from the sale of federal lands in western states. It also authorized the secretary of interior to use the fund to locate and construct irrigation projects to store and distribute water in the western states. Rather than a grant of federal funds, irrigation investments were designed to be self-financing with water use beneficiaries repaying construction costs to the fund without interest, in ten annual installments.

Then, in 1906, Congress authorized the secretary of interior to develop waterpower at reclamation projects where needed for agricultural irrigation. The secretary was also authorized to sell water supplies to towns near water projects.[40]

In the 1930s, the New Deal expanded the federal government's role in the construction of water and wastewater networks to provide jobs for the unemployed, stimulate the construction industries, and meet public needs.[41] The 1933 Public Works Administration (PWA) and the 1935 Works Progress Administration (WPA), later known as the Work Projects Administration, provided federal loans and grants as well as workers for a variety of state and local construction projects.[42]

The PWA made loans and grants to states and localities for a variety of projects, including water supply and wastewater treatment plants. Under the PWA, grants and low-interest loans went to two types of projects: federal and nonfederal. The federal government fully funded so-called federal projects, which comprised slightly more than one-half of the PWA's projects, but which received less than 30 percent of PWA funds. On nonfederal projects, the federal government shared the costs with states, counties, and municipalities, with federal funds accounting for about 56 percent of the total cost of nonfederal projects. The nonfederal project category encompassed waterworks.[43]

Between 1933 and 1939, the PWA financed between about 2,600 water system projects at a cost of approximately $312 million. This sum equaled about one half of total expenditures for waterworks by all levels of government during this period. Between 1933 and 1937, PWA construction awards for nonfederal water and wastewater systems equaled $450 million, out of an aggregate of $3.7 billion awarded for all projects.[44]

In particular, the PWA provided massive financial assistance for the construction of sewage treatment plants. The PWA supported some 1,850 sewer projects with about $494 million in loans and grants compared to nearly 2,600 water system projects funded by about $312 million in loans and grants. Between 1933 and 1939, the PWA constructed about 65 percent of the nation's new (or improved) sewage plants.[45] As a result of these federal efforts, the total American population served by wastewater treatment plants increased by 73 percent between 1932 and 1937.[46]

The WPA (and its predecessors the May 1933 Federal Emergency Relief Administration and the November 1934 Civil Works Administration) spent about $112 million for work relief on public sector water projects.[47] The WPA provided workers and funds for construction projects sponsored by state and local governments. The WPA projects, which were generally smaller than the PWA projects, with the WPA devoting 9.3 percent of its labor effort in the development of water and wastewater systems between 1936 and 1940.[48]

The New Deal grant and loan programs stimulated the expansion of waterworks, especially in smaller communities. Decision-making regarding water supply and wastewater was no longer a purely local (or state) function, with the advent of federal dollars.

Smaller communities experienced the greatest impact of these public funds. For the first time, these communities could finance wastewater treatment facilities and water distribution networks. About three-fourths of the New Deal projects went to communities with less than 1,000 people. Large cities also benefited from federal funds, but not to the same extent.[49]

To obtain matching federal grants and loans on nonfederal PWA projects, localities looked to tax-exempt bonds as a funding source. In 1938, for example, more than 600 cities in some thirty-five states used tax-exempt revenue bonds, paid for with the revenues from sewage-disposal charges, in part, to finance new wastewater projects. PWA funding spurred the increased use of revenue bonds by localities throughout the United States.[50]

Budgets boomed at various federal water agencies. For example, the 1935 Rivers and Harbors Act authorized numerous major reservoir projects.[51] The 1937 Water Facilities Act authorized the construction of agricultural water storage projects in U.S. arid and semiarid regions.[52]

In the 1950s and 1960s, federal construction grant programs continued to make fund available to localities. Under this program, the public sector built many of America's currently aging water and wastewater assets.

By the late 1970s, federal water construction projects, especially water supply facilities, went into eclipse as attention increasingly focused on pollution abatement, discussed in the next section of this chapter. By 1982, for example, annual federal expenditures for public sector water supply systems equaled about $900 million, compared to local and state funds of approximately $11.6 billion spent on capital and operating expenses. As the Reagan administration sought to reduce federal spending on nonmilitary projects, state governmental assistance to municipalities to finance wastewater projects rose so that by 1989 states and localities increasingly handled the funding for water supply and wastewater treatment infrastructure. However, federal grants for wastewater facilities still totaled about $57 billion between 1972 and 1987.[53]

Current federal, non-environmental programs for funding water and wastewater systems, beyond the scope of this book, include the following: U.S. Department of Agriculture, Rural Utilities Services: Water and Waste Disposal Systems Loans for Rural Communities; U.S. Department of Housing and Urban Development, Community Development Block Grant Entitlement Communities Grants; U.S. Department of Housing and Urban Development, State Community Development Block Grants Program for Non-Entitlement Areas; and U.S. Department of Commerce, Economic Development Administration.[54]

Federal Involvement in Water and Wastewater Systems: The Environmental Phase

After World War II, the federal government became increasingly involved promoting water quality. This section discusses the federal government's ever increasing focus on more comprehensive regulation, including wider and deeper water quality standards. The rapidly expanding and complex regulatory machinery became a major cost factor to water and wastewater utilities. The section is divided into three parts: pre-Clean Water Act development; the Clean Water Act and its funding provisions; the Safe Drinking Water Act and its funding provisions.

Pre–Clean Water Act Developments

In 1948, with the passage of federal Water Pollution Control Act,[55] the federal government enacted comprehensive, nationwide water pollution control legislation, beginning its direct involvement in water pollution control. The act provided the first federal government authorization of funds for wastewater treatment facilities in the form of loans. The act empowered the federal government to participate in the abatement of water pollution on interstate rivers, but in a supporting and advisory role, and authorized a modest amount of federal financial assistance via low interest loans for the construction of water pollution mitigation facilities. The act provided $22.5 million annually for five years for loans to construct wastewater treatment facilities. Loans were capped at a maximum of the lesser of 30 percent of a facility's total cost or $250,000.

The 1956 amendments[56] to the 1948 act represented the first permanent federal water pollution control legislation. The 1956 amendments increased federal financial assistance, substituting a 30 percent incentive grant program for the loan arrangement with up to $50 million per year in grants over ten years, for the construction of publicly-owned sewage treatment plants. Although the $250,000 maximum grant amount was too low to attract large projects, the program encouraged a 62 percent rise in sewage treatment plant construction during the program's first five years in comparison to the previous five years.[57]

Beginning in 1961, the federal government became more involved in solving domestic problems with national programs and resources. The Federal Water Pollution Control Act Amendments of 1961,[58] expanded the federal government's jurisdiction to include navigable waters and increased the federal grants program. Appropriations increased for 1962 from $50 million to $80 million, for 1963, $90 million, and $100 million in each year from 1964 through 1967. The prior grant limit of 30 percent of the cost of sewage treatment projects with a $250,000 maximum, was increased to $600,000, more specifically, the lesser of 30 percent of a project's total cost or $600,000. Jointly-sponsored municipal-industrial projects could receive larger grants.

The Water Quality Act of 1965[59] directly involved the federal government in water quality management for the first time. The act created the Federal Water Pollution Control Administration, subsequently renamed, the Federal Water Quality Administration, as the federal agency charged with formulating and enforcing water quality standards for interstate waters. It required states to establish water quality standards for their interstate waters; however, no effective enforcement mechanism existed for those standards.

23

The 1965 act increased the authorized appropriations for the 30 percent grant programs for the construction of sewage treatment plants from $100 million to $150 million per year. It also raised the ceiling on individual grants to $1.2 million to provide incentives for treatment plant construction in large metropolitan areas, which had the largest waste discharges.

The Clean Water Restoration Act of 1966, with a four-year funding authorization, established a new level of federal funding for water quality.[60] The aggregate funding level authorized for the construction grants program rose to $3.4 billion with an increase from $150 million per year to $450 million for fiscal year 1968, to $700 million for 1969, to $1 billion for 1970, and to $1.25 billion in 1971. Despite the increases, funding gaps stalled the construction of wastewater treatment plants. The 1966 act increased the federal share of the construction costs from 30 to 40 percent, provided a state paid 30 percent of the total cost. The federal share would go to 50 percent if a state agreed to pay at least 25 percent of the cost and set enforceable water quality standards for waters into which a project discharged. Also, if a project conformed to a comprehensive metropolitan plan, the federal share would rise to 55 percent.

By removing the previous dollar ceilings and increasing the maximum federal contributions, the 1966 act offered an incentive for the construction of multi-million dollar wastewater treatment facilities and for metropolitan areas to seek federal grants. The act also authorized $200 million over four years for a variety of demonstration projects, including new methods of advanced wastewater treatment, joint municipal-industrial wastewater treatment, and industrial water pollution control.

Thus, by 1969, the federal government had become significantly involved in funding local wastewater treatment needs. Between 1957 and 1969, $5.4 billion in wastewater treatment plants were built in the United States, with $1.2 billion funded by federal grants. Most of the grant funds went to communities with less than 25,000 people. However, the U.S. needs exceeded the combined levels of public sector funding. In particular, America's largest cities faced water pollution problems that outstripped construction.[61]

Following the enactment of the National Environmental Policy Act of 1969,[62] the U.S. government established the Council of Environmental Quality to review federal governmental activities pertaining to the environment, develop impact statement guidelines, and advise the president on environmental matters. Then President Richard M. Nixon created the Environmental Protection Agency (EPA),[63] which began operations in December 1970. Through the EPA, the Nixon administration sought to have environmental policy, regulation, and enforcement considered as one interrelated system. The EPA brought together pollution control programs for water, among other areas, from various federal agencies. Then, in quick order, the federal government increased its role in enhancing water quality.

The Clean Water Mandate and Its Funding

Federal water-related regulation grew, spurred by public demands for tough action to deal with human health problems. In the 1950s and 1960s, with pollution from public and private facilities increasing, the nation's wastewater treatment systems proved ineffective in removing pollutants. Americans wanted to swim without fear and be able to eat the fish caught in their rivers and lakes. In response, Congress enacted the 1972 Federal Water Pollution Control Act, renamed the Clean Water Act in 1977, the main federal law protecting and regulating America's surface water quality. In brief, the legislation established a system of standards, permits, and enforcement designed to reduce the quantity of pollutants discharged into the nation's surface waters. Under the act, the EPA regulates effluent discharges by sewage treatment plants and industrial facilities, technically, point source facilities, to prevent the discharge of harmful quantities of pollutants, as defined, into surface waters. Dischargers must obtain a permit either from the EPA or states with EPA-approved programs. The National Pollutant Discharge Elimination System permit program serves as the main tool for achieving the goal of restoring and maintaining the integrity of the nation's surface waters.

The act provided an increase in federal funding and a larger federal share of municipal wastewater treatment project costs. To help fund the building of publicly-owned wastewater treatment plants, Congress authorized the EPA to make construction grants to the states aggregating $18 billion for fiscal years 1973 through 1975, with the federal share of eligible costs increasing from 50 to 75 percent.[64]

By 1977, Congress recognized that it had underestimated the nation's wastewater treatment needs. The 1977 amendments to the 1972 act continued the emphasis on technology-based water quality standards by increasing the percentage of federal funding from 75 to 85 percent for projects employing innovative technologies.[65]

The 1977 amendments also increased federal construction grant funding for municipal wastewater treatment facilities to $24.5 billion through 1981, by authorizing annual appropriations for five years. As a result, wastewater treatment construction became one of the nation's largest federal domestic public works programs. The public sector built thousands of new wastewater treatment plants and expanded thousands more. Although federal funding helped building publicly-owned treatment works, the expansion of federal monies displaced, to some extent, state and local investment that otherwise would have taken place.

Beginning in 1981, a shift occurred leading to a reduction in federal involvement in many water quality programs, primarily through deregulation and decreased funding. The Reagan Administration and Congress wanted the states and localities to assume major responsibilities for funding new wastewater treatment facilities. As a transitional stage to greater state and local responsibility, the 1981 amendments to the Clean Water Act, the Municipal Wastewater Treatment Construction Grant Amendments of 1981,[66] reduced the eligibility for grants, lowered the federal share of project costs from 75 to 55 percent (thereby increasing the state and local shares), and reduced the annual authorization for federal wastewater construction grants from $4.2 billion to 1981 to $2.4 billion in 1987.

In 1987, Congress changed the way the federal government subsidized wastewater system construction and other water quality projects. The enactment of the Water Quality Act of 1987 signaled the end of the federal funding for municipal and regional wastewater treatment plants through direct construction grants to localities for publicly-owned facilities.[67] By 1994, the federal government terminated any funding for wastewater construction grants, with $1.2 billion annually authorized for fiscal years 1989 and 1990, increasing to $2.4 billion for fiscal year 1991, decreasing to $1.8 billion, $1.2 billion, $600 million for fiscal years 1992, 1993, 1994, respectively.

During the 1970s and 1980s, the construction grants program provided more than $60 billion for the construction of publicly-owned wastewater treatment facilities. Projects funded, which made a significant contribution to the nation's infrastructure, included sewage treatment plants, pumping stations, various types of sewers, and the rehabilitation of sewer systems.

In place of direct construction grants, since 1995, states receive federal grants to capitalize Clean Water State Revolving Fund (CWSRF) loan programs.[68] These state revolving loan programs, funded 80 percent by federal grants and 20 percent by state funds, make low-cost loans available to publicly-owned systems (and in limited situations, to facilities leased to private entities) for a wide variety of high priority projects designed to protect and enhance water quality and compliance with environmental regulations.

State revolving loan programs more efficiently provide federal assistance for wastewater treatment facilities. Through user fees and other dedicated revenue sources, the program's public entity loan recipients pay interest and repay principal to the loan programs. Because the funds revolve over time, capital becomes available to finance new projects.

Although the state revolving loan fund programs prohibit direct loans to privately-owned wastewater treatment works, the system of indirect loans to private entities requires an explanation. CWSRF loans may be made through a municipal lease arrangement allowing the private sector to use the funds. In brief, a CWSRF lends funds to a publicly-owned entity that leases a facility to a private sector entity. The public entity serves as a conduit for funds lent to the private borrower. The private entity makes lease and/or loan payments to the public entity.

The state revolving loan fund programs provide several types of public sector loan assistance, including project construction loans and funds to refinance debt obligations. Construction loans are made at low-interest rates, from zero percent up to market rates, for terms of up to twenty years. States can also use federal monies to repurchase debt obligations and thereby increase loan terms up to thirty years.

Congress made the CWSRF a state-run program with minimal EPA oversight. The CWSRF was designed to allow state programs the flexibility to fund projects based on state water quality priorities. However, states must use CWSRF funds first to ensure that wastewater treatment facilities comply with deadlines, goals, and other federally-mandated requirements. After meeting this first use requirement, states may use the funds to support other types of legally-specified water quality programs.

Since the funding of the inaugural CWSRF program in 1988, by the end of fiscal year 2008, the fifty-one revolving loan programs have provided $68.8 billion in cumulative assistance through 22,700 loans. During this twenty-one year period, federal grants to the program totaled more than $26 billion. To date, publicly-owned wastewater treatment projects have comprised 96 percent of the program's clean water financing, with non-point (undefined) pollution sources, such as agricultural and urban street water runoff, and estuary projects accounting for the remainder.[69]

More than half the states now leverage their funds by using both the federal grants and their respective matching funds as collateral to borrow in the tax-exempt bond market to increase the funds available for project lending. To date, twenty-five states have used this technique to raise an additional $22.4 billion to fund clean water projects.[70]

CWSRF programs fund some 10 to 20 percent of the nation's total, annual public sector wastewater treatment capital investments. Local governments finance the remaining portion of construction costs through user charges, broad-based taxes (such as real estate taxes, sales taxes, or in some cases, a local income tax), other state grants, and borrowing funds by floating tax-exempt bonds.[71] The reliance on public sector funds has made it more difficult to introduce a private asset ownership role in the wastewater treatment sector.

Looking back more than sixty years, the funding of wastewater treatment facilities went through two basic phases, apart from user fees. From 1948 to 1995, money flowed from the federal government and the tax-exempt bond market to localities and states, with states directing funds to localities from 1987 to 1995. Beginning in 1995, money flowed from the tax-exempt bond market and from the states to the localities through revolving loan programs, funded in large part by the federal government.

The Safe Drinking Water Mandate and Its Funding

In the nearly four decades following the enactment of the 1972 clean water legislation, the level of public concern about water purity increased. The American public evidenced a desire for ever-stronger, broader regulatory protection of drinking water. Wanting to know and understand more about the impact of water quality on public health, the growing concern led to broader and more extensive water quality regulation beginning in 1974. Each new, more stringent federal water quality standard resulted in higher costs for water utilities, regardless of ownership.

The Safe Drinking Water Act of 1974 led to the creation National Primary Drinking Water Regulations, through which the EPA establishes and enforces maximum levels for biological, chemical and physical contaminants and for any residuals remaining in drinking

28

water, generally speaking, delivered to users of systems with at least twenty-five persons, regardless of its source, surface or ground water.[72] Recognizing a wide array of threats to drinking water and the need to establish national standards for potable water, the act authorized the EPA to develop enforceable public health protection-based standards for drinking water and to require water system operators to come as close as possible to meeting the standards. The 1974 Act sought to build upon existing state regulatory programs through the concept of primacy. States and sub-state water management districts assumed day-to-day oversight responsibility (if they requested) for implementing the federal standards (and higher state standards, if imposed), and also for enforcing these standards within their borders. Regardless of ownership, private or governmental, water utilities must meet the same standards.

Amendments in 1986 expanded the EPA's authority to regulate a wide range of drinking water contaminants, setting out eighty-three substances for which the EPA had to establish enforceable limits within three years as well as new rules for the treatment of surface water supplies.[73] Communities that had previously failed to treat their surface water supplies were required to do so. However, the EPA, state drinking water programs, and water utilities all struggled to meet the ambitious agenda established in 1986. By the mid-1990s, it was clear that the prescriptive formulation contained in the 1986 amendments was not working well. Although the federal government imposed new burdens, until 1996 Congress failed to provide funding whether through grants or loans to pay for the testing and treatment requirements. The unfunded federal mandate[74] forced localities to meet federal regulations through local revenue sources or state loan funds.

In 1996, Congress again amended the Safe Drinking Water Act.[75] The amendments preserved the public health protection emphasis for standard setting and provided a more focused, science-based approach to identify the contaminants requiring regulation. Repealing the 1986 amendments requiring the agency to regulate twenty-five additional contaminants every three years, the new amendments mandate the EPA to continuously update the list of regulated contaminants. The EPA sets goals, known as Maximum Contaminant Level Goals (MCLGs), for particular contaminants. The goals are set at a level at which no known (or anticipated) adverse human health effects occur. EPA then specifies either standards (Maximum Contaminant Levels) or treatment methods (Treatment Techniques) to come as close to the MCLGs as is feasible, taking costs into consideration.

The 1996 amendments established new programs aimed at preventing unsafe drinking water, including source water protection, operator certification, and water system capacity development. The amendments also directed the EPA to require publicly- and privately-owned water systems to provide their customers with annual consumer confidence water reports, detailing, among other items, the regulated contaminant levels found in their drinking water.

In terms of providing funding, the 1996 amendments authorized the creation of the federal Drinking Water State Revolving Fund (DWSRF) loan program.[76] This program provides publicly- and privately-owned water systems with the financing needed to facilitate compliance with the 1974 Act, as amended. More specifically, the program provides states with grants that may be used for two major purposes: first, to fund state revolving loan funds to provide low-cost loans, with twenty to thirty year terms, to water systems; and second, for states to establish optional set-asides to support the implementation of basic safe drinking water and new contamination prevention programs, among other items. The DWSRF is designed to finance investments in infrastructure and to support the key initiatives introduced by the amendments, including ensuring the technical, managerial, and financial capacity of drinking water systems, achieving sustainable infrastructure, and preventing drinking water contamination. The ongoing program allows drinking water systems to borrow funds at subsidized interest rates. Similar to the clean water revolving funds, as borrowers complete their projects, they must repay their loans, thereby providing funds for new facilities.

Activities eligible for loans include projects to replace or upgrade drinking water treatment, storage, transmission, and distribution facilities. Initiatives funded with set-asides include drinking water source protection and water system operator certification.

States must allocate 15 percent of their respective drinking water revolving loan funds to systems serving 10,000 or fewer people, unless no eligible projects are available for financing. States may combine, coordinate, and jointly administer both their clean water and safe drinking water revolving loan programs and transfer up to 33 percent of the grants between the two accounts.

From the initial $1 billion federal commitment, by the end of fiscal year 2007, DWSRF programs had lent a total of $12.63 billion in the form of nearly 5,200 low-interest loans to fund public sector drinking water protection projects. From fiscal year 1997 through fiscal year 2007, federal grants to DWSRF programs totaled $8.13 billion, with $796 million available in fiscal year 2007.[77]

Today, drinking water systems invest about $10 billion per year in capital improvements. DWSRF financing accounts for approximately 5 percent of the total annual capital investments in drinking water infrastructure. These systems rely mainly on current revenues (39 percent) and tax-exempt borrowings (42 percent). DWSRF financing fills, however, an important niche providing 11 percent of the total capital funds for publicly-owned community water systems (CWSs), including 20 percent of the capital for publicly-owned CWSs serving 10,000 or fewer persons.[78]

The Twenty-First Century Developments on the Federal Level

Two major events marked the first decade of the twenty-first century: the terrorist attacks of September 11, 2001, and the most severe economic downturn since the Great Depression. As a result, water security received increased attention and funding for water and wastewater facilities rose.

Water Security. In the aftermath of 9/11, protecting the domestic water supplies from terrorist attacks became a major priority.[79] When Congress created the Department of Homeland Security (DHS) as part of the Homeland Security Act of 2002,[80] among other items, the DHS received responsibility for assessing and securing the nation's critical infrastructure, through partnerships with the public and private sectors. However, the Act did not transfer EPA's water security functions to the DHS. Although beyond the scope of this book, since fiscal year 2002, Congress has appropriated funds annually for the EPA to work with states and the water sector to improve the security of drinking water supplies.[81]

The 2003 Homeland Security Presidential Directive established a national policy for the federal government to identify, prioritize, and protect critical infrastructure.[82] Under the directive, the DHS assumed the responsibility for the overall coordination and integration of critical infrastructure protection efforts by all governmental levels and the private sector. EPA has the responsibility for developing and providing tools and training for improving security to roughly 53,000 community water systems and 16,000 public sector wastewater treatment facilities. To prevent overlap and duplication by the DHS and the EPA, coordinating entities have evolved.

Congress enacted the Public Health Security and Bioterrorism Preparedness and Response Act of 2002 in response to the 9/11 attacks.[83] The act, in part, aims at improving the security of the nation's drinking water supplies. Mandating protections for the drinking water, the act amended the Safe Drinking Water Act to require some 8,400 community water systems, each serving more than 3,300 people, but in total, more than 240 million people, to conduct and submit vulnerability assessments to the EPA and prepare (or revise) their emergency response plans to address potential terrorist threats to water supplies incorporating the results of the vulnerability assessments. It also authorized funding to community water systems to conduct vulnerability assessments, prepare response plans, and fund basic security enhancements, but did not require water utilities to make security upgrades to address potential vulnerabilities.

As part of its new responsibilities for water security, the EPA created a National Homeland Security Research Center within the Office of Research and Development to develop technology to be used to respond to attacks on the nation's water systems. The agency established a Water Security Division in the Office of Water to train water utility personnel on security issues and provide guidance and tools to utilities as they assess and seek to decrease their systems' vulnerabilities.[84]

Increased Funding. The deep 2007-2009 recession triggered renewed interest in federal funding of water supply and wastewater treatment infrastructure as an economic stimulus and job creation mechanism. As part of a larger stimulus agenda contained in the American Recovery and Reinvestment Act of 2009,[85] the federal government took a step in providing additional funding for water and wastewater infrastructure. However, only a very modest portion, less than one percent of the $787 billion stimulus package will trickle down to America's water and wastewater industry. The act authorized more than $7 billion in federal grants for water infrastructure, consisting of $4.0 billion to the Clean Water State Revolving Fund program, $2.0 billion to Safe Drinking Water State Revolving Fund program, and $1.38 billion for rural water programs. Although pushing forward projects to repair or replace water infrastructure, the funds committed represent only a tiny portion of the capital needed to meet the projected funding shortfall, as analyzed in Chapter 5.

To help get projects moving, the stimulus act waves the 20 percent state matching requirement for state revolving loan funds programs.

It directs states to use not less than 50 percent of the federal grants for additional subsidization to recipients, including loan principal. To the extent that there are sufficient, eligible projects, the act requires at least $1.2 billion of funds appropriated for the revolving loan programs be used for projects to address green infrastructure, water or energy efficiency improvements, or other environmentally innovative projects.

Today, the United States has a mixed, largely publicly-owned, but decentralized, system of water supply and wastewater treatment infrastructure. Public-private partnerships have emerged as an important framework in which public and private entities work together to provide water and wastewater services. The federal government plays an important role in water sector through environmental regulation and providing funding to meet these mandates. Before considering the cost of repairing, replacing, and expanding America's aging water and wastewater infrastructure in Chapter 6, the next chapter considers the threat posed by water scarcity to America's economic growth and way of life.

Notes

1. The early history of private water companies is summarized in Leonard S. Hayman et al., *The Water Business: Understanding the Water Supply and Wastewater Industry* (Vienna, VA: Public Utilities Reports, 1998), 125-127 and Nelson Manfred Blake, *Water for the Cities: A History of the Urban Water Supply Problem in the United States* (Syracuse, NY: Syracuse University, 1956), 63-77.

2. Martin V. Melosi, *The Sanitary City: Urban Infrastructure in America from Colonial Times to the Present* (Baltimore: Johns Hopkins, 2000), 30-32 and Blake, *Water for the Cities*, 18-43. Melosi surveys the early development of major water systems (*Sanitary City*, 36-39) and the subsequent growth of municipal water systems in the U.S. (*ibid.*, 78-83). Hyman et al., *Water Business*, 85-98 traces the development of water supplies in the eastern half of the U.S. See also Ann Durkin Keating, "Public-Private Partnerships in Public Works: A Bibliographic Essay," in *Public-Private Partnerships: Privatization in Historical Perspective*, Essays in Public Works History Number 16 (Chicago: Public Works Historical Society, 1989); Stuart Galishoff, "Triumph and Failure: The American Response to the Urban Water Supply, 1860-1923," in *Pollution and Reform in American Cities, 1870-1930*, ed. Martin V. Melosi (Austin, TX: University of Texas Press, 1980); J. Michael LaNier, "Historical Development of Municipal Water Systems in the United States 1776-1976," *Journal of American Water Works Association* 68:4 (April 1976): 173-180.

3. The statistics in this paragraph are from Melosi, Sanitary City, 36 (Table 1.3 Public and Private Ownership of Waterworks), 74 (Table 4.3 Public and Private Ownership of Waterworks), 120 (Table 7.1 Public v. Private Ownership of Waterworks). See also Keith J. Crocker and Scott E. Masten, "Prospects for Private Water Provision in Developing Countries: Lessons From 19th-Century America," in Thirsting for Efficiency: The Economics and Politics of Urban Water System Reform, ed. Mary M. Shirley (Kidlington, Oxford UK: Elsevier Science, 2002), 324 (Table 9.1 Public and private water-works in the United States, 1800-1896).

4. Melosi, Sanitary City, 120 (Table 7.1 Public v. Private Ownership of Waterworks) and Crocker and Masten, "Prospects," 324 (Table 9.1 Public and private water-works in the United States, 1800-1896).

5. Charles David Jacobson, "Private Firms and Public Goods: An Historical Perspective on Contracting Out for Public Services," in Public-Private Partnerships, 62.

6. Black, Water, 248-264, analyzes the interrelationship between pure water and public health.

7. Ibid., 121-171, discusses the Croton project.

8. Melosi, Sanitary City, 79.

9. Keating, "Public-Private Partnerships," 96 and Melosi, Sanitary City, 120.

10. Keating, "Public-Private Partnerships," 96.

11. Melosi, Sanitary City, 119 (footnotes omitted).

12. Joel A. Tarr, "The Evolution of the Urban Infrastructure in the Nineteenth and Twentieth Centuries," in Perspectives on Urban Infrastructure, ed. Royce Hanson (Washington, DC: National Academy, 1984), 17-18 and 29-31, provides an overview of infrastructure financing.

13. Melosi, Sanitary City, 76, 120-123.

14. Ibid., 122.

15. Gerald R. Ogden, "Agrarianism, Federalism, and Water Development in California," Pacific Historian 27:1 (Spring 1983): 42-56.

16. Melosi, Sanitary City, 120 (Table 7.1 Public v. Private Ownership of Waterworks).

17. Ibid., 217.

18. The statistics in this paragraph are from ibid., 298 (Table 15.1 Ownership of Water Supply Systems), 375.

19. U.S. Environmental Protection Agency (EPA), Factoids: Drinking Water and Ground Water Statistics for 2008.

20. EPA, The Clean Water and Drinking Water Infrastructure Gap Analysis, 2002, EPA-816-R-02-020, 10.

21. Ibid., 11 (Figure 2-2: Percentage of Drinking Water Systems by Type of Ownership).

22. John S. Young, Jr., "The Role of Privatization/Regionalization in Water Resource Management," November 7, 2008, 21, available from www. amwater.com.

23. Jim Carlton, "Calls Rise for the Public Control of Water Supply," Wall Street Journal, June 17, 2008, A6 and Reason Foundation, 2005 Annual Privatization Report, ed. Geoffrey F. Segal, 123.

24. I have drawn on Melosi, *Sanitary City*, 93, 95-98, for the history of waste-water systems in the eighteenth and nineteenth centuries.

25. Joel A. Tarr, "Sewerage and the Development of the Networked City in the United States 1850-1930," in *Technology and the Rise of the Networked City in Europe and America*, eds. Joel A. Tarr and Gabriel Dupuy (Philadelphia: Temple University, 1988) and Jon A. Peterson, "The Impact of Sanitary Reform upon American Urban Planning, 1840-1890, *Journal of Social History* 13:1 (Autumn 1979): 83-103.

26. See, e.g., Samuel A. Greeley, "Organizing and Financing Sewage Treatment Projects," *Transactions of the American Society of Civil Engineers* 109 (1944): 248-263, at 256-258.

27. David T. Beito, "From Privies to Boulevards, The Private Supply of Infrastructure in the United States during the Nineteenth Century," in *Development By Consent: The Voluntary Supply of Public Goods and Services*, eds. Jerry Jenkins and David E. Sisk (San Francisco: Institute for Contemporary Studies, 1993), 25.

28. Melosi, *Sanitary City*, 120.

29. Keating, "Public-Private Partnerships," 98, 102.

30. The statistics in this paragraph are from Melosi, *Sanitary City*, 151-152 (Table 8.1 Estimates of U.S. Population With Sewage Systems).

31. The statistics in this paragraph are from *ibid.*, 172-173 (Table 8.6 Urban Population with Treated Sewage).

32. *Ibid.*, 237.

33. EPA, Gap Analysis, 10.

34. National Association of Water Companies, "Private Water Service Providers Quick Facts" <www.nawc.org/resources/documents /pwsp-quick-facts.html= (June 10, 2009). There are higher and lower estimates of public-private partnerships. The Water Partnership Council estimated 2,400 public-private water and wastewater partnerships in 2002. Water Partnership Council, Establishing Public-Private Partnerships for Water and Wastewater Systems: A Blueprint for Success, 2003, 10-11. The U.S. Conference of Mayor's Urban Water Council placed the number of public-private water and wastewater partnerships at more than 1,800 in 2005. The U.S. Conference of Mayors Urban Water Council, Mayor's Guide to Water and Wastewater Partnership Service Agreements: Terms and Conditions, April 25, 2005, 1. G. Tracy Mehan, III, "Let's Drink to Private Water," *PERC Reports* 26:1 (Spring 2008) (available at www.perc.org) estimated that more than 1,300 government entities in the U.S. contract with private companies to provide water and/or wastewater services. See also Reason Foundation, 2007 Annual Privatization Report, 81.

35. Mike Hudson, "Misconduct Taints the Water in Some Privatized Systems," *Los Angeles Times*, May 20, 2006, A1.

36. I have drawn on Peter Rogers, *America's Water: Federal Roles and Responsibilities* (Cambridge: MIT Press, 1993), 45-73 and Andrea K. Gerlak, "Federalism and U.S. Water Policy: Lessons for the Twenty-First Century," *Publius* 36:2 (Spring 2006): 231-251.

37. Public Law, 57-161.

38. Beatrice Hort Holmes, *A History of Federal Water Resources Programs, 1800-1960* (Washington, DC: U.S. Department of Agriculture 1972), Miscellaneous Publication 1233, 6-7.

39. Michael C. Robinson, *Water for the West: The Bureau of Reclamation, 1902-1977* (Chicago: Public Works Historical Society, 1982) traces the history of the Bureau of Reclamation.

40. Public Law 59-103.

41. See generally, Roger Daniels, "Public Works in the 1930s: A Preliminary Reconnaissance," in *The Relevancy of Public Works History: The 1930s-A Case Study*, Public Works Historical Society, Georgetown University Department of History, September 22, 1975.

42. The National Industrial Recovery Act of 1933, Public Law 73-67, established the Federal Emergency Administration of Public Works (FEAPW). Reorganization Plan No. 1 of 1939 transferred the administration of the FEAPW to the Federal Works Agency and changed its name to the Public Works Administration. Pursuant to the Emergency Relief Appropriation Act of 1935 (Public Resolution 11), Executive Order 7034, May 6, 1935, established the Works Progress Administration. Reorganization Plan No. 1 of 1939 changed its name to the Work Projects Administration and placed it in the Federal Works Agency.

43. Melosi, *Sanitary City*, 219 and Daniels, "Public Works," 8.

44. The statistics in this paragraph are from Melosi, *Sanitary City*, 218-219.

45. *Ibid.*, 240. See also Tarr, "Evolution," 40-41.

46. Holmes, *Federal Water Resources Programs, 1800-1960*, 15.

47. Melosi, *Sanitary City*, 218.

48. *Ibid.*, 219.

49. *Ibid.*, 218.

50. *Ibid.*, 244.

51. Public Law 74-409.

52. Public Law 75-399.

53. The statistics in this paragraph are from Melosi, *Sanitary City*, 378-381, 536, fn 34.

54. See generally, EPA, Environmental Finance Program, Guidebook of Financial Tools: Paying for Environmental Systems, August 2008, EPA-205-R-08-001, Sections 2B and 2C. See also U.S. General Accounting Office, Water Infrastructure: Information on Federal and State Financial Assistance, November 2001, GA0-02-134, 9-16.

55. Public Law 80-845. See also Melosi, *Sanitary City*, 315.

56. Public Law 84-660. See also Melosi, *Sanitary City*, 315-316.

57. Holmes, *Federal Water Resources Programs, 1800-1960*, 30.

58. Public Law 87-88. See also Melosi, *Sanitary City*, 316-317 and Beatrice Hart Holmes, *History of Federal Water Resources Programs and Policies, 1961-70* (Washington, DC: U.S. Department of Agriculture, 1979), Miscellaneous Publication 1379, 30.

59. Public Law 89-234. See also Melosi, *Sanitary City*, 317-318 and Holmes, *History, 1961-70*, 185-186.

60. Public Law 89-753. See also Holmes, *History, 1961-70*, 193-1995.

61. Melosi, *Sanitary City*, 336.
62. Public Law 91-190.
63. Executive Order 11514, March 5, 1970.
64. Public Law 92-500. See also Melosi, *Sanitary City*, 387-389 and Hyman et al., *Water Business*, 146-147.
65. Public Law 95-217. See also Melosi, *Sanitary City*, 389.
66. Public Law 97-117.
67. Public Law 100-4.
68. For the history and background of the Clean Water State Revolving Fund Program see EPA, Clean Water State Revolving Fund Programs, 2008 Annual Report: Clean Our Waters, Renewing Our Communities, Creating Jobs (2008 CWSRF Annual Report), March 2009, EPA-832-09-01, 2-4. See also EPA, Financing America's Clean Water Since 1987: A Report of Progress and Innovation, May 2001, EPA-832-R-00-011, 6-8.
69. The statistics in this paragraph are from the 2008 CWSRF Annual Report, 2, 17 (Figure 5 CWSFR Cumulative Assistance Reached $68.8 billion through 2008), 18 (Figure 7 CWSRFs Provide $68.8 Billion Clean Water Financing through 2008). In absolute dollars, federal funding for the CWSRF between 1989 and 2006, fell six percent; adjusted for inflation, it decreased 39 percent. Northeast-Midwest Institute, Federal Funding Declines Substantially for Clean Water State Revolving Fund, December 2006.
70. The statistics in this paragraph are from *2008 CWSRF Annual Report*, 2, 24.
71. Congressional Research Service, Wastewater Treatment: Overview and Background, Updated March 20, 2008, 98-323, CRS-4.
72. Public Law 93-523. See also Melosi, *Sanitary City*, 392 and Hyman et al., *Water Business*, 151-152. For a review of the history of the Safe Drinking Water Act see Frederick W. Pontius, "SDWA: A Look Back," *Journal of American Water Works Association* 85:2 (February 1993), 22-24, 94-95.
73. Public Law 99-339.
74. Congressional Budget Office, The Safe Drinking Water Act: A Case Study of an Unfunded Federal Mandate, September 1995.
75. Public Law 104-182. See generally, Frederick W. Pontius, "Drinking Water Contaminant Regulation - Where Are We Heading?, *Journal of American Water Works Association* 96:3 (March 2004): 56-59.
76. For the history and background on the Drinking Water State Revolving Fund Program see EPA, Drinking Water State Revolving Fund: Investing in a Sustainable Future: 2007 Annual Report (2007 DWSRF Annual Report), March 2008, EPA-816-R-08-002, 1-25; EPA, The Drinking Water State Revolving Fund Program: Financing America's Drinking Water From The Source To The Tap: Report to Congress, May 2003, EPA-918-R-03-009; EPA, The Drinking Water State Revolving Fund: Financing America's Drinking Water: A Report of Progress, November 2000, EPA-816-R-00-023.
77. The statistics in this paragraph are from 2007 DWSRF Annual Report, 12, 32.
78. The statistics in this paragraph are from *ibid.*, 18.
79. For background on the vulnerabilities and risks facing water systems see Peter H. Gleick, "Water and terrorism," *Water Policy* 8 (2006): 481-503.

80. Public Law 107-296.
81. For funding details, see Congressional Research Service, Safeguarding the Nation's Drinking Water: EPA and Congressional Action, November 26, 2008, RL31294, CRS-6 to CRS-9.
82. The White House, Homeland Security Presidential Directive/HSPD-7, Critical Infrastructure Identification, Prioritization, and Protection, December 17, 2003.
83. Public Law 107-188.
84. Congressional Research Service, Terrorism and Security Issues Facing the Water Infrastructure Industry, November 17, 2008, RL32189, CRS-7 to CRS-9.
85. Public Law 111-5. In March 2009, the U.S. House of Representatives passed H.R. 1262, the proposed Water Quality Investment Act of 2009, 111th Congress, 1st Session, authorizing $19.8 billion over the next five years for wastewater infrastructure and other efforts to improve water quality, including $13.8 billion in federal funding over five years for the Clean Water State Revolving Fund. The proposed Water Infrastructure Financing Act of 2009, S. 1005, 111th Congress, 1st Session would reauthorize both the Clean Water State Revolving Fund (CWSRF) and Drinking Water State Revolving Fund (DWSRF) and provide $38.5 billion for EPA water infrastructure programs over the next five years, boosting the CWSRF to $20 billion and the DWSRF to $14.7 billion, both over five years, and creating a $1.8 billion federal grant program to reduce combined sewer overflows.

Part II
Water Scarcity

3

Water Scarcity in the United States, Climate Change, and Public Sector Conservation Efforts

We are in the midst of a transition from viewing water as an abundant resource to a scarce one. Regions in the United States face a decrease in water availability. Trends in the United States reflect a worldwide theme, as nations throughout the globe face water shortages in the coming decades. One study projects that one-third of the world's countries will likely experience severe water shortages by 2025, with the number of water-deficit countries and regions likely increasing in the future.[1] The study estimates that nearly 1.4 billion people, equal to a quarter of the world's population or a third of the population in developing countries, live in regions that will experience severe water scarcity within the first quarter of this century.

This chapter focuses on water scarcity in the United States. Authorities at the federal, state, and local levels face growing concerns over increasingly inadequate water supplies. Heightened demand, resulting from population growth, and decreasing freshwater supplies, due to drought, among other factors, puts great stress on the nation's water resources. This chapter examines the dwindling supply of freshwater resources in the United States, primarily in the southwest.

Analyzing the impact that increasingly frequent and severe droughts have had on the nation's water supply leads to an investigation for a possible cause. Scientists, in an effort to explain changes in precipitation and runoff patterns, look to climate change as a prime cause for the droughts in the southwestern United States. This chapter examines the global warming concept and the predicted impact future climate change will have on water resources in the United States. Research on global warming by the Intergovernmental Panel on Climate Change and the federal government shows that the impact on the nation's water supply will likely be significant, with changes in precipitation, snowpack melting, mountain runoff, and sea levels. Global climate change may lead to long-term supply/demand imbalances. According to many researchers, protracted droughts and their adverse impacts on water supplies, as well as flooding caused by rising sea levels may represent two of the greatest hazards the United States faces in the foreseeable future. Although many researchers believe that the existence of anthropogenic warming of the planet is unequivocal, critics present scientific data to the contrary. This chapter briefly examines some of the data offered in opposition to the conclusions of the IPCC and the majority of climate researchers.

In the face of dwindling resources, federal, state, and local authorities have implemented conservation efforts in an effort to stretch already stressed water supplies. These measures can take the form of voluntary programs, focused on education or financial incentives, or mandatory water restrictions discussed at the end of this chapter.

The Quantity of Water

When we talk about the quantity of water, there are two types of water supplies: surface freshwater, such as rivers and lakes, and underground freshwater, found in wells and aquifers, a water-bearing stratum of permeable rock, sand or gravel. These basic water resources determine water supplies and the location, quantity, and quality of available freshwater. The cost of transporting surface freshwater or pumping water from aquifers determines the geographical radius of natural freshwater supplies. Concerns about water quantity do not go only to surface freshwater; groundwater, a main U.S. water source, is being extracted in parts of the nation in amounts that exceed long-term replenishment rates.

Water is a renewable resource, as it recycles through its three states of liquid, solid, and vapor; virtually none is gained or lost. Through the hydrologic cycle,[2] water continuously moves back and forth between the Earth's surface and the atmosphere. Evaporation occurs when the sun heats water in streams, rivers, lakes, and oceans, turning the water in vapor that then enters the atmosphere and forms clouds. Evaporation also removes impurities, such as salt, that were picked up naturally or result from human use. When the clouds can no longer hold the moisture, they release water in the form of rain or snow.

Water then returns to the Earth as rain, running into streams, rivers, lakes, and ultimately, the oceans. One hundred and ten thousand cubic kilometers of precipitation, about ten times the volume of Lake Superior, fall from the sky onto the Earth's land surface every year.[3] Of the precipitation that falls on the Earth's surface, about two-thirds rapidly evaporates directly back into the atmosphere; the remainder flows back into the nation's aboveground and underground water sources. Some rain soaks below the Earth's surface into aquifers, allowing the water to pass through and be stored as groundwater. Water also returns to the Earth as snow, usually remaining on the ground until it melts, then following the same path as rain; some snow may turn into glaciers that hold water for hundreds of years before melting. The replenishment rates for these sources vary considerably, water in rivers is completely renewed every sixteen days, on average, but the renewal periods for glaciers, groundwater, and the largest lakes can run from hundreds or thousands of years.[4]

Current and Future Water Scarcities in the United States

Nationwide, the United States currently enjoys plentiful water resources. Rainfall in the continental United States averages about thirty inches annually. This provides a renewable supply of about 1,400 billion gallons per day or 14 times the most recent governmental estimate of the nation's daily consumptive water use.[5]

Despite the abundance and renewability of the nation's freshwater supply, the hydrologic cycle creates uncertainties in the timing, location, and reliability of water supplies. Some regions in the United States are naturally arid and get less than one inch of water per year; while other regions are endowed with more than sixty inches of water a year.[6] Additionally, some regions receive the bulk of their rainfall, or snow melt runoff, at specific times during the year; while others get their rainfall more evenly over the year.

These problems were illustrated in 2002, when warmer than normal temperatures and below-average precipitation, led to a persistent or worsening drought throughout much of the United States. During the early part of the year, a moderate to extreme drought covered one-third of the nation and eventually expanded to cover more than half of the nation during the summer. Subsequently, heavy rainfall during July in Texas alleviated some of the drought conditions but brought about widespread flooding. In addition, above average rainfall from September through November led to significant drought relief in the Southeast, where more than four years of drought had affected much of the region from Georgia to Virginia. However, severe drought

43

conditions persisted over most of the interior western states and the central and northern plains, with the Midwest experiencing abnormal dryness through the end of the year.[7]

Rising demand on the nation's water resources as a result of population gains and economic growth presents supply problem. Estimates indicate that the U.S. population will likely increase to 392 million by 2050, more than a 50 percent rise from the nation's 1990 population size.[8] Most of this growth will occur in the western and southern United States and, more generally, in urban areas. Even prior to this period of population growth, the nation's capacity for storing surface freshwater is already reaching its limits in some areas; many groundwater supplies are being depleted.

A 2003 General Accounting Office study found that freshwater shortages are likely in the near future.[9] Under normal water conditions, state water managers in thirty-six states anticipated encountering local, regional, or statewide water shortages by 2013, if current water use continues unchecked. Under drought conditions, forty-six states could experience shortages during this period.

In particular, the southwestern United States faces "water stress" that occurs when water use outstrips sustainable supplies. These water shortages will result in severe economic and social impacts for this region.[10] The economic negatives include: losses in the agricultural and ranching sector, increased fire hazards, heightened mortality rates for livestock, and damage to fish habitats. These agricultural and ranching losses reduce farm and agribusiness income, increase food prices, contribute to higher unemployment, and require more spending for disaster relief. Water dependent industries, such as nurseries, suffer losses. In addition, hydroelectric power plants lack sufficient water supplies to meet operational needs. Water shortages also raise social concerns, including conflicts between (and among) water users for scarce water resources, threats to the lifestyles of those, such as farmers, whose livelihoods depend on water, and a reduced quality of life for millions of other people.

To begin addressing these concerns, Congress enacted the National Drought Policy Act of 1998.[11] The National Drought Policy Commission issued a report in 2000 recommending policies and programs designed to promote more coordinated responses by all levels of government to future droughts so as to mitigate adverse impacts.[12]

The American southwest, including Los Angeles, Las Vegas, and Phoenix, faces the likelihood an acute water scarcity this century.[13]

Water resources in these semi-arid regions of the United States are already stretched to the breaking point, the development of new water resources is difficult, and the population continues to grow rapidly. It is unclear whether the allocation of 90 percent of the region's water to agriculture is both "sustainable and consistent with the course of regional development."[14] The availability of water in this region will become a critical factor potentially limiting economic activity. Shortages of freshwater will force a reconsideration of water distribution programs; some going back a century ago, in what many now believe was an unusually wet period.

Much of the southwestern United States relies on the Colorado River as a significant water resource. The Colorado River system supplies water to thirty million people in seven states (California, Arizona, Nevada, Utah, Colorado, Wyoming, and New Mexico) and several million acres of crop and ranch land and supports fast-growing cities such as Los Angeles, San Diego, Phoenix, and Las Vegas. Over the years, Colorado River water resources have been allocated following the 1922 Colorado River Compact, which divided water supplies between the upper and lower basin states based on a period of flow unmatched in at least four hundred years. Under the Compact, the Upper Colorado River Basin, consisting of Colorado, New Mexico, Utah and Wyoming, must deliver to the three states in the Lower Basin, namely, Arizona, California, and Nevada, a minimum of 75 million acre-feet of water over each 10-year period. To deal with the lack of water to meet agreed upon allocations, in 2007, the seven states adopted a 20-year plan for the operation of Lake Powell and Lake Mead, and Lower Basin Shortages, reducing water deliveries to Arizona and Nevada but leaving California's water allocation unaffected.[15] The accord provides contingency plans if a shortage occurs to ensure conservation and manage water levels at the two lakes.

Las Vegas is probably the nation's metropolitan area most vulnerable to water shortages. The city has risen out of the barren landscape of the Mojave Desert, a region that receives only four inches of rain a year, becoming almost entirely dependent on water flows from a dwindling Colorado River. By 2007, the two massive reservoirs on the Colorado River, Lake Mead and Lake Powell, were only one half full. Lake Mead, the reservoir supplying 90 percent of Las Vegas' water has dropped about one percent a year since 1999, and could run dry by 2020. By 2012, the lake's surface could fall below an existing pipe that delivers forty percent of the city's water.[16]

Southern Californians in Los Angeles, Orange County, and San Diego must also worry. These centers of immense suburban sprawl exist in arid environments, similar to Las Vegas, dependent, in part, on the Colorado River. In 2009, California faced a third consecutive year of drought, resulting in water cutbacks across the state.[17] Over the past century, droughts lasting three years or more have been rare in California. Until 2009, the state recorded only two notable droughts: the Dust Bowl era from 1929 through 1934 and the six-year drought from 1987 through 1992. A dry 2008 spring in southern California, which followed 2007 when precipitation levels were only 15 and 30 percent of normal, left the runoff feeding the southern part of the state at an estimated 41 percent of typical levels. Snowpacks in the Sierra Mountains measured a meager 25 percent of normal only to return to 80 to 90 percent of average in early 2009. However, the state's major reservoirs remained half full in 2009, a series of storm systems in January 2010 helped replenish the state's water supply.[18]

Hydrology in California depends upon a winter snowpack from the Sierra Nevada mountains as well as water from the State Water Project, which draws on the Sacramento-San Joaquin River Delta in Northern California and the Colorado River, which runs along the state's southeast border. These water sources move water north and, especially, south, with about half of Southern California's water coming from the latter two sources, with the rest cobbled together from groundwater, recycled or surface water and water imports from elsewhere in the state.[19] Seventy-five percent of California's available water typically originates north of the San Francisco Bay area, but 75 percent of its water demand lies south of the bay area.[20]

Environmental restrictions curtail water supplies in California. In 2007, a federal court ordered water managers to protected an endangered species in the Sacramento-San Joaquin River Delta, in part, by limiting how much water is pumped through this source.[21] By forcing water authorities to curtail the use of large pumps in the delta to help preserve dying smelt, this judicial decision cut water shipments from Northern to Southern California by about 30 percent, reducing water flows to agriculture and resulting in dust-bowl-like conditions for many farms.

Looking to the future, snowpack, which feeds reservoirs and key water systems in California, likely will decline. California's Department of Water Resources forecasts a 25 percent Sierra Nevada snowpack reduction by 2050.[22] In addition to providing about fifty percent of

America's fruits, nuts, and vegetables, California has become one of the world's leading agricultural exporters, accounting for 15 percent of the nation's total agricultural exports,[23] by intensively farming a region that receives less than twenty inches of rain per year. A bleak future may lie ahead for the state's lucrative agricultural sector.

In an attempt to deal with the state's gloomy water future, in November 2009, the California legislature passed a sweeping water deal. The plan asks the state's voters in November 2010 to pass $11.1 billion in bonds to help finance new infrastructure and water system ecosystem restoration, with some $29 billion to be paid for by localities largely through new user fees. The bond deal includes about $3 billion for new storage projects, such as dams. The state's water supply will be buttressed through various steps such as mandatory monitoring of groundwater to help the state better manage its water supply and expanded conservation efforts, with a statewide target of a 20 percent reduction in urban per capita water use by 2020. A new state agency will unify efforts to improve the way water from California's north is channeled to the south via the Sacramento-San Joaquin River Delta. The new council will help clear the way for a canal to move water from the Sacramento River around the delta to aqueducts for use in urban and agricultural areas in the south.[24]

Other normally well-watered, fertile regions of the United States, such as Georgia, face water shortages resulting from short-term droughts, demand exceeding supply as a result of population growth, and limited access to new water supplies. Atlanta sucks water from the Chattahoochee River watershed in Tennessee and the Lake Lanier reservoir in Georgia. The quest of Atlanta's city leaders to secure water to feed the sprawling urban region has led to conflict with not only citizens of other portions of Georgia, but also other states, particularly Alabama and Florida.[25] Although metro Atlanta in 2008 came within 90 days of seeing its principal water supply, Lake Lanier, a federal reservoir, dry up, rainstorms eased the drought. Then in 2009, a federal judge ruled that almost all of the water Georgia has withdrawn from Lake Lanier was withdrawn illegally, because the lake was built to provide hydroelectric power.[26] The ruling, if upheld on appeal, means that Atlanta will likely need to find alternate sources of water, unless Georgia, Alabama, and Florida can end their water war.

The building of new, large reservoirs and dams has tapered off, since peaking during the 1960s, thereby limiting the amount of new surface freshwater storage. Throughout the nation, dams that support reservoirs are aging and are in need repairs. Sedimentation also threatens the existing surface freshwater storage. Sedimentary deposits, including soil, rock and other natural materials, continue to fill massive reservoirs constructed during the past century. It is unclear what will happen as U.S. reservoirs fill with sediment and can no longer fulfill their original purpose.[27]

In addition to concerns about the nation's surface water resources, significant groundwater depletion has occurred in many parts of the nation. Groundwater provides about 40 percent of the nation's drinking water supply and 37 percent of the water used for irrigation and livestock.[28] Regions in the United States also pump aquifer water for more high-tech purposes; semiconductor manufacturers use massive quantities of de-ionized freshwater to produce their products. In addition to overpumping, aquifers are also being polluted with chemical runoff from farming and mining, raising a public health concern for the ten of millions of Americans who draw their own drinking water from wells. Groundwater depletion has occurred in many areas of the United States. Aquifers are rapidly being depleted, including the Sparta Aquifer (in Arkansas, Louisiana, and Mississippi), the Cambrian-Ordovician Aquifer (in the Chicago-Milwaukee area), and the High Plains Aquifer, mainly the Ogallala Aquifer.

The Ogallala Aquifer is a deep geologic formation sprawling underneath eight states from South Dakota to Texas. This aquifer underlies a huge 174,000 square mile region, including parts of eight states, Colorado, Kansas, Nebraska, New Mexico, Oklahoma, South Dakota, Texas, and Wyoming. It supplies about 30 percent of all groundwater used in the United States for irrigation.[29]

After World War II, technology enabled pumping the Ogallala Aquifer, turning the High Plains into a productive agricultural region. Its massive water reserves led to the growth of water intensive uses in the area. The Ogallala Aquifer gets little natural replenishment; yet over 200,000 borewells work 24/7 removing water from it.

Intense use of the groundwater from the Ogallala Aquifer has resulted in major water level declines and has reduced groundwater remaining in storage. In the central and southern High Plains, the Ogallala Aquifer holds less than one half the water it held prior to the beginning of groundwater pumping.[30] Water is being drawn down at an unsustainable rate. Estimates place the water depletion in the Ogallala Aquifer at from eight to fourteen times faster than nature can restore it.[31]

Depleting aquifers in coastal areas of the United States may result in saltwater intrusion, making the water unsuitable for drinking and irrigation. In particular, saltwater intrusion has occurred in Florida (the Jacksonville, Miami and Tampa areas), Georgia (the Brunswick and Savannah areas), South Carolina (on Hilton Head Island) and various coastal counties in New Jersey.[32]

Even under normal conditions the United States faces a growing crisis with respect to its water supply. The southwest has experienced droughts in recent years that have grown in both intensity and duration. These droughts have led to major concerns over surface water supplies, for example, the snowpack that feeds the Colorado River. As populations boom in growing cities, such as Los Angeles and Las Vegas, water resources will be stretched even further. In other areas of the country with significant groundwater resources, pumping aquifers at unsustainable levels presents a dangerous game. The next section examines how climate change could put further stress on the nation's water supplies.

The Potential Impact of Climate Change on U.S. Water Supplies

Climate change, many assert, will further exacerbate water stress in the United States. The potential impacts include: changes in snowpack accumulation, melting, runoff patterns, sea-level rise, and droughts. Snowpack may decrease if the climate warms. More precipitation may fall as rain, and snowpacks will develop later and melt earlier. Other potential changes include an increased possibility of winter and early spring flooding, and more summer water shortages. Extended droughts may reduce the reasonably expected safe yields from water sources. Large swaths of the arid southwest may become hotter and drier. Weather changes may affect the hydrological system and the demand for water.

Global warming advocates claim that the buildup of carbon dioxide in the atmosphere, resulting from the burning of fossil fuels, increases the greenhouse effect, leading directly to a warm-up in global temperatures, which will accelerate over time and produce disastrous consequences. Proponents of the global warming apocalypse gained a powerful scientific ally with the publication of the Fourth Assessment Report by the Intergovernmental Panel on Climate Change (IPCC).[33] The 2007 report concluded that human-made climate change is real. Even previous, global warming skeptics, such as Bjorn Lomborg, a

Danish statistician, now concede it is getting hotter and that humanity has caused it, due mainly to emissions from carbon-based fuels.[34]

The World Meteorological Organization and the United Nations Environment Programme established the IPCC in 1988. The IPCC's formation represented an effort by Third World nations to gain restitution from developed nations for pollution resulting from industrial activity. The IPCC strives to assess on a comprehensive basis scientific, technical, and socioeconomic materials relevant to understanding the risk of human-induced climate change, its potential effects, and the options for adaptation and mitigation. The IPCC does not carry out its own research. Its assessment is based primarily on peer-reviewed, published scientific and technical literature. Its mission focuses on proving that there is (and will be) global warming. Once the IPCC was established, it had to document human climate change to validate its existence and gain continued funding for its activities.[35]

The IPCC and former U.S. Vice President Albert (Al) Gore, Jr. jointly received the 2007 Nobel Peace Prize. The Nobel committee praised Mr. Gore and the IPCC for alerting the world to a potential catastrophe resulting from global warming allegedly caused by increasing carbon dioxide emissions.[36]

Global Aspects of the 2007 IPCC Report. With respect to water scarcity, two aspects of the 2007 report are of interest: first, global surface temperatures and second, the impact of global warming on the hydrologic systems. According to the IPCC's 2007 Fourth Assessment Report, the global mean surface temperatures have increased by 0.74 degrees Celsius (C) over the past one hundred years. Additionally, warming rates are accelerating. The warming rate over the past fifty years was nearly twice as fast as over the past 100 years. Eleven out of twelve of the warmest years since 1850 occurred between 1995 and 2006, illustrating an alarming trend.[37]

The report concluded that the warming of the Earth's climate is "unequivocal" based on "observations of increased global average air and ocean temperatures, widespread melting of snow and ice and rising global average sea level."[38] The report also asserted that global warming is producing long-term impacts on natural systems and that human activity is "very likely," with at least a 90 percent confidence level, causing most of the rise in global average temperatures since 1950.[39] In other words, since the mid-twentieth century most of the rise in global average temperatures resulted from an increase in human-induced greenhouse gas concentrations, in particular carbon dioxide.

The IPCC projected a further 1 degree Fahrenheit (0.6 degrees C) increase in the global mean temperature, relative to the 1980-1999 period, by the end of the twenty-first century, even if greenhouse gas concentrations remain at 2000 levels. The IPCC also predicted an average rise in global temperatures of between 2 to 12 degrees F (1.1 to 6.4 degrees C), based on an examination of a range of greenhouse gas emissions scenarios.[40]

The 2007 IRCC Report concluded with "high confidence" that global warming currently impacts the hydrologic system in two ways: first, increasing runoff and earlier spring peak discharge in many glacier- and snow-fed rivers, and second, warming of many lakes and rivers, with an adverse impact on water quality.[41] Looking to the future, freshwater systems are among the most vulnerable sectors as a result of climate change. On a global basis, the report predicted that by the middle of the twenty-first century that annual average river runoff and water availability would increase by 10 to 40 percent at high latitudes, and in some wet tropical areas, but decrease by 10 to 30 percent over some dry regions at mid-latitudes and in the dry topics. Semi-arid subtropical regions could face a further 20 percent drop in rainfall, under a mid-range outlook for greenhouse gas emissions. Drought-affected areas would likely increase in extent. During this century, the report projected that water supplies stored in glaciers and snow would decline, thereby reducing the availability of water in regions supplied by meltwater from major mountain ranges.[42]

Globally, coasts would be exposed to increasing risks, including coastal erosion and sea level rise. Although not providing a best estimate, the IPCC estimated that seas globally will rise somewhere between .18 and .59 meters, depending on greenhouse gas emission levels, during the next 100 years.[43] Additionally, as sea levels rise, they will obliterate more wetlands; wetlands are vitally important because they filter dirt and toxins before they reach rivers, lakes, and aquifers.

Because of higher water temperatures, more floods and droughts will adversely impact water quality. This trend will exacerbate many forms of water pollution, including sediments, pathogens, pesticides, and salt, as well as thermal pollution, resulting in negative conse-quences for ecosystems, human health, and water system reliability and operating costs.[44]

The 2007 IPCC Report and the United States. With respect to the impact of global warming in the United States, the IPCC report forecasted changes in the hydrologic cycle and sea levels. Specifically, in the western United States the snowpack will be smaller and melt earlier, causing stream flows to rise earlier and high flows to dissipate faster. With less snow melting in the spring, less freshwater will be available for capture. Groundwater systems in the southwest will experience decreased recharge. In addition, droughts will become more extensive, accompanied by increased evaporation and even greater demands on water for irrigation. The combination of an earlier snowmelt and more precipitation will likely increase turbidity (water opaqueness), sedimentation, and the risk of flooding.[45]

Rising sea levels will pose a heightened risk of flood damage to coastal water and wastewater facilities in the eastern and western United States, especially resulting from more intense storms. The combination of rising sea levels and lower water flows in freshwater sources will increase the salinity of coastal aquifers and salty (more technically, brackish) surface water sources.[46] Warming temperatures will also adversely impact the operations of existing water infrastructure, including flood defenses as well as drainage and irrigation systems.

U.S. Government Studies of Climate Change

The United States government has conducted its own studies of the impact of climate change on the nation. Three reports by the U.S. Climate Change Science Program, established in 1990 to coordinate the climate research of thirteen different federal agencies, build upon and reinforce the conclusions of the 2007 IPCC report. First, a 2008 scientific assessment by the U.S. Climate Change Science Program, commissioned by the U.S. Department of Agriculture, examined how climate change is reshaping the American landscape. The report highlighted how human-generated carbon dioxide emissions from the burning of fossil fuels had already been translated into a reduced mountain snowpack in the western United States, resulting in an earlier spring snow melt runoff and decreases in annual runoff.[47] The report predicted that from 2040 to 2060 anticipated water flows from rainfall in much of the interior west (Colorado River and Great Basin) may approach a 20 percent drop in the average from 1901 to 1970. In addition to a dearth of water, the west faces large shifts in when it is available. By mid-century, mountain snows that provide a steady flow of spring and summer runoff will dwindle, shifting the availability of water resources in many areas.[48]

Second, subsequent report by the U.S. Geological Survey, commissioned by the U.S. Climate Change Science Program, concluded that the nation faces the possibility of much more rapid climate change by 2100 than previous studies had suggested.[49] The report's worrisome findings projected that in light of recent ice sheet melting, global sea levels could rise by as much as four feet by the end of this century, although recognizing that predictions are uncertain because of shortcomings in existing climate models.[50] Assessing the prospect for prolonged droughts over the next hundred years, the report concluded that the southwestern United States will likely be consistently drier, at least during the next several decades, with severe and persistent droughts possibly lasting more than a decade. Colorado River flow may drop by up to 25 percent. The reduced flow in the Colorado River, among other southwestern rivers, comes when currently the existing flow is fully allocated and the region's population is increasing.[51]

Finally, a 2009 report provided an even more detailed picture of the United States in 2100.[52] It repeated the familiar refrain: warming of the climate is "unequivocal" and human-made greenhouse gases are primarily the cause. The report predicted that average U.S. temperatures nationwide would increase by 4.0 to 11.0 degrees F, under various emission scenarios, by the end of this century, with sea levels rising three feet, and with northern areas becoming wetter and southern areas, especially in the west, becoming drier.[53] This report also provided a forecast of regional climate impacts. By the late twenty-first century, in the Northeast sea levels would rise more than the global averages. In the Southeast, decreased water availability would lead to a decline in groundwater recharging, and depleting aquifers, placing an increased strain on surface water resources, with saltwater intrusion into shallow aquifers as well as sea level rises resulting in the inundation, erosion, and salinity of wetlands and estuaries. The Southwest would face increasingly scarce water supplies and more severe droughts.[54]

The Impact of Global Warming: Additional Studies

Dangerous consequences could be triggered and persist for a long time, even if global emissions are reduced or eliminated. Although several greenhouse gases trap the sun's energy near the Earth's surface, the heat-trapping properties of carbon dioxide are critical. Because of the time scales associated with climate processes and feedbacks, anthropogenic warming, leading to sea level rise and drought conditions,

53

would continue for centuries even if greenhouse gas concentrations are stabilized.[55]

Greenhouse gas levels currently expected by 2050 may produce long-term, Dust-Bowl-like droughts that may persist for 1,000 years even if the world curbs future carbon dioxide emissions. A team of researchers from the United States, Switzerland, and France concluded that carbon dioxide will remain at near peak levels in the atmosphere, far longer than other greenhouse gases. The study projected that if carbon dioxide concentrations peak at 600 parts per million, up from the current, roughly 385 parts per million, the southwestern United States will face major droughts as bad (or even worse than) the 1930s Dust Bowl. For a 2-degree C increase in global warming, the American Southwest could experience a 10 percent drop in rainfall, a precipitous drop seen in major, past droughts, such as the Dust Bowl. Because of the way carbon dioxide, which, according to these researchers, is responsible for one half of greenhouse gas warming, persists in the atmosphere, patterns exist to produce Dust-Bowl-like droughts for at least one thousand years.[56]

The Energy-Water Nexus

The energy-water nexus represents an important consideration as the United States seeks to decrease its reliance on foreign energy sources and fossil fuels. Water is a heavy commodity. Large amounts of energy power the pumps required to extract water from aquifers, move groundwater as well as freshwater supplies through pipelines, and then distribute it for agricultural, industrial, and residential uses. Wastewater treatment and transmission also require high energy levels.

Water and wastewater utilities account for a not insignificant share of the nation's electricity consumption. About 4 percent of the power generated in the United States goes for water supply treatment and distribution as well as wastewater treatment. Because water is pumped over long distances in California, the number closer to 5 percent in that state.[57]

Energy comprises about 75 percent of the cost of drinking water processing and distribution because of the need to maintain pressure in the system. Water and wastewater utilities spend about $4 billion a year to pump, treat, deliver, and clean water. These functions can amount to as much as one-third of a typical municipality's energy bill. The agriculture industry in the United States spends between $1 and

$2 billion a year to pump groundwater for irrigation, which accounts for about 1.5 percent of total U.S. energy consumption, with 20 percent of that total concentrated in California.

The energy-water nexus represents an interesting interplay. As population increases and the demand for water rises, more and more energy will be needed to exploit dwindling water resources. Some of the scarce water resources will be required to produce the energy needed to extract the water. As more energy is used, carbon dioxide emissions in the atmosphere will increase, further exacerbating global warming, according to the IPCC and U.S. government reports. More global warming will lead to even greater water scarcity through long-term droughts and changes in runoff and precipitation, among other impacts.

A number of experts and scientific data support the existence of a global warming trend with its multiplicity of adverse impacts. However, a vocal minority of climate changes researchers have sought to refute the existence of anthropogenic warming.

Criticism of the Global Warming Hypothesis

Two points are not in dispute.[58] First, over the past century or so, global mean temperatures have increased by one degree Fahrenheit, rising significantly from about 1919 to 1940, decreasing between 1940 and the early 1970s, when atmospheric carbon dioxide levels increased rapidly, rising again until the late 1990s, and remaining flat, if not decreasing, since 1998. Over the last four decades, there was probably 0.2 degree C increase in global warming. Throughout the world, great cities were built up. Urban heat islands came into existence. The impact of global warming on cities, according to Lomborg, "will be considerably worse because they will be hit by a double whammy—temperature increases from both CO2 and from still increasing urban hear islands," as "[b]ricks, concrete, and asphalt, which dominate cities, absorb much more heat than vegetation does in the countryside."[59] Second, during the last century, the levels of carbon dioxide in the atmosphere have increased from about 280 parts per million by volume (ppmv) to about 387 ppmv. These two points lead to a key question: does more carbon dioxide result in more trapped warmth?

The global warming hypothesis rests on the correlation between the levels of present and future carbon dioxide emissions and temperature trends. In brief, the hypothesis assumes that the atmosphere, especially water vapor and high clouds, amplify the impact of carbon dioxide, resulting result in a large temperature increase. In other words, the rise in carbon dioxide in the atmosphere greatly magnifies the greenhouse warming of water vapor by letting in sunlight and blocking the escape of some of the resulting heat.

No one denies that carbon dioxide in the atmosphere is increasing. Our modern global economy, powered by fossil fuels, sends carbon dioxide in the atmosphere. We drive gasoline-powered cars and fly in airplanes that release carbon dioxide. We use coal to generate electricity to power our homes and offices. As a result mainly of carbon-based energy sources, atmospheric carbon dioxide is increasing. Humans also produce carbon dioxide when we breathe. As the world's population increases, there is more carbon dioxide. But, what if despite the carbon dioxide increases, global temperatures remain the same, or even cool?

Global Temperature Trends. Recent evidence may refute the linkage between the carbon dioxide increases and average worldwide (and United States) temperatures. At least over the short-term, global temperature may be cooling, not warming. A natural cycle of climate warming and cooling may exist. The earth is either warming or cooling, even without any human forcing.

Nature may be the dominant force in climate change during the late twentieth century. Ocean cycles, not carbon dioxide, may be the single best explanation for temperature variations. The surge in global temperatures starting in 1977 may be attributed, in large part, to a 1976 climate shift in the Pacific Ocean that made warming (El Niño) conditions more likely than they were during the prior thirty years and cooling (La Niña) conditions less likely.[60]

A significant warming trend may have peaked in 1998, an exceptionally hot year, followed by a cooling trend. Observations from weather satellites have not shown any global warming since 1998; rather they reveal a decline, returning the world to the temperatures prevailing in the late 1980s and early 1990s.[61]

The year 2008 was a relatively cool one on Earth. Although average global temperature in 2008 ranked as the tenth warmest in the annuals of reliable record keeping since 1850, it was the coolest since the turn of the twenty-first century.[62] Global temperatures in 2008 ran slightly less than one degree warmer than the mean temperature for the twentieth century.[63] It is uncertain whether the short-term temperature drop signifies a trend lasting decades or only a temporary dip. However, based on the natural cycle of ocean currents, technically, the Atlantic Multidecadal Oscillation, one study predicted that global surface temperatures may not increase over the next decade, with shifting Atlantic Ocean currents cooling parts of North America.[64]

Sea Level Aspects. Researchers, who doubt future catastrophic sea level increases, maintain that the mean rate of global sea level rise has not accelerated recently and probably has fallen.[65] Any increases furthermore, may reflect only periodic fluctuations, not a sustained, long-term increase. With respect to any analysis of global sea level changes, it is important to remember that even if global average sea levels can be estimated accurately, local sea level changes are the most important factor for planners and policymakers.

The poster children for rising sea levels are low-lying coral islands, such as the island nation of the Maldives. Over the past thirty years, sea levels at the Maldives, once condemned to disappear soon into the ocean, have fallen by 20 to 30 centimeters.[66]

Impact of Temperature Trends for Policymakers

Although the impact of global warming may not be as dire as some predict and will likely vary regionally within the United States, climate change will still add complexity and unpredictability to America's water-management efforts. At present, policymakers, however, face a quandary. As we see how complicated atmospheric and climate science is, dependent on many factors, the intense debate over warming has slowed the nation's response. Assuming that we do not face catastrophe in the coming decades, the scientific debate on the extent of global warming and its implications should continue.[67] We need further credible study and more research into the facts. At present, the possible negative impact of temperature increases ought to be addressed through policies designed to facilitate more innovation, new technologies,[68] and enhanced energy efficiency.

Public Sector Approaches to Water Scarcity:
Conservation Measures

Leaving aside the possible impact of global climate change, parts of the United States currently face (and likely will encounter future) water scarcities in the form of intermittent droughts and/or permanent shortages. Shortages will arise from increasing demand resulting from population growth and a variety of human needs, including leisure and amenity uses, as well as a lack of water availability. Aging infrastructure compounds these shortages, a topic considered in more detail Chapter 6.

Basically, there are two possible approaches to deal with water scarcity: the implementation of new technologies developed, manufactured and marketed by private firms (a topic considered in the next chapter) and water demand management, in other words, voluntary or mandatory consumption restrictions. This section briefly surveys water conservation techniques implemented by the public sector.

Voluntary Approaches to Water Conservation. The public sector can take several distinct, but reinforcing, approaches to promote water conservation. Conservation incentives increase customer awareness regarding the benefits of reducing water use. Incentives that motivate water users to implement efficiency measures consist of three categories: educational, financial, and regulatory.[69]

Education makes the public aware of the benefits and opportunities of adopting water-saving technologies and strategies, including improved hardware and behavior-driven usage modifications. In a move to educate the public on water-saving opportunities, the U.S. Environmental Protection Agency created the WaterSense program to help consumers identify water efficient products and services.[70] For example, the program labels toilets and faucets that use less water but perform as well or better than standard models. By replacing older toilets with WaterSense labeled models, individuals can save 4,000 gallons of water per year, and a family of four can reduce their water bills by some $90 per year. Among other conservation possibilities, the program provides suggestions for reducing outdoor watering uses.[71] States and localities have also undertaken numerous programs to educate consumers on a water-use ethic.

The public sector uses financial incentives to promote conservation. For example, the Southern Nevada Water Authority instituted its Water Smart Landscapes Rebate program in 1999 to reduce water use. The voluntary program provides incentives for existing residential and commercial property owners to replace aesthetic turf with water efficient landscaping.[72] In 2009, following the lead of the Southern Nevada Water Authority, the Los Angeles Department of Water and Power's (DWP) implemented a Residential Drought Resistant Landscape Incentive Program. Single-family homes served by the DWP will receive one dollar for every square foot of turf they replace with less water thirsty alternatives, including drought tolerant plants, mulch, or permeable ground cover.[73]

The public sector also uses the price mechanism to reduce the demand for water.[74] Effective rate structures play an essential role in signaling to customers the cost of providing water and promoting more efficient use. The traditional declining block rate structure, which charged lower rates per incremental volume of water used, rewarded the highest water users with the lowest rates. Conversely, increasing water rates provide a strong incentive for users to reduce use. Through an increasing block rate design, for example, the unit price for water rises as the volume use increases, with prices set for each "block" of water over the allotted amount. Localities implement a price structure in which a specified percentage, say 75 percent, of the water a business or residence uses is kept at current rates; while a premium rate is imposed on any water use over that percentage. Other types of pricing to encourage conservation include seasonal rates.

Mandatory Approaches to Water Conservation. Beyond voluntary consumption reduction campaigns and financial incentives designed to decrease water usage, the public sector has imposed mandatory restrictions that require the use of efficient technology or limit water use. Federal laws provide national water-efficiency standards for plumbing fixtures. To reduce wasteful water use, the Energy Policy Act of 1992[75] established mandatory national allowable water-flow rates for plumbing fixtures. For example, all toilets manufactured in the United States after January 1, 1994 must be low-volume fixtures that use no more than 1.6 gallons per flush, about one-quarter of the amount of water traditionally used. Shower heads manufactured after that date cannot pump out more than 2.5 gallons of water per minute, less than one half the flow that was common until then.

Facing acute shortages, states and localities have implemented mandatory restrictions on water use, including prohibiting outdoor watering during the hottest times of the day. Failure to follow these mandatory regulations can result in adverse financial consequences to those who disobey them.

In 2008, for example, Los Angeles approved revisions to its existing Water Conservation Ordinance to discourage water misuse by expanding the prohibited uses of water and increasing penalties. Customers were barred from watering lawns or outdoor landscape during the daytime (between 9 a.m. and 4 p.m.). The ordinance doubled the fines for residential first-time offenders.[76] Then, in 2009, the city limited residents' sprinkler usage to two days a week.[77] The Los Angeles Department of Water and Power resorted to having civil representatives issue citations, only a few of which carry a fine, to those who violate the city's water ordinances. These citations increase the awareness of the water ordinances, but are not designed to raise revenues.[78]

Water Management Approaches. States and localities have also undertaken broader measures focused on more comprehensive conservation efforts and water management planning. The Atlanta, Georgia region offers an example of a broad conservation program, along with implementation difficulties.

Prior to 2003, half of the local water districts in the Atlanta region lacked any conservation programs. Those districts with programs focused on education.

Then, in 2003, in response to a growing drought, the Metropolitan North Georgia Water Planning District, planners for the Atlanta region, developed a comprehensive water management approach to coordinate water, sewage, and storm water plans across a jumble of bureaucracies within its sixteen county border. With respect to conservation, the plan recommended implementation of the following measures: establishing conservation pricing; enacting legislation to require plumbing retrofits on home sales and low-flush urinals for non-residential buildings; enacting legislation to require rain sensor shut-off switches on new irrigation systems; requiring sub-unit meters in new multi-family buildings; assessing and reducing distribution system losses; conducting residential and commercial water audits; distributing low-flow retrofit kits to residential users; and developing education programs.[79] Public education, conservation pricing, and leak detection programs were implemented. However, as of December 2007, even in the midst of a severe drought, only a handful of counties had established residential plumbing retrofit programs. Incentive programs to replace appliances, such as dishwashers and clothes washers, had not been created. A 2009 update introduced only two new conservation measures, requiring government buildings to install ultra-low-flow toilets and urinals and mandating newly built carwashes recycle their water.[80]

Jurisdictions may coordinate the management of surface and groundwater resources to assist in meeting current and future needs. In January 2008, the Georgia Water Council and then the Georgia General Assembly adopted the state's first-ever water management plan.[81] The plan requires a three-year assessment of the state's supply-demand requirements before deciding on how to allocate water from the state's rivers, lakes, and aquifers among its eleven water districts.

The assessment will determine how much water can be removed and how treated sewage can be returned to a water source without ruining the resource. On completion of the study, the Georgia Environmental Protection Division and the regional water districts will use the information, together with population projections, to divide the available water among the districts, with each district allocating the allotted water among various users, residential, agricultural, and industrial.

Water Conservation and Usage

Until the late 1970s, total U.S. freshwater withdrawals rose rapidly in the post-World War II era.[82] The term "water withdrawal" refers to the removal of water from a surface water or groundwater source to meet a human need with some return to the original source despite changes in quantity and quality. Over the past three decades or so, water withdrawals nationally have leveled off. Since the late 1970s, in the face of a U.S. population increase of some one hundred million people per capita withdrawals have declined by about 25 percent. Two major factors account for less water use per person (and also less water use in the United States in total): first, changes in water use efficiency; and second, changes in the structure of the American economy. Consumers became more efficient water users. As noted in the prior section, national standards have reduced the amount of water required to flush a toilet, among other plumbing fixtures. Competitive economic pressures and federal water quality discharge regulations (the latter discussed in Chapter 2) led to water-use decline in steel production, among other processes. Reducing the volume of water used offered one of the least costly ways of meeting federal water quality standards. The drop in per capita water use also resulted from decreases in water withdrawals for irrigation and various industrial uses, such as power plant cooling. Those reductions significantly outweighed the modest, regular increases in water withdrawals for residential uses.

Changes in the U.S. economy played a part in reducing industrial water use. The economy became less dependent on water-intensive industries, such as manufacturing, and more a function of sectors requiring less water per unit of output, such as telecommunications and services.

Despite these gains, achieved, in part, by conservation, the United States remains the world's most wasteful water user, as ranked by the Water Poverty Index.[83] The United States achieved its bottom level ranking as a result of the nation's inefficient use of its water resources.

Despite the nation's water wastefulness, a water conservation ethic is gradually seeping into the country's consciousness. Conservation and demand management programs reduce or postpone the need for system expansion and the accompanying capital financing considered in Chapter 6. Water conservation is generally less expansive than developing new supplies. Even the U.S. Bureau of Reclamation has in recent years concentrated more on promoting water use efficiency than on building new dams and reservoirs, a marked departure from the past. As the main operator of federal water projects in the western United States, the bureau encourages efficient water use through a variety of programs.[84] The bureau's new focus on water resource management includes a series of water conservation initiatives undertaken by its Water Conservation Field Services Program designed to improve the reliability of existing water supplies and reduce drought impacts as well as limit point and non-point sources of pollution.

Conservation does, however, have one possible drawback. Conservation and demand management increase the financial risks for water utilities. As users work smarter to use less water, revenues paid to public sector water agencies in some U.S. regions have fallen leading to declining revenues, a new and an unanticipated problem. Revenue shortfalls place an even greater financial burden on the public sector. Fewer funds are available to invest in badly needed water supply infrastructure, a topic considered in Chapter 6.

We next consider how water scarcity drives technological development and private sector efforts in this sector. Technologies can boost water supplies and offer improved efficiencies in water use. Smarter, more efficient, more sustainable use of existing water resources will serve as a new supply sources and postpone the day of reckoning in the United States.

Notes

1. David Seckler et al., World Water Demand and Supply, 1990 to 2025: Scenarios and Issues, International Water Management Institute, 1998, Research Report, 19 and David Seckler, Randolph Barker, Upali Amarasingshe, "Water Scarcity in the Twenty-First Century," *Water Resources Development* 15:1/2 (March-June 1999): 29-42.
2. For background on the hydrological cycle see Leonard S. Hyman et al., *The Water Business: Understanding the Water Supply and Wastewater Industry* (Vienna, VA: Public Utilities Reports, 1998), 6-11.

3. Peter Rogers, "Facing the Freshwater Crisis," *Scientific American* 299:2 (August 2008): 46-53, at 48.

4. U.S. General Accounting Office (GAO), Freshwater Supply: States' Views of How Federal Agencies Could Help Them Meet the Challenges of Expected Shortages, July 2003, GAO-03-514, 15.

5. The statistics in this paragraph are from *ibid.* at 13.

6. *Ibid.*, at 15.

7. *Ibid., at 17.*

8. U.S. Census Bureau, "Population Profile of the United States," <www.census. gov/population/www/pop-profile/natproj.html> (March 17, 2009).

9. GAO, Freshwater Supply, 5, 8, 64.

10. *Ibid.*, 5, 67-74.

11. Public Law 105-199.

12. National Drought Policy Commission, Preparing for Drought in the 21st Century, May 2000.

13. Edward R. Cook et al., "Long-Term Aridity Changes in the Western United States," *Science* 306:5 (November 5, 2004): 1015-1018. For a history of water in the western United States see Marc Reisner, *Cadillac Desert: The American West and Its Disappearing Water,* Revised edition (New York: Penguin, 1993). Jon Gertner, "The Future is Drying Up," *New York Times Magazine*, October 21, 2007, provides an overview of the drought in the American West.

14. U.S. Climate Change Science Program and the Subcommittee on Global Change Research, Abrupt Climate Change, Final Report Synthesis and Assessment Product 3.4, December 2008, 148.

15. U.S. Secretary of the Interior, Record of Decision, Colorado River Interim Guidelines for Lower Basin Shortages and Coordinated Operations of Lake Powell and Lake Mead, December 2007. See also Randal C. Archibold, "Western States Agree To Water-Sharing Pact," *New York Times,* December 10, 2007, A18 and Ashley Peters, "Colorado River water deal is reached," *Los Angeles Times*, December 14, 2007, A16.

16. Urban Land Institute and Ernst & Young, *Infrastructure 2008: A Competitive Advantage* (Washington, DC: Urban Land Institute 2008), 37; John Lippert and Jim Efstathiou Jr., "Running Dry," *Bloomberg Markets* 18:4 (April 2009): 98-108, at 98-99, 103, 105; Felicity Barringer, "Lake Mead Could Be Within a Few Years of Going Dry, Study Finds," *New York Times*, February 18, 2008, A18; Felicity Barringer, "Water Use in Southwest Heads for a Day of Reckoning," *New York Times*, September 28, 2010, A14.

17. Jim Carlton, "Shrinking Water Supplies Imperil Farmers," *Wall Street Journal*, February 10, 2009, A4 and Hector Becerra, "'Rain year' comes up dry, *Los Angeles Times,* June 30, 2009, A3.

18. I have drawn on *Economist*, "Dust to dust" 390:8621 (March 7, 2009):39; Bettina Boxall, "Drought yes, but it's not that bad," *Los Angeles Times*, March 3, 2009, A1; Stu Woo, "In California, Hot Dry Conditions Stir Drought Concerns," *Wall Street Journal*, January 14, 2009, A4; Heather Cooley, "Every Drop Counts," *Los Angeles Times*, February 10, 2008, M9;

Bettina Boxall, "By every measure, its been dry," *Los Angeles Times*, March 31, 2007, A1.

19. Sabrina Shankman, "California Gives Desalination Plants a Fresh Look," *Wall Street Journal*, July 9, 2009, A4.

20. Wade Graham, "A Hundred Rivers Run Through It," *Harper's* 296: 1777 (June 1998): 51-60, at 51.

21. Natural Resources Defense Council v. Kempthorne, 506 Federal Supplement 2d 322, Case No. 1:05-CV-01207 OWW (TAG), United States District Court, Eastern District of California, May 25, 2007 and Natural Resources Defense Council v. Kempthorne, 2007 WL 4462391 (E.D. Cal.), United Stated District Court, Eastern District of California, December 14, 2007. See also Jim Carlton, "Parched State Searches for Ways to Expand Water Supply," *Wall Street Journal*, July 9, 2009, A4; Bettina Boxall, "U.S. tightens tap on water from N. Calif.," *Los Angeles Times*, December 16, 2008, B3; Eric Bailey, "Smelt ruling may cut into water supply," *Los Angeles Times*, September 1, 2007, B1; Bettina Boxall, "State shuts off delta water to protect smelt," *Los Angeles Times*, June 1, 2007, B4; Bettina Boxall "Judge rules against water system," *Los Angeles Times*, May 26, 2007, B3.

22. State of California, Department of Water Resources, Climate Change in California, June 2007.

23. Heather Cooley, Juliet Christian-Smith, Peter H. Gleick, More with Less: Agricultural Water Conservation and Efficiency in California, Pacific Institute, June 2008, 11.

24. Jennifer Steinhauer, "California Water Overhaul Caps Use and Paves Way for a Canal," *New York Times*, November 5, 2009, A16; Jim Carlton, "California Passes Water Deal," *Wall Street Journal*, November 5, 2009, A3; Bettina Boxall, "Legislators strike major water deal," *Los Angeles Times*, November 5, 2009, A1.

25. Cornelia Dean, "Southeast Drought Study Ties Water Shortage to Population, Not Global Warming," *New York Times*, October 2, 2009, A13; Alison Young, "Georgia's Water Crisis," *Atlanta Journal-Constitution*, December 5, 2007, A1; Stacy Shelton, "'Historic' Drought," *Atlanta Journal-Constitution*, June 29, 2007, A1; Stacey Shelton, "Atlanta water supply precarious," *Atlanta Journal-Constitution*, June 27, 2005, E1. For a summary of water resource development in Atlanta see Thomas W. Fitzhugh and Brain D. Richter, "Quenching Urban Thirst," *BioScience* 54:8 (August 1, 2004): 741-654, at 749-750.

26. In re Tri-State Water Rights Litigation, Case No. 3:07-md-01 (PAM/JRK), 639 Federal Supplement 2d 1308 (Middle District of Florida, July 17, 2009). See also Shaila Dewan, "A Dispute Over a River Basin Is Pitting Atlanta Against its Neighbors," *New York Times*, August 16, 2009, 12 and Dan Chapman and Leon Stafford, "Will water ruling dry up growth?" *Atlanta Journal-Constitution*, July 24, 2009, A1.

27. GAO, Freshwater Supply, 48-50.

28. *Ibid.*, 50.

29. Maude Barlow, *Blue Covenant: The Global Water Crisis and the Coming Battle for the Right to Water* (New York: New Press, 2007), 12. For a history

of the Ogallala Aquifer and High Plains farming see John Opie, *Ogallala: Water for a Dry Season*, Second Edition (Lincoln: University of Nebraska, 2000).

30. GAO, Freshwater Supply, 5, 52.

31. *Economist*, "Irrigate and die" 368:8333 (July 19, 2003): 11-13, at 12 and Maude Barlow and Tony Clarke, *Blue Gold: The Fight to Stop the Corporate Theft of the World's Water* (New York: New Press, 2002), 16.

32. GAO, Freshwater Supply, 56.

33. Intergovernmental Panel on Climate Change (IPCC), *Climate Change 2007: Synthesis Report*, 2008 *(Synthesis Report)* and IPCC, *Climate Change 2007: The Physical Science Basis, Contribution of Working Group I to the Fourth Assessment Report of the Intergovernmental Panel on Climate Change* (New York: Cambridge University, 2007)*(Working Group I Report)*. See also Elizabeth Rosenthal and Andrew C. Revkin, "Science Panel Says Global Warming is 'Unequivocal,'" *New York Times*, February 3, 2007, A1 and Sharon Begley, "Latest Report Shows Climate Pessimists Were Climate Realists," *Wall Street Journal*, February 9, 2007, B1.

34. Bjørn Lomborg, *Cool It: The Skeptical Environmentalist's Guide to Global Warming* (New York: Knopf, 2007), xi, 11-13. See also, Bjørn Lomborg, "A Chilling View of Warming," *Wall Street Journal*, September 13-14, 2008, W1.

35. For a critical view of the IPCC held by many climate change skeptics see Robert Cheetham, "IPCC History" <appinsys.com/Global Warming/GW History.htm> (February 27, 2009), who argued that United Nations bureaucrats created the IPCC to entrench themselves in power.

36. Nobel Prize, Press Release, "The Nobel Peace Prize 2007," October 12, 2007. See also Elizabeth Bumiller and Jim Rutenberg, "With Prize, Gore is Vindicated Without Having to Add President to Resume," *New York Times*, October 13, 2007, A13.

37. IPCC, *Synthesis Report, Summary for Policymakers*, 2; IPCC, *Synthesis Report*, 30; IPCC, *Working Group I Report, Summary for Policymakers*, 5; IPCC, *Working Group I Report, Physical Science Basis*, 237, 241-243.

38. IPCC, *Synthesis Report, Summary for Policymakers*, 2 and IPCC, *Working Group I Report, Summary for Policymakers*, 5.

39. IPCC, *Synthesis Report, Summary for Policymakers*, 5 and IPCC, *Working Group I Report, Summary for Policymakers*, 10. Climate change skeptics take issue with the manner by which the IPCC adopted its conclusions. For example, a study dealing with the IPCC reviewers of IPCC, *Working Group I Report*, Chapter 9, "Understanding and Attributing Climate Change," indicates there were only a limited number of independent reviewers, 23 individual reviewers and 8 government reviews, of that chapter and of these only 4 explicitly supported the overall chapter and its hypothesis that "very likely" greenhouse gas forcing represented the dominant cause of global warming over the past fifty years. John McLean, "Peer Review? What Peer Review?: Failures of Scrutiny in the UN's Fourth Assessment Report," Science and Public Policy Institute, September 2007, 20-21, 24. The scientific "consenses" that human activity is warming the plant came

under fire in late 2009 after a series of embarrassing events. See Jeffre Ball, "Climate Panel Details Its Review Plan," *Wall Street Journal*, March 11, 2010, A10; John M. Broder, "Scientists Take Steps to Defend Climate Work," *New York Times*, March 3, 2010, A1; Jeffrey Ball, "Climate Group Plans Review," *Wall Street Journal*, March 1, 2010, A11; Jeffrey Ball and Keith Johnson, "Push to Oversimplify at Climate Panel," *Wall Street Journal*, February 26, 2010, A1; Gautam Naik and Keith Johnson, "Controversies Create Opening for Critics," *Wall Street Journal*, February 17, 2010, A4; Juliet Eilperin and David A. Fahrenthold, "Missteps weigh on agenda for climate," *Washington Post*, February 15, 2010, A1; John M. Broder, "Climate Fight Is Heating Up In Deep Freeze," *New York Times*, February 11, 2010, A1; Jeffrey Ball and Keith Johnson, "Climate Group Admits Mistakes," *Wall Street Journal*, February 10, 2010, A10; Elizabeth Rosenthal, "U.N. Climate Panel and Its Chief Face a Siege on Their Credibility," *New York Times*, February 9, 2010, A1; Andrew C. Revkin and John M. Broder, "In Face of Skeptics, Experts Affirm Climate Peril," *New York Times*, December 7, 2009, A1.

40. IPCC, *Synthesis Report, Summary for Policymakers*, 7-8 (Table SPM.1 Projected global average surface warming and sea level rise at the end of the 21st century); IPCC, *Working Group I Report, Summary for Policymakers*, 13-14 (Table SPM.3 Projected global average surface warming and sea level rise at the end of the 21st century); IPCC, *Working Group I Report, Physical Science Basis*, 749, 764-766. One IPCC participant, Patrick J. Michaels, using a revised temperature record, concluded that the warming by the end of this century would be about 2.5?F (1.4?C). Patrick J. Michaels, "Global Warming: Correcting the Data," *Regulation* 31:3, no. 3 (Fall 2008): 46-52. According to Michaels, the sensitivity of temperature to carbon dioxide is about two-thirds of what it was thought to be. Michaels based his conclusion on temperature data collected from industrialized and non-industrialized areas, attributing a significant portion of the increased "global" temperatures on local land use changes, primarily, urban heat islands. Michaels argued that the IPCC's data was flawed because it was impossible to take truly global temperature readings, stating that research suggested that the IPCC's geographic selection for temperature readings resulted in an overestimation of warming by 33 percent. Patrick J. Michaels and Robert C. Balling Jr., *Climate of Extremes: Global Warming Science They Don't Want You to Know* (Washington, DC: Cato Institute, 2009), 59-62. However, a report Climate Change 2009: Science Compendium, September 2009, 11, by the United Nations Environment Programme predicted that the planet may warm by 6.3°F by the end of this century. This may occur even if nations fulfill their most ambitious pledges concerning the reduction of carbon emission. Juliet Eilperin, "New Analysis Brings Dire Forecast Of 6.3-Degree Temperature Increase," *Washington Post*, September 25, 2009, A4.

41. IPCC, *Synthesis Report, Summary for Policymakers*, 2; IPCC, *Synthesis Report*, 31; IPCC, *Climate Change 2007, Impacts, Adaption and Vulnerability, Contribution of Working Group II to the Fourth Assessment Report of the IPCC (Working Group II Report), Summary for Policymakers*, 8, 11; IPCC, *Working Group II Report*, 182-185, 186-189.

42. IPCC, *Synthesis Report, Summary for Policymakers*, 8-9; IPCC, *Synthesis Report*, 49; IPCC, *Working Group II Report, Summary for Policymakers*, 8, 11; IPCC, *Working Group II Report*, 182-185; IPCC, *Climate Change and Water, IPCC Technical Paper VI (Climate Change and Water)*, 2008, 3, 19-22, 25-30. See also Heather Cooley, "Water Management in a Changing Climate," in *The World's Water 2008-2009: The Biennial Report on Freshwater Resources*, ed. Peter H. Gleick et al. (Washington, DC: Island Press, 2009), 43.

43. IPCC, *Synthesis Report, Summary for Policymakers*, 7-8 (Table SPM.1 Projected global average surface warming and sea level rise by the end of the 21st century); IPCC, *Working Group I Report, Summary for Policymakers*, 13-14 (Table SPM.3 Projected global average surface warming and sea level rise by the end of the 21st century); IPCC, *Working Group I Report, Physical Science Basis*, 812-822; IPCC, *Working Group II Report, Summary for Policymakers*, 12; IPCC, *Working Group II Report*, 317, 322-324, at 323 (Table 6.3 Projected global mean climate parameters relevant to coastal areas at the end of the 21st century for the six SRES marker scenarios), 328-330, 331. See also Cooley, "Water Management," 43. The United Nations Environment Programme report, Climate Change 2009, 9, 28, predicted sea levels may rise by as much as six feet by 2100.

44. IPCC, *Climate Change and Water*, 3, 43, 70-71. See also Cooley, "Water Management," 44.

45. IPCC, *Synthesis Report, Summary for Policymakers*, 11 (Table SPM.2 Examples of some projected regional aspects); IPCC, *Synthesis Report*, 52; IPCC, *Working Group II Report, Summary for Policymakers*, 14; IPCC, *Working Group II Report*, 627-629; IPCC, *Climate Change and Water*, 102-103. See also John E. Cromwell III, Joel B. Smith, Robert S. Raucher, "No Doubt About Climate Change and Its Implications for Water Supplies," *Journal of American Water Works Association* 99:9 (September 2007): 112-117, at 114.

46. IPCC, *Working Group II Report, Summary for Policymakers*, 12 and IPCC, *Working Group II Report*, 630. See also Cromwell, Smith, Raucher, "No Doubt," 114-115 and Cooley, "Water Management," 44. The influx of warm water could raise sea levels in the northeastern United States by as much as one or two feet more than in other coastal regions by the end of this century. Aixue Hu, et al., "Transient response of the MOC and climate to potential melting of the Greenland Ice Sheet in the 21st century," *Geophysical Research Letters* 36 (May 29, 2009): L10707 <doi:10.1029/2009GL037998>. See also Cornelia Dean, "Sea's Rise May Prove Greater in the Northeast," *New York Times*, May 28, 2009, A15 and David A. Fahrenthold," East Coast May Feel Rise in Sea Levels the Most," *Washington Post*, June 8, 2009, A4.

47. U.S. Climate Change Science Program and the Subcommittee on Global Change Research, The Effects of Climate Change on Agriculture, Land Resources, Water Resources, and Biodiversity in the United States, Synthesis and Assessment Product 4.3, May 2008, 3, 8, 82-86, 96-103, 121-150. See also Juliet Eilperin, "Report Details Effects of Climate Change Across U.S.,"

Washington Post, May 28, 2008, A2 and Andrew C. Revkin, "U.S. Report Foresees Effects of Climate Shift," *New York Times,* May 28, 2008, A14.

48. U.S. Climate Change Science Program, The Effects of Climate Change, 137, 139-140.

49. U.S. Climate Change Science Program, Abrupt Climate Change, 7-14, 23-43, 60-257. See also Juliet Eilperin, "Faster Climate Change Feared," *Washington Post,* December 25, 2008, A2.

50. U.S. Climate Change Science Program, Abrupt Climate Change, 8-9, 10-12, 23-28, 60-62.

51. *Ibid.,* at 12-14, 143-145, 196-200.

52. U.S. Global Climate Change Research Program, Global Climate Change Impacts In The United States, June 2009, 9, 10, 12, 13, 27-52, 129-134. See also David A. Fahrenthold, "Report on Warming Offers New Details," *Washington Post,* June 17, 2009, A3 and John M. Broder, "Government Study Warns of Climate Change Effects," *New York Times,* June 16, 2009, A12.

53. U.S. Global Climate Change Research Program, Global Climate Change Impacts, 29-31.

54. *Ibid.,* 107-116, 129-139.

55. IPCC, *Synthesis Report, Summary for Policymakers,* 12-14; IPCC, *Synthesis Report,* 46-47; IPCC, *Working Group I Report,* 822-831.

56. Susan Solomon et al., "Irreversible Climate Change Due to Carbon Dioxide Emissions," *Proceedings of the National Academy of Science* 106:6 (February 10, 2009): 1704-1709. See also Juliet Eilperin, "Long Droughts, Rising Seas Predicted Despite Future CO2 Curbs," *Washington Post,* January 27, 2009, A4; Cornelia Dean, "Emissions Cut Won't Bring Quick Relief, Scientists Say," *New York Times,* January 27, 2009, A21; Thomas H. Maugh II, Climate change has a firm grip," *Los Angeles Times,* January 27, 2009, A1.

57. The statistics in this and the next paragraph are from Janney Montgomery Scott LLC, "Key Themes in Water Technology," Industry Report, October 6, 2008, 5 and U.S. Department of Energy, Energy Demands on Water Resources, Report to Congress on the Interdependency of Energy and Water (December 2006), 25-27.

58. The statistics in this paragraph are from Richard S. Lindzen, "There Is No 'Consensus' on Global Warming," *Wall Street Journal,* June 26, 2006, A14.

59. Lomborg, *Cool It,* 20, 18.

60. J.D. McLean, C.R. de Freitas, R.M. Carter, "Influence of the Southern Oscillation on tropospheric temperature," *Journal of Geophysical Research* 114 (July 2009): D14104 <doi:10.1029/2008JD0 11637,2009>.

61. Craig Idso and S. Fred Singer, *Climate Change Reconsidered* (Chicago: Heartland Institute, 2009), 4, 111. See also Nature, Not Human Activity, Rules the Climate: Summary for Policymakers of the Nongovernmental International Panel on Climate Change, ed. S. Fred Singer (Chicago: The Heartland Institute, 2008), 27. See also Jeffery Ball, "The Earth Cools, and Fight Over Warming Heats Up," *Wall Street Journal,* October 30, 2009, A21.

62. United Nations World Meteorological Association, WMO Statement on the Status of the Global Climate in 2008, WMO-No. 1039 (2009). See also David Deming, "Global Warming Freeze?," *Washington Times,* December 10,

2008, A16. However, the U.S. National Oceanic and Atmospheric Administration Goddard Institute for Space Studies indicated that 2009 tied for the second warmest year in modern records, based on an analysis of global surface temperatures. NASA Goddard Institute for Space Studies, *Research News*, 2009: Second Warmest Year on Record, January 21, 2010. See also Juliet Eilperin and David A. Fahrenthold, "Winter offered as proof of warming," *Washington Post*, January 28, 2010, A10. According to the United Nations World Meteorological Organization, 2009 was the fifth warmest year on record and the 2000-2009 decade was the warmest decade on record. World Meteorological Organization, WMO statement on the status of global climate in 2009, WMO-No. 1055 (2010).

63.   Robert Lee Hotz, "The Warming Earth Blows Hot, Cold and Chaotic," *Wall Street Journal*, January 2, 2009, A8.

64.   N.S. Keenlyside et al., "Advancing decadal-scale climate prediction in the North Atlantic sector," *Nature* 453:7191 (May 1, 2008): 84-88.

65.   Idso and Singer, *Climate Change Reconsidered*, 4, 187. See also Nature, ed. Singer, 17, 28. Bruce C. Douglas, Michael S. Kearney and Stephen P. Leatherman, *Sea Level Rise: History and Consequences* (San Diego: Academic Press, 2001), surveyed sea level changes and how low sea level rise in the twentieth century has impacted coastal habitability.

66.   Nils-Axel Mörner, Michael Tooley, Göran Possert, "New Perspectives for the future of the Maldives," *Global and Planetary Change* 40:1-2 (January 2004): 177-182.

67.   Richard S. Lindzen, "The Climate Science Isn't Settled," *Wall Street Journal*, December 1, 2009, A19. For the arguments climate change skeptics make and proponents respond see Michael Totty, "What Global Warming?," *Wall Street Journal*, December 7, 2009, R4.

68.   J. Eric Bickel and Lee Lane in An Analysis of Climate Engineering as a Response to Climate Change, Copenhagen Consensus on Climate, 2009, advocate solar radiation management, specifically, cloud brightening technology designed to reflect more sunlight away from the Earth. See also John Tierney, "The Earth Is Warming? Adjust the Thermostat," *New York Times*, August 11, 2009, D1; Bjorn Lomborg," Technology Can Fight Global Warming," *Wall Street Journal*, August 28, 2009, A15; Bjorn Lomborg, "Time for a Smarter Approach to Global Warming," *Wall Street Journal*, December 15, 2009, A21. Legendary physicist Freeman Dyson, "The Question of Global Warming," *New York Review of Books*, June 12, 2008, 43-45, at 45 offered the idea of genetically engineered trees to "eat" carbon and either bury it underground or convert it into liquid fuels.

69.   Amy Vickers, *Handbook of Water Use and Conservation* (Amherst, MA: WaterPlow Press, 2001), 5-6.

70.   U.S. Environmental Protection Agency (EPA), WaterSense, "Questions & Answers About the WaterSense Program," June 2008, EPA-832-F-06-009; EPA WaterSense, "Frequently Asked Questions: WaterSense Product Certification and Labeling, June 2009; EPA WaterSense, "WaterSense Labeled Toilets," February 2008, EPA-832-F-06-018.

71. EPA, WaterSense, "Watering Can Be Efficient!" June 2008 and EPA WaterSense, "Tips for Landscaping."

72. Southern Nevada Water Authority (SNWA), "Water Smart Landscapes Rebate" <www.snwa.com/html/cons_wsl.html> (June 23, 2009); "Program Conditions-Water Smart Landscapes" <www.snwa.com/html/cons_wsl_conditions.html> (June 23, 2009); SNWA Conservation Plan 2009-2013, May 2009, 10; SNWA, Water Resource Plan 09, 17; SNWA, Water Resource Plan, 18. See also Heather Cooley and Peter H. Gleick, "Urban Water-Use Efficiencies," 107 and Heather Cooley et al., Hidden Oasis: Water Conservation and Efficiency in Las Vegas, Pacific Institute and Western Resource Advocates, November 2007, 29; Henry Brean, "Landscape conversations spur rebate changes through 2009," *Las Vegas Review-Journal*, November 21, 2008, B4; Henry Brean, "Water authority ready to pay for bigger grass conversions," *Las Vegas Review-Journal*, December 7, 2007, B1; Henry Brean, "Rebates doubled for lawn removal," *Las Vegas Review-Journal*, December 8, 2006, B1; Henry Brean, "EPA honors water authority," *Las Vegas Review-Journal*, December 5, 2006, B3; John Przybys, "Making the change," Las *Vegas Review-Journal*, May 23, 2006, E1; Henry Brean, "Authority takes aim at turf," *Las Vegas Review-Journal*, March 17, 2006, B5; Joan Whitely, "Hold your water," *Las Vegas Review-Journal*, January 31, 2005, E1; Sonya Padgett, "Xeriscape incentives," *Las Vegas Review-Journal*, March 10, 2003, E1.

73. See, e.g., Los Angeles Department of Water and Power, Press Release, "LADWP To Offer Incentive to Residential Customers Who Replace Traditional Lawns with Drought Tolerant Plants," June 2, 2009. See also Emily Green, "An incentive to uproot," Los Angeles Times, June 13, 2009, E3 and Alexandra Zavis, "DWP offers incentives for removing lawns," *Los Angeles Times*, June 3, 2009, A8.

74. Regulatory incentives to promote water demand management were considered in Patrick Carvel Mann, Assessing the Applicability of Selected Financial Incentive Regulation Methods for Water Utility Regulation, National Regulatory Research Institute, February 1997, NRRI 97-09, 26-30, 44-45. See generally, Janice A. Beecher et al., Revenue Effects of Water Conservation and Conservation Pricing: Issues and Practices, National Regulatory Research Institute, September 1994. See also Cooley and Gleick, "Urban Water-Use Efficiencies," 112-118 and Vickers, *Handbook*, 143-144.

75. Public Law 102-486.

76. Water Conservation Ordinance, Los Angeles Ordinance No. 180148, August 14, 2008; Mayor's Office, Press Release, "Mayor Villaraigosa Cracks Down on Excessive Water Use," August 14, 2008; Los Angeles Department of Water and Power (LADWP), Press Release, "LADWP Strengthens Water Use Ordinance to Encourage Conservation," June 4, 2008. See also Rich Connell, "Water wasting by city angers mayor," *Los Angeles Times*, August 21, 2008, B3 and David Zahniser, "'Drought Buster' Plan Up for a Vote," Los Angeles Times, June 3, 2008, B3.

77. Water Conservation Ordinance, Los Angeles Ordinance No. 180823, August 5, 2009 and LADWP, Press Release, "Mandatory Water Conservation Is Here," June 1, 2009. See also William M. Welch, "L.A. mows down water

usage," *USA Today*, December 23, 2009, 3A; Sabrina Shankman, "Water Cops Crack Down in Drought Areas," *Wall Street Journal*, August 24, 2009, A5; Nicole Santa Cruz and David Zahniser, "Demand for water drops to 32-year low, DWP says," *Los Angeles Times*, July 28, 2009, A10; Susan Carpenter, "How the rationing will work," *Los Angeles Times*, April 25, 2009, E3.

78. Stu Woo, "In California, Hot and Dry Conditions Stir Drought Concerns," *Wall Street Journal*, January 14, 2009, A4 and Esmeralda Bermudez, "Please step away from the hose, sir," *Los Angeles Times*, August 16, 2009, A1.

79. Water Supply and Water Conservation Management Plan, Prepared for Metropolitan North Georgia Water Planning District, September 2003, ES-12, 8-1 to 8-5. The Metropolitan North Georgia Water Planning District was established by the Metropolitan North Georgia Water Planning District Act, Official Code of Georgia §§ 12-5-570 to 12-5-586, in 2001.

80. Metropolitan North Georgia Water Planning District, 2007 Activities & Progress Report, December 2007, 6-9 and Cooley and Gleick, "Urban Water-Use Efficiencies," 108-109. See also Pacific Institute for Studies in Development, Environment, and Security, A Review of Water Conservation Planning for the Atlanta, Georgia Region, August 2006; Stacy Shelton, "Metro water plan," *Atlanta-Journal Constitution*, January 18, 2009, B1; Stacy Shelton, "Plug is pulled on plumbing plan," *Atlanta-Journal Constitution*, February 3, 2006, E5; Stacy Shelton, "Water mandate runs dry," *Atlanta Journal-Constitution*, January 30, 2006, B1.

81. Georgia Comprehensive State-wide Water Management Plan, Water Council Approval, January 8, 2008. See also Stacy Shelton, "Georgia's Water Crisis," *Atlanta Journal-Constitution*, January 20, 2008, D1. The water management plan was adopted by the Georgia Water Council pursuant to the Comprehensive State-wide Water Management Planning Act, Official Code of Georgia §§ 12-5-520 to 12-5-525.

82. I have drawn on National Research Council, *Desalination: A National Perspective* (Washington, DC: National Academies Press, 2008) 41-46. See also Michael Spector, "The Last Drop," *New Yorker* 82:34 (October 23, 2006): 60-71, at 69-70.

83. Peter Lawrence, Jeremy Meigh, Caroline Sullivan, The Water Poverty Index: An International Comparison, Keele Economics Research Papers 2002/19 (revised March 2003), Appendix 1 (The Water Poverty Index and Sub-Indices Compared with the Falkenmark and the Human Development Indices (Preliminary Estimates)).

84. U.S. Department of the Interior, Bureau of Reclamation, 2008 Annual Report, Reclamation: Managing Water in the West, 13-14 and Bureau of Reclamation, Water Conservation Field Services Program <www.usbr. gov/waterconservation> (July 1, 2009).

4

Technology Commercialization by the Private Sector Increases Water Supplies and Facilities Conservation

Water scarcity helps drive technological innovation and the role of private firms as product and service vendors. The private sector can increase the supply of water through its cleanup and treatment as well as reduce demand through conservation. The reality (and the future threat) of water scarcity in the United States provides a marketing opportunity for firms, large and small, to expand their reach. Both new and adapted technologies provide innovative responses to the emerging scarcity problem.

New technologies, including water reuse and desalination, will help boost water supplies and help overcome scarcities. Water reuse represents an innovative supply enhancer with industrial reuse currently easier to implement than direct sewage reuse for residential drinking water. With more acute water shortages looming and enhanced management of costs through better membranes and energy saving devices, desalination has become a more viable technique to increase water supplies.

As analyzed in Chapter 3, supply shortages are forcing both water purveyors and users to become more serious about conservation. This chapter examines water saving technologies, including pipe rehabilitation, water-free urinals, and innovative irrigation techniques, for residential, commercial, and agricultural uses. Before focusing on the technologies that can increase water supplies and facilitate conservation, the role of venture capitalists and other financing arrangements is briefly considered.

Supplying Capital: The Role of Venture Capitalists and Others

Capital sees scarcity as an opportunity. Established corporations, venture capitalists, and private investors have provided capital to new firms as well as marketing skills to help overcome declining water quantity and quality in the United States.[1]

Smaller firms entered into joint ventures and various types of licensing arrangements with larger companies to obtain capital and marketing help. Major companies, needing new products and services they cannot develop in-house, look to start-ups for items to add to their offerings.

Venture capitalists are early stage equity investors in businesses. They enter when a technology development venture becomes more proven and as its products (or services) become more commercially viable.

Venture capitalists raise funds from institutions and wealthy individuals. In return for their investments, venture capital firms receive stock and decision-making participation through seats on a company's board of directors. Venture capitalists bring networking contacts, credibility in the financial community and the marketplace, as well as valuable business acumen and expertise by having been through many past efforts.

Venture capital firms aim to profit subsequently from their investments when the entities they invested in go public or sold. Up until September 2008, for most of the first decade of this century, venture capital firms took in huge amounts of cash, spawning numerous start-ups. The hunt for fresh investment sectors, such as clean technology, led to many of the businesses profiled in this chapter.

Increasing Water Supplies

Increasing supplies can help meet the current and future demand for water in the United States. This section considers the use of technology to purify (and thus recycle) wastewater and desalinate seawater.

Purifying Wastewater

The boundary between water and wastewater continues to fade. In the coming years, wastewater will come to be viewed as another source of primary water. Customers ingest only two percent of water delivered to residences, with about 30 percent of the water flowing to houses being used outdoors for watering lawns, washing cars, and filling swimming pools.[2] Given the urgency of water shortages, now and in the near term, the treatment of wastewater to augment water supplies is gaining traction. Indirect reuse and direct reuse must, however, be distinguished.

Indirect Water Reuse

In most residential, commercial, and industrial applications, wastewater is treated to meet environmental requirements and then discharged by sewer plants into local waterways where it may be used downstream by primary drinking water plants and ultimately run out to the ocean through indirect water reuse.[3] For indirect reuse, multiple barriers, including source protection, distribution system integrity, and monitoring programs, help ensure the safety of the reused water. In some major U.S. river systems, water is used and re-used up to twenty times as it travels to the sea.[4] As a result of the impact of, and the progress under, the federal Clean Water Act, discussed in Chapter 2, some discharged water from wastewater treatment plants is cleaner than the rivers into which they flow.

Indirect water reuse offers numerous benefits. It creates a source of high quality water. Indirect reuse returns water to reservoirs or groundwater basins, thereby maximizing the value of these storage assets. It also eliminates, or at least defers, the need to build new, costly reservoirs. Because water is delivered via existing pipes, it avoids the cost of new infrastructure.[5]

Critics assert, however, that recycled water may not be safe for humans. Treated water may contain residues from toxic substances, such as pharmaceuticals, hormones, antibiotics, and chemotherapy medication.[6] The term "xenobiotics" includes a whole range of synthetic water contaminants, including medical treatment drugs, pharmaceutical compounds, personal hygiene and beauty products, and modern household chemicals, that may have a harmful, but yet poorly understood, impact on human endocrine and reproductive systems. Several studies lend credence to these fears.

A study by the U.S. Geological Survey and the Centers for Disease Control and Prevention of the surface water and treated water at one plant in New Jersey found at least eleven and as many as seventeen unregulated contaminants in each of four samples.[7] However, the levels found were far below a daily dose. Another study of effluents found a number of unregulated pharmaceutically active compounds, personal care ingredients, and plasticizers in reclaimed and retreated wastewater.[8] At a minimum, a need exists to measure accurately what is in recycled water and to understand the impact of these compounds on human health through testing.

New technologies can deal with these contaminants.[9] Mechanical filters can eliminate pollutants. The most advanced ultra-filtration purification technologies can remove most of these contaminants, while widely available membrane-based filtration technology can filter out health hazards, including viruses and bacteria, to the sub-micron level, treating wastewater to potable water standards for reuse. Other approaches degrade pollutants and treat storm water.

Membrane Filtration. Membrane filtration technology focuses on nanotechnology, specifically nanomembranes. Nanotechnology is an emerging field of technology dealing with engineering at the molecular level (a nanometer is a billionth of a meter). Nanoparticles are very small and are smaller than anything ever put into commercial products.[10]

Argonide Corp., a privately-held firm, was founded in 1994 by its current CEO, Frederick Tepper, to invest in a Russian process that produces nanopowder. The firm's current mission focuses on the development of nanotechnology products, particularly filtration technology and devices.[11]

In 2000, Tepper and his associate Dr. Leonid A. Kaledin invented a nano alumina filter. The electropositive charge of the filter attracts negatively-charged bacteria and viruses. The filters remove bacteria and viruses, along with other biological hazards, from the water supply. The filter consists of nanofibers so small that it takes more than 250,000 to equal the thickness of one strand of human hair. In 2002, *R & D Magazine* recognized Argonide's nano alumina fibers and the filters derived from them as one of the top 100 most technologically significant new products.[12] The R & D 100 awards program honors significant commercial promise in products, materials, or processes developed by the international research and development community.

Argonide was originally self-funded by Tepper. The firm has also received federal government grants. In 2001, it received a Small Business Innovation Research (SBIR) Program grant from the National Aeronautics and Space Administration (NASA). The grant funded the development of the nano alumina ceramics filter and enabled the firm to demonstrate its feasibility for sterilizing water. The 2001 grant led to a 2002 Phase II SBIR small business grant from NASA that provided additional funds to further develop the filtration technology for recycling and purifying space cabin drinking water, including increasing the filter size and determining methods for renewing the filter. Argonide also received a 2002 grant from the U.S. Environmental Protection Agency to create a filter using a new type of activated aluminum to remove arsenic from water. Then, in 2007, the company received a Phase III small business grant from the U.S. Air Force for the development of an improved air filter.[13]

Recognizing that it was difficult to be a stand-alone nanotech company, in 2002, Argonide granted a worldwide exclusive license to Ahlstrom Corp., a publicly-held Finnish company, to manufacture and sell filters, based on its patented nano alumina fiber technology.[14] Ahlstrom, a global leader in the development, manufacture, and marketing of high performance fiber-based material, now sells the filter, which grafts alumina nanofiber onto a microglass filter, under the Disruptor PAC label.

Post-9/11, as discussed in Chapter 2, terrorist threats may compromise the microbiological safety of U.S. water supplies. Security concerns exist regarding potentially widely introduced compounds into U.S. water distribution systems as a result of terrorist activities. Although it is unlikely that terrorists could develop sufficient doses of injurious or fatal agent contamination for reservoirs, these contaminants could be developed and used in water supplies closest to the consumer, such as water storage facilities or vulnerable points in the distribution system. Some biological agents, such as anthrax spores, resist chlorine used to treat water supplies. Argonide's technology could eliminate these biological agents from drinking water and also collect and concentrate these agents for analysis.

Pollutant Degradation. Another approach degrades pollutants, thereby facilitating indirect reuse. Microvi Biotech Inc. (Microvi), founded in 2004 by Dr. Fatemeh Shirazi, its current CEO, chief technology officer, and chair of its Board of Directors, developed patented biological reactors that house natural microorganisms that feed off and eat particular pollutants in water, including perchlorate (a rocket fuel additive), PCE (the chemical used in dry cleaning), and nitrates.[15] These microorganisms are packaged in materials and configurations protecting them from the secondary stream of pollutants that otherwise must be disposed of. This system is self-cleaning. When the microbe population reaches a critical stage, it stops growing. Living organisms feed off dead ones. No fouling or build-up occurs inside a reactor. There is no sludge, secondary wastes, or other harmful by-products to dispose of, thereby eliminating post-treatment costs.

Microvi markets its product to water and wastewater facilities as a treatment for currently unregulated pollutants. A market also exists in treating water discharged by various industries, including food and beverage firms, which produce water high in organic pollutants and nitrates, and paper companies, which generate wastewater high in toxic chlorinated phenols.

With a $1.8 million in grants from various federal agencies, including the National Science Foundation and the National Institutes for Health, Dr. Shirazi worked to perfect the technology to modify organisms that degrade water pollutants. The firm also received support for its unique biotechnology solutions from Pratt & Whitney, a division of United Technologies Corp., the American Petroleum Institute, and the U.S. Department of Defense.[16] Then, in August 2009, Microvi announced the completion of its first round of equity financing. Although the terms were not disclosed, the company used the proceeds to expand its product development, grow its team, enhance its R & D pipeline, and pave the way for the commercialization of its water technologies.[17]

Storm water Treatment. Although not an example of indirect reuse, storm water runoff, which consists of rainwater plus anything else it gathers up after hitting the ground, such as oil and grease from cars and trucks, brake dust, road salt, pathogens from animal waste, presents another concern because of its impact on surface freshwater and groundwater. Treating storm water runoff removes an additional burden from America's aging wastewater treatment facilities.

AbTech Industries Inc. (AbTech) manufactures water filters and sponges used in street-level storm drains and catch basins that clean road runoff water passing through streets.[18] Glenn R. Rink, the founder and CEO of AbTech, a privately-held company, began using his Smart Sponge Technology in 1997 to clean up oil spills from tankers in the ocean. Smart Sponge Technology, made from a synthetic polymer, bonds permanently hydrocarbons. When deployed in filtration mechanisms, it removes hydrocarbons, among other contaminants, from water.

In 1999, Rink turned his attention to storm water. When rain water hits sidewalks and streets, hydrocarbons run largely unfiltered into the nation's storm sewers along with traces of heavy metals and pesticides. It then washes into nearby rivers or offshore. He recalled, "No one was really doing anything about dealing with the billions of gallons of rain that come down on the roads and go into our flood-control devices and are contaminated on the way through."[19]

The Ultra-Urban Filter with Smart Sponge manufactured by AbTech ensures that the water flowing through the product is properly and completely treated for federal environmental regulatory purposes. The sponge material is molded into different shapes that fit into street-level storm drains and catch basins. The product treats storm water runoff from curb inlet openings and catch basin drains by absorbing oil and grease and capturing trash and sediment, thereby removing contaminants and pollutants from storm water runoff. In other words, the Smart Sponge filter acts as a super-size sink trap. According to Rink, "Compared with building new storm-water treatment plants or upgrading already existing facilities to handle runoff pollution, which would cost in the millions of dollars, our products are very affordable."[20] For example its Ultra-Urban filters are sold in a dozen sizes and cost between several hundred and one thousand dollars each.

To further develop its product, in 2002, AbTech entered into a strategic alliance with BioShield Technologies, Inc. AbTech coats its sponges with an antimicrobial agent developed by BioShield, so that the system disinfects water without releasing chemicals or leaching.[21]

As of the end of 2008, AbTech had some 13,000 Smart Sponge installations in 36 states. Municipalities comprise 70 percent of its business, with commercial entities an increasing part of the mix. For example, in 2004, Long Beach, California installed some 2,000 of AbTech's filters in more than 500 of its storm drains, thereby eliminating pollutants from entering local waterways, especially the city's beaches. An analysis showed that the filters in Long Beach had captured 92,000 pounds of various contaminants, such as debris, sediment, oil, grease, and heavy metals, and an additional 25,000 pounds of hydrocarbons and oil products.[22] Private firms can also install an AbTech system to treat runoff at their facilities.

With respect to financing, in November 2006, AbTech completed a $6.8 million private financing that enabled the firm to significantly expand its sales and marketing efforts and commit additional resources to broaden the application of its technology to new markets. The round was led by the legitimate part of the now infamous Bernard L. Madoff Investment Securities LLC along with several other institutional investors. Previously, the firm had raised a total of $15 million during the previous nine years in $1 million units from wealthy individuals.[23]

Direct Water Reuse

Direct reuse of water involves the more immediate treatment and recycling of wastewater for primary uses, such as drinking and cooking.[24] Existing purification systems can recycle wastewater for direct reuse purposes. Recycled wastewater can also be used in the workplace or gardens, in toilets and for housecleaning.

Treating wastewater and reusing it on-site (or nearby) serves two purposes. First, it reduces the demand for available water supplies. Second, it eliminates the cost of transporting water over long distances.

At the residential level, direct reuse is technologically feasible. For example, new home construction could install a dual piping system for more expensive potable recycling and less treated, less expensive nonpotable water.[25] The barrier to direct water reuse is psychological. It encounters the "yuck" factor.[26] Thus, putting a "black box" treatment system outside a residence to treat sewage and recycle it directly back to the tap (toilet-to-tap) is currently unacceptable to most Americans. Customers remain hesitant about toilet-to-tap as a source of drinking water.

In contrast to the barriers encountered for residential reuse, water reuse plays a role in industrial settings, where decisions on process purity and costs turn on rational and financial, not emotional, factors.[27] Specifically, who will pay for the upfront capital expenditures to build a reuse system and who will buy the end product created? Targeted treatment to recover not only water but also other fluids and waste stream by-products makes reuse a more viable financial proposition for industrial water users that also wish to display their "green" credentials.

Companies are active in the direct reuse for non-residential purposes. For example, MIOX Corp., founded in 1994, uses mixed-oxidant technology, originally developed in 1982 by Los Alamos Technical Associates, to purify water with the goal of replacing traditional water treatment chemicals.[28] The first patent for MIOX technology was issued in 1988. MIOX makes and sells chemical-free water purification products that replace traditional wastewater treatment techniques, such as chlorine.[29]

The MIOX technology involves mixing untreated water with salt. An electric current separates the salt into its components, sodium and chloride. The resulting, chlorine-based mixed oxidant water disinfectant destroys all pathogenic microorganisms in the water, with less chlorine and less buildup of biofilm and algae in the treatment system. Production of the solution on-site eliminates the need to store or transport hazardous chemicals and avoids the development of undesirable chlorine by-products. Industrial and commercial customers are looking to use MIOX equipment as part of a self-contained recycling system to disinfect water for non-drinking uses, such as landscaping maintenance.

Total venture capital investment in MIOX stands at nearly $50 million. In August 2008, just prior to the stock market collapse, the firm raised $19 million from DCM, Sierra Ventures, and Flywheel Ventures, to go with the $14.5 million obtained prior from Sierra Ventures, Tao Capital, New Mexico Community Capital, and Flywheel Ventures. Previously, it had raised $16 million in 2005 led by Flywheel Ventures, Altira Group, and a group of new and existing private investors as part of a takeover of the firm by principals from Entrada Ventures, a fund created in 2004 for the sole purchase of buying and restructuring one manufacturing company.[30]

Converting wastewater to potable drinking water remains, however, rare in the residential market. In high water demand states, such as California and Florida, reclaimed wastewater is starting to be more widely used to replenish dwindling groundwater supplies rather than allowing it to run downstream to the ocean via discharges into rivers. For example, the Orange County (California) Sanitation District's Groundwater Replenishment Project, one of the world's largest, came online in 2008. The $500 million dollar advanced filtration system treats 70 million gallons of sewage a day with microfiltration, reverse osmosis, and ultraviolet disinfection. The water is then pumped to spreading grounds, where it filters through purifying substrate to mix with the county's underground water supplies.[31]

As analyzed in Chapter 6, many investor-owned water utilities centrally consolidate water treatment creating economies of scale for advanced treatment applications in larger facilities. However, the high cost of transporting treated water and repairing (or replacing) pipes has led to an interest in decentralized treatment via smaller systems or even onsite treatment for residential and commercial uses.[32]

About 30 percent of U.S. homes are off the water grid as a result of the rise of the suburban sprawl, in addition to rural areas.[33] Many developers put residences on septic systems rather than hooking them into a centralized system. Treating wastewater onsite reduces the potential for contamination by fluids otherwise percolating into the surrounding soil. The thousands of small decentralized publicly-owned systems in the United States that may have only a handful of homes and businesses on their water and wastewater facilities are for practical purposes also off the grid. These small systems generally remain behind in implementing the advanced water and wastewater treatment technology adopted by larger, centralized systems.

The environmental footprint and the economic impact of in-house water treatment units are far superior to bottled water. The rising opposition to bottled water because of the energy costs involved in transporting water and the billions of non-biodegradable plastic bottles going to landfills will likely spur the demand for home and commercial water treatment systems. High tech, small-scale water treatment systems, using ultra filtration technology, exist for home water use. However, the upfront expense of these sophisticated home water treatment systems, which currently can cost from $2,000 to $5,000, remains a barrier to their use.[34]

On a larger scale, onsite treatment can offer opportunities for water reuse, with wastewater (and even "gray water," such as bathroom sink water) treated and recycled back into the home. Because many people have a gut-level aversion to deriving drinking water from sewage, residences, rather than recycling wastewater for drinking water purposes, can deploy it for other uses, such as toilet flushing.[35] Making even these small incremental gains in terms of nonpotable water reuse could substantially improve overall water availability.

A leader in nonpotable water reuse, the AQUS System, manufactured by WaterSaver Technologies, Inc. (WaterSaver) recycles water from the bathroom sink to the toilet tank. In American homes, the 70 percent of water is used indoors. The bathroom is the largest consumer of indoor water, with toilets accounting for about 27 percent of indoor household water use (or about 19 percent of total household use).[36]

In 2003, Mark Sanders founded the privately-held WaterSaver firm.[37] Previously in 2000, Sanders had made a sketch of a water recycling system that would take used bathroom sink water and route it to the toilet tank for flushing. He took the drawing to a friend. Two weeks later, the friend had a working prototype that Sanders patented.

After founding WaterSaver, Sanders and his business partner spent years testing more prototypes and raising money from individual investors. In 2006, the system, called the AQUS Greywater Recycling System, debuted at a water industry trade show. It was designated as one of the 100 best innovations of 2007 by *Popular Science* magazine.[38] In addition to conserving water, the system saves money in reduced water charges and wastewater treatment fees.

AQUS uses standard plumbing parts, can be installed by a plumber in about two hours, is priced at under $400, and can save up to 5,000 gallons of water a year in a two-person residence. The AQUS system consists of two parts: the fill control unit and the vanity tank. The fill control unit clips onto the back of a toilet and holds the fill valve up, in the off position, which allows the vanity tank, located under the bathroom sink, to fill the tank with treated and recycled sink water. The system does not shut off the freshwater supply or cross connect to it. The system holds the freshwater in an off position until it is needed to supplement the toilet fill.

In 2009, the firm joined forces with Sloan Valve Co., a leading manufacturer of flush valves that deliver a predetermined, metered volume of water to fixtures, such as a toilet, to provide the AQUS technology to the commercial/residential marketplace. The strategic marketing partnership will leverage both WaterSaver's products and Sloan's market position and distribution channels to provide efficient solutions to businesses and homeowners. According to Sanders, "Sloan's position in the industry will bring much needed attention to this low-maintenance, low-cost, and highly effective water-saving solution."[39]

Looking to the future, it is not necessary to treat all recycled residential water to stringent regulatory standards for drinking water. Nonpotable water used for watering lawns and washing cars need not meet these standards. Most of the roughly 100 gallons Americans use per person per day could be recovered and treated without anyone drinking directly recycled wastewater. Of the 100 gallons of water used per capita in the United States that is currently treated to drinking water standards, most individuals drink less than one gallon per day.[40] Most of the rest goes to flushing toilets, watering lawns, washing cars, and filling swimming pools. These applications do not require water to be treated to drinking water standards.

More onsite residential wastewater treatment can help reduce water use and thus the need to find new freshwater supplies and build high volume, massive, centralized wastewater treatment facilities. In sum, systems to treat and reuse wastewater may be one of the least costly and most efficient methods to increase supplies. Water reuse systems likely represent a far less expensive source of additional water than huge desalination plants. However, more advanced desalination techniques, including the next-generation membranes and energy recovery techniques, can facilitate the implementation of this effective, but power-hungry, solution to America's water supply needs.

Water Desalination

New water sources and production methods focus on desalination. Noting the possibilities for desalination decades ago, President John F. Kennedy at his April 12, 1961 press conference stated: "[I]f we could ever competitively, at a cheap rate, get freshwater from salt water, that . . . would really dwarf any other scientific accomplishments."[41] That time may be near.

Desalination is a process that removes salt from seawater by evaporation or by forcing the salty water through membrane filters to create fresh, drinkable water. Although desalination has become more viable as localities run out of other choices, it represents a controversial solution to water shortages because of intake issues, the creation of a concentrated brine waste stream that the plant must dispose of, and high energy usage.[42]

There are two intake issues. First, water fed into a desalination system may contain contaminants not filtered out. These include biological contaminants (viruses and bacteria), chemical contaminates, pharmaceuticals, and personal-care products. Second, as a result of impingement, marine life gets sucked into the intake screens and is killed. Small organisms that pass through the intake screens are killed during the processing of the saltwater, more technically, they suffer entrainment. Technological and operational measures together with design considerations, beyond the scope of this book, can reduce impingement and entrainment.

As a by-product, desalination plants generate a combination of concentrated brine mixed with the chemicals used in the production of freshwater and those that clean and maintain the membrane filters. The plants discharge this concentrate into the ocean. The discharge also contains the decomposed remains of aquatic life, fish, larvae, and eggs that are killed during the intake process. These remains reduce the oxygen content of the water near the discharge pipes creating an additional stress on marine life. A number of less ecologically harmful brine disposal options, beyond the scope of this book, are available.

Desalination plants are highly energy-intensive, putting a huge burden on local power grids. Large-scale desalination would increase greenhouse gas emissions and may exacerbate global warming. Despite critics' assertions, desalination of seawater has become economically feasible because of the improved efficiency of reverse osmosis membranes. Also, energy costs connected with desalination are declining.[43]

Membrane filters use reverse osmosis, a separation process that uses high pressure to drive salt water through membranes, leaving the concentrate behind. Advances in the reverse osmosis process, such as the use of better membranes and more efficient energy recovery devices, have decreased the associated energy costs, making this technique the preferred desalination method, especially where energy costs are high.

With reverse osmosis desalination technology, seawater is forced, under intense pressure, about 800 pounds per square inch, through a spiral of porous membrane sheets consisting of a dense polymer film. The membranes have a dense barrier layer at the surface where the separation of water and salt takes place. Under pressure, water molecules pass through the pores of the semi-permeable membrane, but salt ions and other impurities do not. About 50 percent of the incoming water is collected as freshwater on the other side of the membranes and taken to its intended use. The other 50 percent, now twice as salty, exits the system as concentrated brine wastewater to be dumped back into the sea.

Although the reverse osmosis membranes can remove particles as small as one molecule, they are more energy-intensive than traditional filtration techniques. Also, membrane-based water treatment requires pressure to move water through membranes, resulting in high energy costs.

Two technology keys exist to desalination efficiency and cost effectiveness: better membranes and enhanced energy efficiency.

Better Membranes. Companies focus on bringing down the cost of reverse osmosis desalination through better membranes that can do the job with less pressure and/or power, thereby reducing energy costs and making the desalination of seawater more economically feasible. Nanotechnology facilitates the making of enhanced membranes.

Water nanotechnology, previously discussed in this chapter, includes nanomembranes. Nanotechnology research focuses on improving the permeability of membranes, increasing their intake effectiveness, and reducing their energy requirements. With their ability to control the pore size within a polymer membrane, nano-enhanced membranes offer the promise of greater energy efficiency.

In November 2006, researchers at the University of California at Los Angeles (UCLA) announced the development of a reverse osmosis membrane designed to reduce the cost of seawater desalination and wastewater reclamation.[44] The UCLA scientists are working with NanoH$_2$O Inc. to develop the patent-pending nanocomposite membrane technology into a low energy, fouling resistant membrane for desalination and water reuse.

NanoH$_2$O was founded by Robert Burk in 2005.[45] Its current CEO is Jeff Green, a serial entrepreneur who previously founded two software start-ups.

The firm seeks to mass produce a nanocomposite membrane based on the technology developed by the UCLA researchers. Nano H$_2$O secured its intellectual property through UCLA's technology transfer program. The new membrane developed by UCLA researchers uses a cross-linked matrix of polymers and nanoparticles to draw in water ions but repel nearly all contaminants. The polymer-based membranes embedded with nanoparticles create molecular tunnels through which water flows more easily than the contaminants. The nanoparticles attract and thus draw in water. Highly porous like a sponge, they soak up water, while repelling dissolved salts and other impurities and contaminants.

With these improvements, less energy is needed to pump water through the membranes. Because they repel particles that ordinarily stick to the surface of conventional membranes, the new membranes foul more slowly than other ones where bacteria and other particles build up on the surface and clog them. With conventional membranes, the fouling results in higher energy demands on the pumping system and leads to the costly clean up of membranes and their replacement.

By exploiting chemical attraction, the NanoH$_2$O thin-film nanocomposite membrane technology reduces the amount of mechanical-induced pressure required for reverse osmosis desalination. As a result, the water purification process is more effective than current methods, more energy efficient, and potentially much less expensive. With the new membranes consuming 50 percent less energy, the process may reduce the total cost of desalinated water by up to 25 percent. The firm claims its technology can process up to 70 percent more water with 20 percent less power than conventional reverse osmosis plants.[46]

NanoH$_2$O has received two rounds of venture capital funding. In 2007, it obtained $5 million from Khosla Ventures. Then in August 2008, it secured $15 million more from Khosla Ventures and Oak Investment Partners.[47] The firm devoted the funds to commercialize its seawater reverse osmosis membrane product and to expand its research and development activities.

In the reverse osmosis process, sucking and pressurizing consumes a considerable amount of electricity to push the water through the membranes. Power expenses typically account for one-third to one-half of the operating costs of a seawater desalination plant. Thus, a need exists for technology to reduce energy expenses.

Enhanced Energy Efficiency. On the energy cost reduction side, the PX Pressure Exchanger, manufactured by Energy Recovery, Inc., a publicly-held company, helps reduce desalination costs by capturing energy in a ceramic-based pressure exchange system and recycling it back to the feed water system.[48] The device, according to the firm, can cut a desalination plant's energy costs by 60 percent. The firm was founded in 1992 with the goal of making seawater desalination affordable by reducing energy costs.

Energy Recovery went public in July 2008, prior to the stock market collapse, raising $119 million. After underwriting commissions, but before expenses, the firm and selling shareholders received slightly more than $63 million and $46 million, respectively. Prior to going public, it raised capital by the private placement of its shares of common stock. During three years, 2005-2007, it issued common shares for a total net proceeds of $6.6 million.

Today, the firm is the world's largest manufacturer for energy recovery devices, with a 70 percent market share. Specifically, it manufactures and sells the PX Pressure Exchanger that became commercially available in 1997. This technology recovers energy from a high-pressure wastewater stream at up to 98 percent efficiency, thereby reducing the cost of water production to less than half the cost without the device. Its proprietary design uses one moving part, a corrosion-resistant, cylindrical rotor with long, narrow ducts. The rotor spins inside a sleeve between two end covers with port openings for both streams. Pressure energy is transferred from the high-pressure concentrate (the reject stream) to the low-pressure feed (the seawater stream). In a typical desalination plant, 50 percent of the water that does not pass through the reverse osmosis membranes carries away the rejected salt that pours out of the reverse osmosis cartridges at high pressure and is otherwise wasted. The PX Pressure Exchanger pipes the high pressure concentrated brine water into a series of open cylinders in a spinning column; thereby recycling the energy that otherwise would have been lost in the high-pressure reject stream of the seawater and applying it to the low-pressure incoming seawater. In other words, it captures the pressure trapped in the left-behind brine and recycles that energy into repressurizing the next batch of seawater destined to be slammed against the reverse osmosis membranes, thereby reducing the desalination energy requirements.

As a result of the combination of better membranes and lower energy usage, the cost of producing a cubic meter (246 gallons) of freshwater from seawater using reverse osmosis technology is now under 46 cents per cubic meter. With tightening freshwater supplies and increasing shortages, this cost figure begins to make desalination a more attractive supply option, even in comparison with ten or twenty cents per cubic meter for water obtained from a reservoir or a well.[49] However, the cost of producing desalinated may rise in the future if the cost of energy increases faster than cost decreases resulting from technological improvements.

The improved desalination technology may help meet California's water supply needs. In May 2009, the San Diego Regional Water Quality Control Board, the last of four agencies whose assent was required, approved the construction $320 million dollar desalination plant. The facility to be built north of San Diego will be the West Coast's first large-scale desalination plant and the largest in the Western Hemisphere. It will serve as a test case for whether this type of large project, using reverse osmosis membranes and the Energy Recovery's pressure exchanger, can meet its financial and technical goals while safeguarding the environment.[50]

Conservation and Low Water Use Technologies

Conservation and low water use technologies can help manage demand. Various technologies, including pipe rehabilitation, water-free urinals, and innovative irrigation techniques, save water.

Pipe Rehabilitation. A need exists to rehabilitate existing underground transmission and distribution infrastructure, such as pipes.

Water loss management represents both an important problem and a commercial opportunity. Beneath most cities and towns, miles and miles of water and sewer pipes are deteriorating, a topic discussed in more detail in Chapter 6, some almost to the point of collapse. The result: millions of gallons of lost drinking water, dangerous sewer overflows, and unnecessary threats to human health.

The cost of pumping water focuses attention on leakage in water distribution systems. In the United States, leaky pipes result in an average water loss of about 10 to 25 percent in water transmission systems with rates running as high as 40 percent in some older urban systems.[51] For example, Atlanta loses more than 5 billion gallons of water each year, about 15 percent of the water it takes from the Chattahoochee River.[52] Throughout the nation, losses result into foregone revenues and higher costs may jeopardize water safety and reliability. Losses typically grow as systems age.

Historically, municipalities did not fix pipes until a water main break resulted in a major rupture to the system. In the future, increasing attention will focus on leak detection and targeted pipe repair. It can cost up to five times more to build a new underground water main than to rehabilitate it in place.[53] It is also easier, cheaper, and more environmentally sound to fix existing water mains and pipes than to build new water mains and pipes, new dams and reservoirs, or seek new supply sources.

In addition to water transmission and distribution facilities, throughout the nation concrete sewer lines installed after World War II are nearing the end of their fifty-year lifespan. Holes, breaks, and joint failures in pipes allow water runoff to seep inside. After large storms, the volume of rainwater that enters damaged pipes can overwhelm sewage treatment plants. The plants often discharge the sewage overflows into local waterways, causing human health threats.

Insituform Technologies, Inc. (Insituform), a publicly-held corporation, enjoys a steady flow of business from a growing number of cities and private firms seeking to repair aging water and sewer pipes.[54] Its trenchless techniques enable public and private entities to give their decaying pipes a new lease on life without digging or disruption. Founded in 1971, Insituform has become a leading worldwide provider of proprietary technologies and services for rehabilitating deteriorating water and sewer pipes.

The firm's most important innovation allows it to repair sewer pipes without digging into the ground.[55] Its Cured-In-Place Pipe (CIPP) technology lines a damaged pipe with a watertight material that sticks to the inner surface, covering cracks. The company installs a customized synthetic liner saturated with a resin mixture in a host sewer pipe by various processes. After heating, the resin hardens, forming a new pipe within the old pipe. The jointless, seamless pipe-within-a-pipe renews structural integrity while increasing flow capacity and reducing long-term maintenance costs. With its sanitary sewer and storm sewer repair technology, Insituform helps wastewater treatment systems avoid the large capital cost of expanding facilities and prevents the environmental problems caused by sewer overflows.

Beyond relining existing sewer pipes, the firm's Insituform Blue family of rehabilitation products restores structural integrity to damaged drinking water system pipes, thereby resolving leaks and water main breaks and preventing the loss of treated water.[56] Its products increase flow capacity with minimal disruptions. A part of the Insituform Blue family, Thermopipe is a thin polyester-reinforced polyethylene structural lining system for the rehabilitation of water distribution mains and other pressurized piping systems. Once the liner, which is winched into a host pipe from a reel, is inflated with air and heated with steam, it forms a close-fit within the host pipe, creating a jointless, leak-free lining system. The polyethylene liner stops leakage by building and sealing holes and joints. It extends the life of water distribution infrastructure and also helps improve the quality of water within a water main.

The company also deploys a robotic device, iTAP, which restores and upgrades connections from inside a pipe without digging. Unlike robotic equipment that uses closed-circuit television cameras, in iTAP employs non-visual, electric current to identify service locations.

Water-Free Urinals. Thinking about conservation technology often focuses on plumbing fixtures, specifically, toilets. Beyond low-flow toilets, which Congress mandated in 1992 (as discussed in Chapter 3), Falcon Waterfree Technologies, Inc. (Falcon) manufactures water-free urinals.[57] The firm, a privately-held company, was founded in 2000. Building on the existing sales and distribution networks of its established partners in the sanitary equipment industry, it claims about 90 percent of the worldwide market for water-free urinals. With a 100 percent water reduction, each urinal saves about 40,000 gallons of water a year.[58] Furthermore, this amount of water need not be transported to the urinal or away from it to a treatment facility, saving energy. By reducing the total load on treatment plants, water-free urinals reduce the need to build new water treatment capacity and lower the incidences of overflow events at treatment facilities.

Falcon's founder and lead investor is Marc Nathanson, a cable entrepreneur. In 2006, Capricorn Management, an investment group founded by Jeffrey S. Skoll, eBay's first president, bought a 25 percent stake in Falcon. Mapleton Investments, LLC, a venture capital firm, is another major investor.[59] Members of Falcon's advisory board include former U.S. Vice President Albert (Al) Gore, Jr. and Richard Riordan, the former mayor of Los Angeles.

The technology behind a water-free urinal is simple. Falcon manufactures a urinal with a drain, a bowl with a hole that funnels urine through a biodegradable liquid sealant layer in a sealed, replaceable cartridge. Instead of water, it relies on gravity to force urine through the cartridge installed at the bottom of the urinal, which is connected to a drainpipe. The liquid layer of sealant floats in the top of the cartridge, allowing urine to pass through to the drain line. The sealant provides an airtight barrier between a restroom environment and the sewer line to prevent any odors from escaping. When urine passes through the cartridge, which contains a liquid having a specific gravity lighter than water, the liquid covers and seals it, blocking any escaping odor caused when urine reacts with water creating ammonia oxide and releasing sewer gases in the drain line. Unlike conventional urinals, no flush plume spreads bacteria. No moving parts require maintenance. No flush valves break down and there are no worries about leaks or continuous flushing. The cartridge, with a list price of about $40, must be replaced about every 7,000 uses because it collects sediment.

Some doubts exist, however, regarding water-free urinals. A drain line buildup problem focuses on the impact that significantly reduced water flows from high-efficiency urinals may have on the buildup of urine solids in the drain line, resulting in a restricted flow or clogging. The feature in question regarding increased maintenance requirements and longevity is the urinal's trap into which urine drains.

No-flush urinals require distinct cleaning procedures, thereby posing another problem. With high turnover among maintenance staff, some commercial and institutional buyers find it difficult for their personnel to keep the no-flush urinals in an odor-free, efficient operation. Maintenance staffs also tend to change cartridges whenever urinals back up, which can happen far more often than every 7,000 uses. A sudden surge of water, for example, if a staff member empties a mop bucket into a no-flush urinal, can destroy the urinal's seal by flushing the trap. There is also the "yuck" factor involved in changing cartridges calcified with others' urine as sediment builds up inside over time.[60]

Innovative Irrigation Techniques. Agricultural, recreational, and landscaping water use offer water conservation possibilities. One of the leaders, The Toro Company (Toro), a huge publicly-held firm with revenues in 2008 of nearly $1.9 billion, makes lawn mowers and other products for professional and residential use. Toro is active in water conservation in three areas: agricultural irrigation, golf course irrigation, and residential and commercial landscape irrigation.

Agricultural irrigation cries out for efficiency improvements. Freshwater use for agricultural and horticultural irrigation (including golf courses) equals about 40 percent of total freshwater withdrawals.[61] Irrigation for crop production claims a big chunk of total water consumption, upwards of 80 percent in many arid western states.[62] The amount of water devoted to irrigation impacts on supply in two ways. It restricts the water available to urban consumers, forcing system owners to find more distant, and thus more expensive, supplies. It also lowers groundwater (aquifer) levels by withdrawing more water than sparse rainfalls can recharge, thereby reducing the water available to meet future needs and increasing the cost of obtaining water.

Agricultural irrigation as typically practiced is highly wasteful. The resulting salt buildup also can lead to less fertile soils, unless properly managed. In the United States, salt has damaged about 23 percent of irrigated farmland.[63] Minor irrigation improvements could considerably extend existing U.S. freshwater supplies.

New and more efficient technologies for water use in irrigation, such as drip irrigation, offer great promise.[64] Toro's drip (or micro) irrigation products line, which regulates the flow of water, involves the firm in more efficient agricultural irrigation.[65] One product consists of long tapes that can extend for one thousand feet with evenly spaced tiny holes. Water drips through each hole and directly irrigates certain plants' roots, rather than in the form of a spray on top of plants where some of it will evaporate. Thus, drip irrigation applies smaller amounts of water directly to plants and their root system. Water is distributed more slowly and precisely, avoiding unnecessary wetting of plant leaves, reducing water loss from wind or evaporation, and minimizing moisture wasted on weeds, unplanted areas, and runoff. Depending on the crop, drip irrigation can produce a 30 percent drop in water usage and a more than 50 percent increase in yields.

In short, water-saving drip irrigation systems will facilitate more efficient agricultural irrigation.

Because the aesthetics of a golf course remain integral to attracting customers, greens must continue to be watered, despite decreased allocations in some U.S. regions. Golf courses turn to technologies provided by firms, such as Toro, to maximize their constrained water allocations. Toro provides sprinkler heads with greater flexibility in terms of spray angle and direction, thereby reducing the possibility for overwatering and water runoff. These sprinklers provide enhanced water distribution control together with greater uniformity, nozzle flexibility, and system efficiency.[66]

Toro also offers its TurfGuard wireless monitoring technology, which it purchased from JLH Labs LLC in 2007.[67] With this technology, sensors measure moisture, temperature, and salinity in the ground and wirelessly send the data to an Internet-connected computer so better decisions can be made on how to irrigate, among other turf management activities. The system tells the user if an area is in an acceptable moisture level range. It helps reduce water usage without risking turf quality, promotes root growth by avoiding overwatering, and detects dry areas before they impact on the turf's health. It also aids in taking the guesswork out of monitoring and managing salinity levels.

About 30 percent of household water use is devoted to outdoor activities, primarily, on the order of 80 to 90 percent, lawn and landscape irrigation.[68] Outdoor water use varies greatly in the United States, largely as a result of differences in climate. Water withdrawals for landscaping are highest in the arid regions of the west and southwest.

As much as 58 percent of the U.S. urban water supply is applied to landscapes, both residential and commercial, which are generally over-watered by 30 to 300 percent. Upwards of half of all that water is lost or wasted because of evaporation or inefficient practices.[69] Each day, millions and millions of gallons of water, laden with various pollutants, such as fertilizers and pesticides, runoff these over-watered landscapes. However, proven technologies exist to enhance efficiencies in the outdoor use of water for lawns and landscape.

Through a November 2003 agreement with HydroPoint Data Systems Inc. (HydroPoint), Toro supplies "smart" irrigation controllers to the residential and commercial landscape market. Toro and HydroPoint Data Systems co-developed and market intelligent, weather-based irrigation controllers using HydroPoint's Weather-TRAK technology.[70]

The WeatherTRAK system uses real-time meteorological data to tell sprinklers when and how much to water lawns, plants, and crops to prevent over-watering. Toro's Intelli-Sense controllers system, the brand under which it markets the WeatherTRAK system, determines how much moisture a landscape needs for ideal turf and plant growth. Controllers do the management tasks for the property owner, precisely and automatically. These tasks involve dispensing the amount of water different plants need, applying the sprinkler at different rates, and adjusting watering schedules to changes based on current weather conditions. The system irrigates automatically and precisely using the WeatherTRAK scheduling engine, which combines site-specific information with real-time ET (evapotransportation) data from weather stations nationwide and site-specific parameters to calculate exactly how much water a landscape needs.

Toro's Intelli-Sense controllers connect customers' sprinkler systems with weather satellites to create an individualized weather-based schedule that adjusts irrigation needs to local weather changes. After customers set their respective controllers with information about their plants, soil, slope, and sun exposure on their site, the WeatherTRAK system creates and calculates a customized watering schedule. The product adjusts irrigation scheduling in real-time according to weather conditions and plant needs, not preset times, as with traditional controllers. The controllers prevent irrigation when it is raining and hold off watering if several days of cloud cover will follow a storm because under these conditions water will likely evaporate a slower rate.

As mentioned, Toro entered into a 2003 agreement with Hydro-Point, a privately-held company, founded in 2002.[71] HydroPoint uses its database and servers to provide localized weather conditions, such as wind, humidity, temperature, down to one square kilometer for every neighborhood in the United States. This real-time data is sent to adjust the WeatherTRAK's satellite-linked controllers based on actual site and environmental conditions. Thus, smart controllers match water application with the changing water needs of plants and lawns. They eliminate water waste through the automated adjustment of water output based on various environmental parameters, such as plant type and local weather.

Independent studies have concluded that the WeatherTRAK system has produced water savings of up to 59 percent and protected water quality by reducing runoff.[72] For example, the Irvine (Orange County, California) Residential Runoff Reduction Study concluded that WaterTRAK achieved an average 10 percent total household water use savings and reduced landscape runoff by 71 percent in comparison to a control group.[73] A two-year study in Santa Barbara County, California showed an average overall decrease of about 26 percent in residential water usage with the WeatherTRAK system.[74]

The WeatherTRAK product line has received perfect scores on the Irrigation Association's Smart Water Application Technology (SWAT) performance test.[75] SWAT, a consortium of water purveyors and irrigation industry leaders, performance results measure the degree to which controllers maintain root zone moisture levels within an acceptable range. Controllers are evaluated for both irrigation adequacy and excess. Irrigation adequacy reflects the percentage of water required for turf plant material supplied by rainfall and the controller-scheduled irrigation. Irrigation excess represents how much water is applied beyond the needs of the turf or plant material.

Good technology helps raise capital. HydroPoint has received four rounds of venture capital funding.[76] In November 2004, in a first round; it obtained $11.9 million in funding from The Toro Company, Shea Ventures (a division of Shea Homes), Monitor Venture Partners, Firelake Strategic Technology Fund, Scenic Ventures, and various private individuals. The funding helped accelerate the firm's nationwide rollout of its WeatherTRAK irrigation management solutions for commercial and residential landscapes. In November 2005, it raised $5 million in second round of venture capital funding to support its sales, marketing, and product initiatives. Then, in February 2007, it secured a third round of venture capital funding totaling $19 million, led by RockPort Capital Partners, with support from Chrysalix Energy Venture Capital, Firelake Strategic Technology Fund, Monitor Ventures Partners, Shea Ventures, and The Toro Company. The financing enabled the company to expand its sales and marketing efforts throughout North America. Finally, in September 2007, Sustainable Development Investments of Citi Alternative Investments, a division of Citi Group Inc., provided a material investment in the firm.

Supplying Capital to Start-up Private Entities Revisited

As examined in this chapter, innovative technologies exist to increase water supplies and conserve water. Investors want to see solid, independently verified operating data. However, it is difficult for a weakly capitalized start-up firm to obtain credible data without a pilot-scale demonstration unit. Development funds are difficult to obtain because customers do not want to purchase an unproven product, but the product cannot be developed and proven without sufficient investment capital. Thus, funding a new technology is difficult.

Venture capitalists and other investors remain skeptical of investing in ideas. During the deep 2007-2009 recession, as venture capital companies scrambled to preserve cash, funding dried up for start-up and expansion-stage enterprises, hurt by the plunge in initial public offerings and acquisitions. With the 2008-2009 stock market collapse, pension funds, endowments, and wealthy investors in venture capital funds became more cautious about the sector, thereby curtailing the raising of new cash. Taking a hard look at their portfolios and the returns generated by their venture capital investments, they did not have funds to invest or did not want to risk their cash. In the context of a credit crunch that resulted in a very limited bank debt market and constrained, if not nonexistent, initial public offering and acquisition markets, venture capital funds sought the best companies, so-called green-light companies. Available, but limited, resources went into firms having great business models, predictable revenues, and a high return on capital. Venture capital firms continued to invest in the small number of businesses that met those criteria and allowed them to go to scale. In contrast, no money went to so-called red-light companies. The in-between, yellow-light companies, which include the vast majority of firms seeking venture capital, faced a difficult problem as many venture capital firms sought to sell or merge these entities.[77]

"Water scarcity," a phrase that currently does not strike fear into the hearts of most Americans, has spurred action by inventors, entrepreneurs, and investors to take advantage of the growing need for technological advances to increase supplies and conserve water. New technologies continue to be developed; existing technologies are applied to water and wastewater applications. New firms emerge; older companies reshape themselves as players in the water market. Up until the 2008 stock market crash, venture capital firms regularly made investments in private entities developing and marketing various water and wastewater technologies.

The private sector plays an important role in another aspect of the water and wastewater industry. We turn and consider the viability of infrastructure privatization as a financial tool and managerial technique. We begin with an analysis of the various modes of privatization.

Notes

1. See, e.g., Mickey Meece, "Partnerships Bolster the Big and the Small, *New York Times,* April 30, 2009, Business Section, B4 and Edward Iwata, "Venture capitalists today look far and wide for start-ups," *USA Today,* August 27, 2008, B1.

2. *The Water Encyclopedia: Hydrologic Data and Internet Resources,* Third Edition, eds. Pedro Fierro, Jr. and Evan K. Nyer (Boca Raton, FL: Taylor and Francis, 2007), 7-101 (Table 7E 40 Typical Urban Water Use by a Family of Four).

3. For background on indirect portable water reuse see Takashi Asano et al., *Water Reuse: Issues, Technologies, and Applications* (New York: McGraw Hill, 2007) 933, 1248-1254, 1305-1321. See also Water Environment Foundation (WEF) and American Water Works Association (AWWA), *Using Reclaimed Water to Augment Potable Water Resources,* Second Edition (Alexandria, VA: Water Environment Federation and Denver, CO: American Water Works Association, 2008), 2-1 to 2-22.

4. Steve Maxwell, The State of the Water Industry: Blood of the Earth.... Store of Economic Value: A Concise Review of Challenges and Opportunities in the World Water Market, TechKNOWLEDGEy Strategic Group, 2009, 16.

5. WEF and AWWA, *Using Reclaimed Water,* 6-3 to 6-4 and John D. Borrows and Todd Simpson, Water Reuse: Consideration for Commissions, National Regulatory Research Institute, June 1997, 13-20.

6. For technical background on emerging contaminants see Asano, *Water Reuse,* 108-114, 117-120 and WEF and AWWA, *Using Reclaimed Water,* 3-13 to 3-16.

7. Paul E. Stackelberg et al., "Persistence of pharmaceutical compounds and other organic wastewater contaminants in a conventional drinking-water-treatment plant," *Science of the Total Environment* 329: 1-3 (August 15, 2004): 99-113. See also Dawn Fallik, "Drinking water holds surprises," *Philadelphia Inquirer,* November 28, 2004, B1.

8. Mary A. Soliman et al., "Human Pharmaceuticals, Antioxidants, and Plasticizers in Wastewater Treatment Plant and Water Reclamation Plant Effluents," *Water Environment Research* 79:2 (February 2007): 156-167. See also A.J. Watkinson, E.J. Murby, S.D. Constanzo, "Removal of antibiotics in conventional and wastewater treatment: Implications for environmental discharge and wastewater recycling," *Water Research* 41:18 (October 2007): 4164-4176, who report small amounts of antibiotics passing through sophisticated wastewater treatment plants.

9. For background on various removal methods, See Asano, *Water Reuse,* 425-439, 463-473, 529-591 and WEF and AWWA, *Reclaimed Water,* 4-3 to 4-18.

10. Critics of nanotechnology point to seemingly unfounded, potential negative health and environmental impacts of nanotechnology. Maude Barlow, *Blue*

Covenant: The Global Water Crisis and The Coming Battle for the Right to Water (New York: New Press, 2007) 97-99; Jennifer Sass, Nanotechnology's Invisible Threat: Small Science, Big Consequences, National Resources Defense Council Issue Paper, May 2007; Royal Society and Royal Academy of Engineering, Nanoscience and Nanotechnologies: opportunities and uncertainties, July 2004, 3-5-50, but see HM Government in Consultation with the Devolved Administrations, Response to the Royal Society and Royal Academy Report, 'Nanoscience and Nanotechnologies: opportunities and uncertainties', February 2005. See also Barnaby J. Feder, "As Uses Grow, Tiny Materials' Safety Is Hard to Pin Down," *New York Times*, November 3, 2003, C2 and Barnaby J. Feder, "From Nanotechnology's Sidelines, One More Warning," *New York Times*, February 3, 2003, C1.

11. I have drawn on Argonide Corp. (Argonide), "Bioseparations" <www.argonide.com/bioseparations.html> (February 26, 2009); Argonide, "Industrial Water Purification" <www.argonide.com/turbidity.html> (February 26, 2009); Argonide, "Collection and Removal of Biological Warfare Agents <www.argonide.com/biowarfare.html> (February 26, 2009); Argonide, "Ultra-Pure Water Production" <www.argonide.com/pure-water.html> (February 26, 2009); Ahlstrom Corp., Press Release, "Ahlstrom's water filtration media named for INDA 2009 Visionary Award," November 7, 2008. See also Feliza Mirasol, "Fiber holds it together," *ICIS Chemical Business* 278:8 (September 1, 2008): 23-25; Fred Tepper and Leonid Kaledin, "A High-Performance Electropositive Filter," *BioProcess International* 4:6 (June 2006): 64-68; *Product News Network*, "New Low Cost-High Efficiency Virus Sample Hits Market," January 10, 2006 <LexisNexis>; *Flame Retardancy News*, "Argonide Stays Lean and Mean to Commercialize Filters," 15:1 (January 2005) <LexisNexis>; Danielle Sidawi, "Water Testing and Treatment Reflect the Times," *R and D* 46:5 (May 1, 2004): 52-55; *Nanoparticle News*, "Nanosize Fibers Are Found To Have Unusual Bioactivity" 4:9 (October 2001) <LexiNexis>; Jamie J. Anderson, "Business Employs Russian Scientists," *Orlando Sentinel* (Florida), July 29, 2001, K1; *High Tech Ceramics News*, "Argonide Launches Nano-Alumina Fibers" 12:11 (February 2001) <LexisNexis>.

12. *R & D Magazine*, "R & D 100 Awards: Fiber Filters Microbes, Metals," September 2002, 40. See also *Nanoparticle News*, "News Briefs" 5:7 (August 2002) <LexisNexis>.

13. Argonide, "About Argonide" <www.argonide.com/company.html> (February 26, 2009); National Aeronatics and Space Administration (NASA), Small Business Innovation Research (SBIR) Program, Press Release, "NASA Selects 325 Innovative Small Business Projects," September 11, 2001; NASA, SBIR Program, Press Release, "2001 SBIR/STTR Phase 2," July 18, 2002; NASA, Scientific and Technical Information, "Freeing Water From Viruses and Bacteria," updated February 27, 2009 <www.sti.nasa.gov/tto/Spinoff2004/hm_3.html> (June 12, 2009); NASA, NASA SBIR Success, "Nano Ceramic Sterilization Filter," March 21, 2005 <http://sbir.gsfc.nasa.gov/ SBIR/successes/ss/9-072text.html> (June 12, 2009); U.S. Environmental Protection Agency (EPA), National Center for Environmental Research (NCER), Press Release, "Contracts Awarded for Technologies to

Remove Arsenic from Drinking Water," December 6, 2002; EPA, NCER, "Final Report: Nano Alumina Arsenic Filter," updated June 12, 2009 <http://cfpub.epa.gov/ ncer_abstracts/ index.cfm/fuseaction/display.abstract-Detail/abstract/56> (June 12, 2009); Argonide, Press Release, "Argonide Wins Air Force Contract to Improve Hepa Filters, May 10, 2007. See also *Advanced Ceramics Report*, "Water filter systems for space" (September 1, 2002):8; *Nanoparticle News*, "Grants and Contracts" 5:7 (August 2002) <LexisNexis>; *Environmental Laboratory Washington Report*, "1.15 million in grants awarded, for environmental technologies" 13:22 (December 19, 2002):12; U.S. Newswire, "Latest Developments from the Environmental Protection Agency," December 4, 2002 <LexisNexis>; *U.S. Fed News Service*, "Argonide Wins $372,605 Contract," April 23, 2007.

14. Ahlstrom Corp. (Ahlstrom), Press Release, "Ahlstrom introduces Disruptor nanoalumina filter technology," November 30, 2006 and Ahlstrom, Press Release, "Ahlstrom introduces new powdered activated carbon media for water filtration," March 27, 2008.

15. I have drawn on Microvi Biotech Inc.(Microvi), "Our Company" <www.microvibiotech.com/company.html> (March 30, 2009); Microvi, "Markets We Serve" <www.microvibiotech.com/markets.html> (March 30, 2009); Microvi, "Our Solutions" <www.microvibiotech.com/ olutions.html> (March 30, 2009); Microvi "Our Groundwater Solutions" <www.microvi-biotech.com/ groundwater.html> (March 30, 2009); Microvi, "Our Drinking Water Solutions" <www.microvibiotech.com/drinkingwater.html> (March 30, 2009); Microvi, "Wastewater Solutions" <www.microvibiotech.com/ wastewater.html> (March 30, 2009). See also Adam Bluestein, "Blue is the New Green," *Inc. Magazine* 30:11 (November 2008): 117-128, at 128.

16. Microvi, Press Release, "Microvi Biotech Receives a National Institutes of Health Grant for the Demonstration of its Patented Clean Technology, July 24, 2006; Microvi, Press Release, "Microvi Biotech Gains Significant Support for Pilot-Scale Demonstration of In-situ Patented Process for Destruction of MTBE at Port Hueneme, California," February 1, 2006; Microvi, Press Release, "Microvi Biotech Gains Significant Support for the Demonstration of its Patented Clean Technology for the Destruction of MTBE in Groundwater," January 31, 2006. See also National Institutes of Health, Research Portfolio Online Reporting Tool, Institution Detail for 2008 and 2007 <http://report.nih.gov/award/trends/FindOrg_Detail.cfm?OrgID=10006109> (June 11, 2009).

17. Microvi, Press Release, "Microvi Biotech Inc. Raises Series A Equity Financing," August 26, 2009.

18. I have drawn on AbTech Industries Inc. (AbTech), "About AbTech" <www.abtechindustries.com/index.asp?mid2=181> (February 19, 2009); AbTech, "Products" <www.abtechindustries.com/under.asp?mid=66> (February 19, 2009); AbTech, Press Release, "Long Beach City Council Approves Million-Dollar Contract to Reduce City's Stormwater Pollution Using AbTech Industries' New Patented Antimicrobial Technology," August 25, 2004. See also Coeli Carr, "Absorbing a setback, *Time* 173:18 (May 11, 2009):8; Bluestein, "Blue," 126, 128; Tony Natale, "Filter company cleans up environment," *The Tribune* (Mesa, Arizona), October 6, 2008, A10; *Journal*

of Environmental Health, "AbTech's Smart Sponge® Plus Takes on Health-Threatening Bacteria" 67:9 (May 1, 2005): 81; *Water World*, "Stormwater filtration (New Products)" 20:9 (September 1, 2004): 97; *Business Week*, "Making Storm Drains the Last Stop for Toxins" 2784 (May 27, 2002): 95.

19. Quoted in Bluestein, "Blue," 126, 128.
20. Quoted in Carr, "Absorbing."
21. BioShield Technologies, Inc.(BioShield), Press Release, "BioShield and AbTech Industries [Strike] Alliance Which Will Result in First Antimicrobial Solution in Rapidly Growing Stormwater Market," December 21, 2001; BioShield, Press Release, "BioShield Secures $2.45 Million Agreement with AbTech Technologies, Inc.," January 15, 2002.
22. Carr, "Absorbing."
23. AbTech, Press Release, "Competes Financing of $6.8 Million," November 14, 2006. See also Jane Larson, "Scottsdale company whose technology sucks bacteria and other contaminants out of storm water has found a believer in a New York investment house," *Arizona Republic* (Phoenix), October 27, 2006, 6.
24. For background on direct water reuse see Asano, *Water Reuse*, 934, 1346-1349.
25. *Ibid.*, 902-919.
26. See, e.g., Bettina Boxall, "Doubts Still Swirl to Surface," *Los Angeles Times*, May 7, 2009, B1 and D.J. Waldie, "Los Angeles' Toilet-to-Tap Fear," *Los Angeles Times*, December 1, 2002, M2.
27. Industrial uses of reclaimed water are discussed in Asano, *Water Reuse*, 1105-1155.
28. Bluestein, "Blue," 120-121.
29. Disinfection with chlorine is considered in Asano, *WaterReuse*, 622-654 and WEF and AWWA, *Using Reclaimed Water*, 4-24 to 4-25. For a historical overview of disinfection with chlorine see M.N. Baker, *The Quest for Pure Water: The History of Water Purification from the Earliest Records to the Twentieth Century* (New York: American Water Works Association, 1948), 326-343. See also Martin V. Melosi, *The Sanitary City: Urban Infrastructure in America from Colonial Times to the Present* (Baltimore: Johns Hopkins, 2000), 303, 382 and Steve Hoffman, *Planet Water: Investing in the World's Most Valuable Resource* (Hoboken, NJ: Wiley, 2009), 94-120.
30. MIOX Corp. (MIOX), Press Release, "MIOX Announces $19 Million Investment to Accelerate Growth in Global Markets," August 26, 2008; MIOX, Press Release, "MIOX Corporation Set to Expand with Investment from Sand Hill Road Venture Capital Firm," January 22, 2007; Flywheel Ventures, Press Release, "MIOX Corporation Set to Expand with Investment from Sand Hill Road Venture Capital Firm, January 22, 2007. See also *Albuquerque Journal*, "Water treatment firm, investor strike deal," September 8, 2008, 8; *Journal of American Water Works Association*, "Business Briefs" 99:4 (April 2007): 6; *New Mexico Business Weekly*, "MIOX gets $14.5 private equity boost," January 26, 2007 <albuquerque.bizjournals.com/albuquerque/stories.2007/01/29st...<; Andrew Webb, "Water disinfection

tech company MIOX to get new management, marketing," Knight Ridder Tribune Business News, October 4, 2005; *New Mexico Business Weekly,* "Investors take control of Miox for $16 million," September 30, 2005, <albuquerque.bizjournals.com/albuquerque/stories/2005/10/03/story>.

31. Frank Mickadeit, "I knock back a cup of Calcutta Crude," *Orange County Register* (California), January 25, 2008, Local Section, 2; Pat Brennan, "Sewer-to-tap system kicks off," *Orange County Register* (California), January 11, 2008, Local Section, 1; Dan Weikel, "Sewage in O.C. goes full circle," *Los Angeles Times,* January 2, 2008, A1; Pat Brennan, "Pumping up the volume," *Orange County Register* (California), News Section, 3. See also Randal C. Archibold, "From Sewage, Added Water for Drinking," *New York Times,* November 27, 2007, A29.

32. For background on onsite and decentralized water reuse systems see U.S. Environmental Protection Agency (EPA), Office of Water, Decentralized Wastewater Treatment Systems: A Program Strategy, January 2005, EPA 832-R-05-002 and Asano, *Water Reuse,* 766-821.

33. John Montgomery Scott, Key Themes in Water Technology, Industry Report, October 6, 2008, 11.

34. For background on decentralized water treatment see Hoffman, *Planet Water,* 127-144.

35. The urban nonirrigation water reuse applications, such as toilet flushing, are considered in Asano, *Water Reuse,* 1171-1197.

36. EPA, "Indoor Water Use in the United States," June 2008, EPA-832-F-06-004 and Peter W. Mayer and William B. DeOreo et al., Residential End Uses of Water, American Water Works Association Research Foundation, 1999, xxv-xxvi, 106-111. See also WaterSaver Technologies Inc. (WaterSaver), "Introducing AQUS," <www.watersavertech.com/AQUS-Water-Conservation.html> (February 19, 2009), 7.

37. WaterSaver, "FAQ about the AQUS" <www.watersavertech.com/AQUS-Water-Conservation-Questions.html> (February 19, 2009). See also Bluestein, "Blue," 122, 124.

38. *Popular Science,* "Guilt-Free Flushing" 271:6 (December 2007) :104.

39. Quoted in *Journal of the American Water Works Association,* "Business Briefs" 100:9 (September 2008): 196-199, at 199. See also WaterSaver, "WaterSaver Technologies partners with Sloan Valve Company to distribute AQUS System" <www.watersavertech.com/Sloan-Valve.html> (June 23, 2009).

40. EPA, "Water Wastewater Pricing, Introduction" <www.epa.gov/waterinfrastructure/pricing /index.htm> (March 3, 2009); Amy Vickers, *Handbook of Water Use and Conservation* (Amherst, MA: WaterPlow Press, 2001), 12, 15; Maxwell, State of the Water Industry, 16.

41. *Public Papers of the Presidents of the United States,* John F. Kennedy (Washington DC: Government Printing Office, 1962), 261.

42. Heather Cooley, Peter H. Gleick, Gary Wolff, Desalination, With a Grain of Salt: A California Perspective, Pacific Institute for Studies in Development, Environment, and Security, June 2006, 41-43, 53-66, 71-74, provide a critical view of desalination, but see Nikolay Voutchkov, "California

Desalination Report with More than a Grain of Salt," *Water Conditioning & Purification* 49:1 (January 2007): 30-36. See also Phil Dickie, Making Water: Desalination: option or distraction for a thirsty world?, World Wildlife Federation Global Freshwater Programme, June 2007, 13-20; Joseph A. Cotruvo, "Water Desalination Processes and Associated Health and Environmental Issues," *Water Conditioning & Purification* 47:1 (January 2005): 13-17; John Eric Edinger and Venkat S. Kolluru, "Power Plant Intake Entrainment Analysis," *Journal of Energy Engineering* 126:1 (April 2000): 1-14. See generally National Research Council, *Desalination: A National Perspective* (Washington, DC: National Academies Press, 2008), 5-7, 61-65, 97-105, 107, 108-146, noting the considerable uncertainties about the environmental impacts of desalination.

43. *Ibid.*, 4-5, 7-9, 65-97, 150-170, 179-181. For background on desalination see Hoffman, *Planet Water*, 220-226.

44. Melissa Abraham, "Today's Seawater Is Tomorrow's Drinking Water," *UCLA News*, November 6, 2006<http//newsroom.ucla.edu/ portal/ucla/ PRN-Today-s-Seawater-Is-Tomorrow-s7410.aspx>(February 25, 2009).

45. Bluestein, "Blue," 119-120 and Michael Kanellos, A Guide to the Water World (Greentech Media), November 17, 2008.

46. NanoH$_2$O Inc. (NanoH$_2$0), "Technology" <www.nanoh20.com/Technology. php5> (February 19, 2009) and NanoH$_2$O, "Water Opportunity" <www. nanoh2o/wateropportunity.php5?category=BetterDesalination> (February 19, 2009).

47. NanoH$_2$O, Press Release, "NanoH$_2$O Secures $15 Million. Investment Round from Oak Investment Partners and Khosla Ventures," September 8, 2008 and NanoH$_2$O, Press Release, "NanoH$_2$O Secures Funding from Khosla Ventures," April 11, 2007. See also *Filtration Industry Analyst*, "NanoH$_2$O Secures US$5MN From Khosla Ventures," June 2007, 2.

48. I have drawn on Energy Recovery, Inc. (Energy Recovery), "About ERI" <www.energyrecovery.com/company/who_is_eri.php4> (February 19, 2009); Energy Recovery, "Company Overview" <www.energyrecovery.com/ phoenix.zhtml?c=221013&p=irol-homeprofile> (February 24, 2009); Energy Recovery, "Products Overview" <www.energyrecovery.com/ products/ products_overview.php4> (February 19, 2009); Energy Recovery, "How It Works" <www.energyrecovery.com/px_technology/how_how_it_works. php4> (February 24, 2009); Energy Recovery, SEC Form S-1, April 1, 2008, 1, 24-25, 40-49; Richard L. Stoner, "Seawater reverse osmosis with isobaric energy recovery devices," *Desalination* 203:1-3 (February 2003): 168-175. See also Jennifer Hoyt, "Firm Wagers Desalination Can Pay Off," *Wall Street Journal*, May 6, 2009, B2B; Jeff Hull, "Water, Water Everywhere," *Fast Company* 132 (February 2009): 66-71, 100, at 70; Tom Abate, "New pump desalinates water as it saves money," *San Francisco Chronicle*, August 3, 2008, D1; John P. MacHarg and Stuart A. McClellan, "Pressure Exchanger Helps Reduce Energy Costs in Brackish Water RO System," *Journal of American Water Works Association* 96:11 (November 2004): 44-48.

49. Energy Recovery, SEC Form S-1, 2, 41; Bluestein, "Blue," 119.

50. Sabrina Shankman, "California Gives Desalination Plants a Fresh Look," *Wall Street Journal*, July 9, 2009, A4; Michael Burge, "Desalination plan at

defining moment," *San Diego Union-Tribune*, May 24, 2009, N1; Felicity Barringe, "In California, Desalination of Seawater, As a Test Case," *New York Times*, May 15, 2009, A15.

51. The U.S. General Accounting Office, Water Infrastructure: Information on Financing, Capital Planning, and Privatization, August 2002, GAO-02-764, 51, indicated that many communities cannot account for 25 percent of more of the water they produce. Maxwell, "State of the Water Industry," 16, places the leakage of drinking water at 20 to 40 percent. See also National Research Council, *Privatization of Water Services in the United States: An Assessment of Issues and Experience* (Washington, DC: National Academy Press, 2002), 85; Steve Maxwell, "Where Are We Headed? Ten Key Trends and Developments in the Water Industries," *Journal of the American Water Works Association* 93:4 (April 2001): 114-118, at 117; Thomas Rooney, "Water crisis," *Natural Life* (September-October 2007): 4 and 6.

52. D.L. Bennett, "Pipe Replacement for Atlanta Water Mains Is In the Works," *Atlanta Journal and Constitution*, March 30, 2003, F3. See also Pacific Institute for Studies in Development, Environment, and Security, A Review of Water Conservation Planning for the Atlanta, Georgia Region, August 2006, 15.

53. Maxwell, "State of the Water Industry," 16.

54. I have drawn on Insituform Technologies Inc. (Insituform), SEC Form 10-K, March 2, 2009, 4-5 and Insituform, "Company Information" <www.insituform.com/content/137/company-information.aspx> (February 19, 2009). See also Marilyn Much, "Acquisitions Strengthen Company That Maintains Water, Energy Pipes," *Investor's Business Daily*, February 9, 2009, A6; Jack Naudi, "Chesterfield, Mo., pipe repair firm takes a costly swat at an industry gnat," *St. Louis Post-Dispatch*, December 10, 2004, C1; Casey Smith and Blaine Robinson, "The Great Phoenix Bypass," *Public Works* 135: 10 (September 2004): 76-80; J. Bonasia, "Clean Water, Air Plans Hinge on Technology," *Investor's Business Daily*, August 30, 2004, A22; *Public Works*, "Sewer Rehab Results In Dramatic Infiltration Drop" 133:1 (January 2002): 48-50.

55. Insituform, "Insituform CIPP [Cured-In-Place Pipe] Sanitary/Sewer Storm Repair" <www.insituform.com/content/ 342/cipp_technology.aspx> (February 24, 2009) and Insituform, "How Insituform Cured-in-Place Pipe (CIPP) is Installed" <www.insituform.com/ content/190/insituform_cipp_process.aspx> (February 24, 2009). Limitations exist, however, on trenchless sewer rehabilitation techniques see *Water Encyclopedia*, 9-23 (Table 9B.29 Limitations of Trenchless Sewer Rehabilitation Techniques).

56. Insituform, "Thermopipe" <www.insituform.com/content/344 /about_thermopipe.aspx> (February 24, 2009) and Insituform," How Thermopipe is Installed" <www.insituform.com/content/209/how_thermopipe_is_in-stalled_.aspx> (February 24, 2009).

57. Falcon Waterfree Technologies Inc. (Falcon), "Background," November 2004 and Falcon, "About Us." See also Bluestein, "Blue," 124-125 and Robert Kravitz, "Building Goes Water-Free," *Maintenance Supplies* 50:5 (July 2005): 34-35. For background on urinals see Vickers, *Handbook*, 76-86.

58. Falcon, "Background." November 2004.

59. Falcon, Press Release, "Capricorn Management Makes 'Green' Investment in Falcon Water Technologies," April 25, 2006 and Capricorn Management, Press Release, "Capricorn Management Makes 'Green' Investment in Falcon Waterfree Technologies," April 25, 2006. See also Bluestein, "Blue," 124-125 and Stephanie Strom, "What Wrong with Profit?", *New York Times*, November 13, 2006, F1.

60. Frank Greve and Queenie Wong, "No thanks to no-flush urinals," *Seattle Times*, November 17, 2008, A2 and Katherine Yung, "Cascade Twp. Firm Rides Next Wave With Waterless Urinals," *Detroit Free Press*, October 26, 2008, Business Section, 3.

61. U.S. Geological Survey, Estimated Use of Water in the United States in 2000, U.S. Geological Survey Circular 1268, 2004, 20. See also Vickers, *Handbook*, 330 and Noel Gollehon and William Quinby, "Irrigation Resources and Water Costs," in *Agricultural Resources and Environmental Indicators*, eds. Keith Daniel Wiebe and Noel R. Gollenhon (New York: Nova Science, 2006), 24-32.

62. Nicholas Spulber and Asghar Sabbaghi, *Economics of Water Resources: From Regulation to Privatization*, Second edition (Boston: Kluwer Academic, 1998), 196, 283. See also Maxwell, "State of the Water Industry," 13, 16 and Janney Montgomery Scott Key Themes, 3.

63. Vickers, *Handbook*, 334.

64. For innovations in irrigation see Hoffman, *Planet Water*, 214-215.

65. The Toro Company (Toro), What Is Drip Irrigation? <www.toromicroirrigation.com> (March 3, 2009) and Toro, SEC Form 10-K, December 22, 2008 (2008 SEC Form 10-K), 4. For background on drip irrigation see Vickers, *Handbook*, 197-198, 200, 377-383.

66. Toro, "Sprinklers" <www.toro.com/irrigation/golf/sprays_ micro/index. html> (March 3, 2009); Toro, Press Release, "Toro Introduces New Line of Durable Swing Joints That Optimize Golf Sprinkler Alignment and Performance," February 5, 2009; Toro, Press Release, "Toro Introduces Precision Series Spray Nozzles With Toro H_2O Chip Technology," November 2, 2008; Toro, Press Release, "Toro Adds High-Tech Enhancements To Improve Irrigation Nozzle Efficiency," January 31, 2008. For background on the maintenance of sprinkler components see Vickers, *Handbook*, 191-195.

67. Jeffrey Kanige, "M & A briefly noted," *Daily Deal*, December 7, 2007 (2007 WLNR 24152295); Toro, "Turf Guard Sensors" <www.toro.com/irrigation/ golfturfguard/index.html> (March 3, 2009); Toro, "Turf Guard" <www. turfguard.net> (March 3, 2009); Toro, 2008 SEC Form 10-K, 4; Toro, Press Release," Toro Introduces Turf Guard Wireless Soil Monitoring System," January 31, 2008.

68. EPA, "Outdoor Water Use in the United States," August 2008, EPA-832-F-06-005 and Vickers, *Handbook*, 140-141.

69. Leonard S. Hyman et al., *The Water Business: Understanding the Water Supply and Wastewater Industry* (Vienna, VA: Public Utilities Reports, 1998), 60 and HydroPoint Data Systems (HydroPoint), "WeatherTRAK: The Proven Leader in Smart Water Management" <www.weathertrak. com/company-info/abouthydropoint .php> (February 19, 2009). See also Bluestein, "Blue," 126.

70. Toro, Press Release, "The Toro Company Introduces Weather TRAK Technology for Commercial and Home Irrigation Control," November 12, 2003; Toro, Press Release, "Water Management and Conservation are Driving Forces for the Toro Company," November 18, 2003; Toro, Press Release, "Toro Unveils Intelli-Sense: The Smarter Way to Water," November 14, 2004; Toro, Press Release, "Toro Intelli-Sense 'Smart' Controllers Reduce Water Waste and Irrigation Costs," November 2, 2008; Toro, "Small Turf Controllers," www.toro.com/irrigation/res/smturfcont /index.html> (March 3, 2009); "Intelli-Sense Series" <www.toro.com/irrigation/res/ smturfcont/intelli.html> (March 3, 2009); Toro, 2008 SEC Form 10-K, 4. See also Georgia Tasker, "Smart Irrigation," *Miami Herald*, December 9, 2007, H4; Jeff St. John, "Smart Irrigation," *Fresno Bee* (California), April 8, 2007, F1; Joe Provey, "Lawn Irrigation Gets Smarter," *Popular Mechanics* 183:8 (August 2006): 92-93; *Landscape & Irrigation*, "Tracking the Weather" 28:1 (January 1, 2004): 21.

71. HydroPoint, "WeatherTRAK: The Proven Leader in Smart Water" <www. weathertrak.com/company-info/about-hydropoint.php> (February 19, 2009); HydroPoint, Press Release, "HydroPoint Data Systems Closes Strongest Q4 in Company History," January 21, 2009; HydroPoint, Press Release, "HydroPoint Enhances Web-Based WeatherTRAK Application to Facilitate Smart Water Management from Any Location," October 31, 2008; HydroPoint, Press Release, "California Cities Implement Smart Water Management System to Protect Water Supply," April 28, 2008; Hydro Point, Press Release, "WeatherTRAK Smart Water Management Provides Answer to Rocky Mountain Water Shortage," January 23, 2008; HydroPoint, Press Release, "HydroPoint Extends WeatherTRAK Smart Irrigation Solution from Single-Family Homes to Community Common Areas," July 28, 2006; HydroPoint, Press Release, "NWP Services Corporation to Provide WeatherTRAK Irrigation Management to the Multi-Housing Industry," March 29, 2006. See also Bluestein, "Blue," 126; *Wireless News*, "HydroPoint Gets 5 Awards for Smart Water Management Technology," November 23, 2008; Steve Hart, "Petaluma Irrigation System Company Poised To Cash In If 'Smart' Watering Bill Wins Governor's Approval," *Press Democrat* (Santa Rosa, CA), September 8, 2006, E1.

72. See generally HydroPoint, "Independent Research Studies" <www.weathertrak.com/smart-irrigation/research- studies.php> (March 5, 2009).

73. Municipal Water District of Orange County, Irvine Ranch Water District, The Residential Runoff Reduction Study, July 2004, ES-3, ES-6. See also Anil Bamezai, ET Controller Savings Through the Second Post-Retrofit Year: A Brief Update, April 2001 and Irvine Ranch District, Municipal Water District of Orange County, Metropolitan Water District of Southern California, Residential Weather-Based Irrigation Scheduling: Evidence Residential Weather-Based Irrigation Scheduling: Evidence from the Irvine "ET Controller" Study, June 2001.

74. Santa Barbara County ET Controller Distribution and Installation Program, Final Report, June 30, 2003. For other studies see Anil Bamezai, LADWP [Los Angeles Department of Water and Power] Weather-Based Irrigation Controller Pilot Study, Western Policy Research, August 3, 2004; Aquacraft, Inc., Analysis of Operation of WeatherTRAK Controller in Field Conditions

During 2002, April 23, 2003; AquaCraft, Inc., Performance Evaluation of WeatherTRAK Irrigation Controllers in Colorado, n. d.

75. HydroPoint, Press Release, "WeatherTRAK Receives Irrigation Association's First Perfect Score on SWAT Performance Test," January 26, 2006; Irrigation Association, Smart Water Application Technology (SWAT) Performance Report, January 9, 2006. See also Jill Hoyenga and Robert Reaves, "Smart Water Application Technology," *Journal of American Water Works Association* 98:2 (February 2006): 112-121.

76. HydroPoint, Press Release, "HydroPoint Secures $11.9 in Venture Funding," November 11, 2004; HydroPoint, Press Release, "HydroPoint Receives $5 Million in Venture Funding," November 1, 2005; HydroPoint, Press Release, "HydroPoint Secures $19 million in Series C Financing," January 21, 2007; HydroPoint, Press Release, "HydroPoint Secures Investment Citi Alternative Investments," September 25, 2007. See also Steve Hart, "Petaluma Firm Raises $5 Million," *Press Democrat* (Santa Rosa, CA), November 26, 2005, E1.

77. Pui-wing Tam, "Venture-Capital Firms Caught in a Shakeout," *Wall Street Journal*, March 9, 2010, B1; Brian Deagon, "Venture Capital Investing Rises 17% From Q2, But Still Ailing," *Investor's Business Daily*, October 20, 2009, A4; Brian Deagon, "Venture Capitalists to Entrepreneurs," *Investor's Business Daily*, June 10, 2009, A4; Pui-Wing Tam, "Venture Capitalists Head for the Door," *Wall Street Journal*, June 5, 2009, C1; Doug Tsuruoka, "'Yellow Light' Issues for VC, Equity Field," *Investor's Business Daily*, March 10, 2009, A4.

Part III
Infrastructure Privatization, Comparative Background, and Privatization Incentives

5

Modes of Privatization, Comparative Background, and Privatization Incentives

This chapter considers the various forms privatization may take in the United States, namely, asset sales, contractual arrangements, and design-build-operate-transfer agreements.[1] It identifies the key characteristics of the British (England and Wales) and French approaches to the privatization of water and wastewater systems. Although an analysis of the impact of privatization in these two nations is beyond the scope of this book, these two countries typify the alternative approaches to drinking water and sewage management. This chapter forms the backdrop for a detailed discussion of the benefits and potential disadvantages of privatization in Chapter 6, and an analysis of privatization in practice in the United States considered in Chapters 7 and 8, respectively. The impact state utility regulation on privatization transactions and federal tax and non-tax incentives to facilitate privatization are also reviewed.

Before analyzing the various forms privatization may take, it is helpful to have a working definition of the term. Privatization involves shifting some degree of responsibility for water supply and wastewater treatment services from the public sector to the private sector. One group of experts stated that privatization connotes the transfer of "some or all of the assets or operations of public water systems into private hands."[2]

Privatization can involve a spectrum of arrangements between the private firms and public entities. Numerous permutations exist involving various ownership and operational possibilities. Localities can explore a variety of options with private entities before settling on one to match their own unique needs. Each arrangement involves a different sharing of responsibilities, revenues, risks, rewards, and accountabilities.

Besides the numerous forms privatization transactions can take, the private sector "privatizers" consist of a variety of entities from giant multinational corporations, to U.S.-based shareholder-owned firms, to mom-and-pop operations, all seeking an expanded role in providing water supply and wastewater treatment services. There are also third-party service providers, private vendors that enter into contractual arrangements with public agencies. These private vendors market their engineering or management expertise to public sector infrastructure owners.

The privatizers exhibit a range of business strategies including creating new entities, restructuring existing firms, and entering into partnerships (or joint ventures) to buy assets or compete for contracts. Some of the most active privatizers are affiliated with larger firms, which are, in turn, often controlled by multinational corporations. Greater access to capital gives these larger firms a significant advantage over smaller entities in bidding for privatization projects.

Asset Sales

In an asset sale, a government unit sells and thus divests itself of an asset to the private sector. A private firm then owns the facility or system. More specifically, a transfer of ownership occurs when a private firm purchases a public agency's assets, assumes the locality's franchise and operating certificates, and takes control over (and responsibility for) operations, financing, planning, and construction.

An asset sale releases a locality from direct responsibility for managing and financing operations as well as complying with environmental requirements. As discussed later in this chapter, in the United States, a governmental agency, a state public utility commission, typically has economic regulatory oversight and monitoring responsibilities with respect to privately-owned utilities, such as water suppliers. In addition to the capital invested by the new owner in the asset acquisition and subsequent operations, as well as a long-term financial commitment, the ownership model may facilitate the consolidation of fragmented water supply and wastewater treatment services, with the expectation of achieving operational efficiencies and improved access to capital.

One advantage of an asset sale for a municipality (or locality) is that it can use the proceeds for various public purposes. In addition, the private buyer becomes subject to taxation, thereby generating revenues for the public sector.

Potential disadvantages of privatization through asset divestitures include private control of vital assets, lack of local control and responsiveness, the possibility of foreign ownership, and future ownership instability resulting from a facility or system's sale from one private entity to another. The valuation of assets can also be difficult. Once sold, if a locality wishes to reacquire the assets it may need to exercise its power of eminent domain.[3]

Several barriers to asset sales exist. First, localities are not necessarily interested in selling their assets. In turn, private firms may not be interested in buying assets as opposed to entering into contractual arrangements. Second, asset purchases require substantial capital investments funded by equity and/or debt. Finally, if a facility is sold to a private party, debt funding is no longer tax-exempt, raising the cost of capital typically by about four percent.[4] In many cases, the cost of capital differential makes contractual arrangements the more attractive option.

In the United States, asset sales generally have occurred because of a municipality's difficulty in raising capital for modernization or expansion by floating tax-exempt bonds. In addition to contractual arrangements for existing infrastructure, in the United States, privatization efforts have tended to focus on the construction of new facilities through design-build-operate-transfer arrangements, discussed later in this chapter. However, the British model is instructive on the mechanics of the privatization of water and wastewater services through an asset sale.

Asset Sales: The British Model

In 1989, the Conservative Government, led by Prime Minister Margaret Thatcher, transferred the assets of nationally-owned, regional water authorities in England and Wales to private providers. The private firms assumed ownership of the infrastructure and received licenses to run their respective systems for twenty-five years. Elsewhere in the United Kingdom, water utilities remain publicly-owned in Scotland and Northern Ireland.

England and Wales typify a top down, total privatization approach, where the subsequent financial benefits (and accompanying risks) go to the shareholders of private firms that own the water assets. Privatization in England and Wales was achieved in one bold stroke. In 1989, water supply and wastewater treatment services went from almost wholly public ownership and management to totally private ownership and management. The sale of water supply- and wastewater-related assets in 1989 in England and Wales represented the

111

world's largest privatization to date, with the assets privatized serving some fifty million people.

Prior to the 1989 privatization, ownership of water and wastewater infrastructure in England and Wales passed through three phases: private; municipal; and then regional, public ownership and management. A shift occurred from private to decentralized, municipal ownership beginning in the mid-1800s and was mostly completed by the early twentieth century. In the mid-nineteenth century, sporadic outbreaks of cholera and typhoid linked to polluted water buttressed the consensus that the public sector ought to provide water and especially sanitation, particularly in view of large, required capital investments coupled with the low rates of profitability. At the same time, a need existed to build large-scale waterworks in Britain as a result of industrialization and urbanization; however, the universal provision of water to residences made water supply less profitable for private firms. Cognizant of these realities and the ineffectiveness of the regulation of private companies from 1840 to 1870, the Gas and Water Facilities Act of 1870 spurred the development of municipal water systems. The act enabled the establishment of municipal water entities by administrative decision, not parliamentary act. With the enactment of the Public Health Act of 1875, municipal ownership grew in importance as localities took over private systems on public health grounds. The act made local authorities responsible for the quantity and quality of water supplies.[5] By the early decades of the twentieth century, a majority of Britons obtained their water from local, publicly-owned entities. So that by 1939, municipalities controlled the British water industry, although some private water supply companies, generally in urban areas, in and around London, continued to exist.

The National Water Act of 1945 encouraged the amalgamation of the British water industry, significantly reducing the number of public water and sewerage bodies. The subsequent 1973 Water Act continued the rationalization and consolidation approach by restructuring the largely publicly-owned industry into nationally-owned, but regionally operating, authorities.[6] The act placed management of the existing publicly-owned water and sewage systems in ten multipurpose, regional water authorities, each covering a river basin area in England and Wales. In addition to providing urban and rural water and sewage services and becoming responsible for their operations, the new water bodies administered some environmental regulations, focusing on pollution control and the protection of aquatic ecosystems. Although the restructuring took a territorial approach to water resources management, investment in the water and wastewater sector, as well as rates, came under the central government's control. To generate funds for repairs and maintenance, infrastructure renewal and upgrades, and water pollution remediation and prevention, the regional water authorities could only borrow funds from the central government, negatively impacting both the industry's infrastructure and the quality of its services.

From the mid-1970s onward, problems soon developed on two fronts.[7] Underinvestment deteriorated infrastructure, which resulted in declining water quality and increased pollution. Between 1974 and 1984, after a massive International Monetary Fund loan, the United Kingdom heavily cut public investment. Underground sewage facilities came near the bottom of the political priorities. As a result, wastewater infrastructure suffered from severe underinvestment. Problems plagued the under funded regional authorities, including both leakage in water distribution and supply pipes, and wastewater systems discharging untreated sewage directly into the ocean. At the same time, concern for the environment assumed greater importance, following the introduction of strict European Union (EU) water quality standards in 1976 and 1980 for swimming and drinking water. The public desired an improvement in water quality. Worries surfaced about various potential public health hazards. The water quality of Britain's beaches presented a pressing problem as a result of sewage contamination in excess of the maximum levels set by the European Union. British rivers were also in poor condition, polluted by industrial waste, agricultural runoff, and untreated sewage. Drinking water in many parts of England and Wales did not meet EU standards.

To deal with these problems, in 1989, privatization of water services was imposed from the top down. Through the Water Act of 1989, the central government privatized, via asset sales, the publicly-owned regional water supply and sewage systems in England and Wales.[8] The government transferred the property rights, most of the infrastructure owned by the ten regional water authorities, and most, but not all, of their functions to ten new, privately-owned, regionally-based water service companies, with little enterprise or managerial reorganization. Ten private, vertically integrated firms extract, process, and deliver water, collect revenues, process sewage, own the assets, reservoirs, treatment plants, and provide operations and maintenance services to their respective networks, initially each covering the same geographical areas as the old regional water authorities. No company operates as a contractor, concessionaire, or lessee. They are each subject to a license agreement, given by the central government that includes conditions for, and obligations of, the public service they provide. However, at the outset they each functioned as a territorial monopolist on water supply and wastewater treatment within their respective geographical areas, river basins within a region; they did not compete with each other.

The new firms provided sewage services to all of the connected population within their respective regions and water services to about three-quarters of the connected population in England and Wales. The remaining one-quarter continue to be served by one of the twenty-nine previously existing private water supply companies. In 1989, these private (so-called statutory) water companies, which provided water, but not sewage services, were renamed water-only companies. These companies became subject to the same economic and environmental regulations as the newly privatized firms.

Apart from ideology, namely, government disengagement from the economy, financial factors motivated privatization. The industry's infrastructure had decayed significantly since the mid-twentieth century under governmental ownership and management. Massive new capital expenditures were required for repairs, maintenance, and upgrades. Policymakers knew of the need for capital infusions and rate hikes, but wanted to avoid responsibilities for both. The costs of meeting new, stringent environmental rules also encouraged privatization. An estimated £24 to £30 billion would be required to raise British water quality to EU standards.[9] Although water quality and environmental outlays had become key drivers of the industry's capital investment program, the Thatcher government did not to want the public sector to finance the requisite massive expenditures. The British Treasury insisted that public sector borrowing for environmental upgrades be reduced. Privatization of water services freed the central government from meeting the financial burdens of environmental compliance.

Privatization would not only provide the framework for the huge capital investments in the water industry to take place but also eliminate the need for public sector borrowing to provide the necessary capital. The private firms would obtain capital for new infrastructure, in part, by charging consumers more realistic prices. Through privatization, the central government sought to distance itself from the public displeasure that would result from the rate hikes needed to fund the requisite capital expenditures.

Privatization was conducted by the central government's sale of shares in the new water service companies. The initial public offering of shares generated £5.2 billion for the British Treasury. To improve water quality to EU standards and ensure a successful public issuance by the new firms on the stock market, the government added a variety of financial sweeteners. The financial package included three key elements. First, the government wrote off the water industry's debt of £5.2 billion. Second, the industry received an additional cash injection of £1.5 billion from the central government. Third, the new companies received £7.7 billion in tax benefits. The firms also received guaranteed price increases, above the rate of inflation, for a specified time period, thereby enabling the generation of the financial resources required for modernization of aging infrastructure pursuant to a ten-year capital spending program for each new company.[10]

Privatization thus provided a mechanism for funding capital expenditures for improving services and water quality. Post-privatization, capital investment in the water and wastewater section in England and Wales roughly doubled averaging slightly more than £3.0 billion per year. By 1998-1999, cumulative capital expenditures amounted to some £33 billion.[11] The capital infusion led to an extensive program of construction of new wastewater treatment plants, upgrades of water supply and wastewater treatment facilities, and thousands of miles of new water pipes and sewers. These paid off in a dramatic improvement in the level of service and environmental performance. Freshwater and drinking water quality improved; coastal beaches became swimmable. Progress was made at stemming water leakages. There were negative consequences, of course, including rate increases as well as the post-privatization restructuring and consolidation of the water industry, but these matters are beyond the scope of this book.

As part of the privatization program, powerful new, national regulatory watchdogs were created to encourage efficiency, protect consumers, and promote environmental improvements.[12] Privatization led to the separation of the national economic and environmental regulators. The core businesses of the private firms, namely, water supply and sewage treatment, are licensed by the nationwide economic regulator, Office of Water Services (OFWAT), for twenty-five years. Technically, the operating licenses are subject to periodic renewal with the governmental required to give ten-years' (subsequently increased to twenty-five years') notice of a termination. In addition to functioning as the economic regulator, having responsibility to set price limits,

115

OFWAT also serves as auditor of the private entities and as a consumer protection service. Two other new nationwide regulatory bodies were established, the National Rivers Authority to regulate wastewater disposal, water conservation, and river basin management, and the Drinking Water Inspectorate, a national body to monitor and regulate drinking water quality based on EU environmental directives.

Britain chose a full privatization program of its water and wastewater services in the face of growing financial and environmental concerns. Its regulatory approach took a centralized turn. The United States has taken a different, decentralized approach to utility regulation.

Economic Regulation of Privately-Owned Water and Wastewater Systems in the United States

Water storage, transmission, and distribution have the characteristics of a natural economic monopoly, particularly with respect to water capture and transportation. Water supplied to a locality by one firm generally entails lower costs than if supplied by more than one provider. With the distribution of water highly localized, marked by one seller in a market, problems associated with monopoly power exist, namely, the potential for high prices and poor service.

Because water distribution and wastewater treatment are natural monopolies, the United States uses decentralized regulation on the state, not national, level to check the power of private firms and protect customers from potential abuse. These economic regulators set price levels and rate structures, typically using a rate of return approach.[13]

Effective regulation seeks to balance the interests of consumers and private operators. It strives to protect consumers lacking competitive alternatives from excessive charges resulting from a monopoly situation, while allowing firms to earn a "fair" return on their investments. To maintain current service levels, meet new demands for service, maintain existing infrastructure, and provide for future infrastructure needs, water and wastewater utilities need sufficient revenues. The rates charged customers must finance operating and maintenance expenses as well as capital costs, pay taxes, and provide a return to shareholders.

In the United States, the regulatory structure overseeing the privately-owned water supply and wastewater treatment companies, among other utilities, is decentralized. State public utility commissions typically regulate investor-owned utilities. These state commissions do not exercise uniform authority over all systems under their jurisdiction. Usually, state commissions most comprehensively regulate investor-owned utilities, with the specific oversight areas varying from state to state. In some states, regulatory authority jurisdiction also extends to certain types of publicly-owned utilities. More generally, for publicly-owned utilities, accountability is achieved through local electoral channels.

State utility regulation generally does not extend to private firms' contractual operations. Local governments continue to regulate private firms and consumer rates by contract as well as ongoing monitoring and enforcement processes.

State policies or requirements can facilitate or impede privatization arrangements via asset sales or have no direct (or apparent) impact. Generally speaking, private entities desire to avoid state public utility commission regulation. An asset sale transaction, including the financial arrangements, typically requires commission review and approval. In a few states, a regulatory commission must approve both asset sales and contractual arrangements. Generally, however, states maintain oversight over asset sales and, in some cases, long-term leases, but not with respect to private firms entering into service or operations and maintenance contracts with public entities. Various types of contractual arrangements are examined in the next section of this chapter.

After an asset sale, state regulatory commissions subject privately-owned water utilities to allowable rates-of-return regulation, thereby determining the rate of return a utility can achieve. For investor-owned utilities, economic regulation represents a threat to profitability. Private firms do not want states to constrain their ability to earn profits. Furthermore, they do not want to be inhibited by regulatory procedures that are often costly, time-consuming, cumbersome, and bureaucratic. Additionally, regulatory disputes involving contested administrative proceedings are heard by courts often lacking sufficient technical expertise.

Rate-of-return represents the key regulatory consideration in the state-based model of economic regulation of investor-owned utilities. Although an extended discussion of regulation is beyond the scope of this book, a state public utility commission begins by analyzing a firm's rate base, specifically, the value of assets on which a firm can earn a return. It authorizes a rate of return to allow a company to cover both its capital costs and its allowable operating expenses during a specified time period. Capital costs include a firm's debt service obligations, both interest and principal payments. Thus, if a private firm owns a water system, for example, no economic incentive exists to ignore water quality regulations. The regulatory framework allows for the cost recovery of expenses incurred in complying with water quality standards. After setting a utility's total revenue requirements, regulators then set the rates the utility can charge various classes of its customers. A regulated firm must operate within the boundaries approved by its regulator during its most recent rate case.

In attempt to escape the strictures imposed by rate-of-return regulation, larger water utilities have created holding companies to provide both regulated and unregulated services. For regulators, holding company structures raise issues regarding cost allocation and related-party transactions. With respect to risk allocation, regulators do not want a regulated utility's customers to bear the risks associated with the unregulated ventures.

Asset sales are just one avenue localities may explore in attempting to reduce the burden of providing water and wastewater services. Many cities turned to various forms of contractual arrangements in which localities retain ownership over their facilities while contracting out functions to private companies.

Contractual Arrangements

Unlike asset sales, which result in for-profit corporations owning water and/or wastewater systems, through contractual arrangements (also called public-private partnerships) governments hire private firms to provide services, operate, or lease public sector-owned facilities. Under these contracted arrangements, asset ownership remains with the government.

With a public-private partnership, the public partner fulfills its responsibility for providing residents with safe drinking water and adequate wastewater treatment in a new way. The public partner takes on the role of ensuring that its private partner operates in the best interests of the public.

Privatizers enter into contractual arrangements with public agencies to provide services or operate facilities they do not own. Because of the greater institutional constraints on assets sales than contractual arrangements, including state regulatory approval and supervision, the privatization of existing U.S. water supply and wastewater treatment facilities (or systems) typically occurs through contractual mechanisms. Various contractual arrangements involve different levels of private sector responsibilities and commitments by for-profit firms. After briefly providing an overview of the contract model, this section considers three types of arrangements for existing assets: outsourcing; operations and maintenance; and long-term leases. Design-build-operate-transfer arrangements for the construction of new infrastructure are then discussed.

The Contractual Model: An Overview

Under the contractual model, infrastructure remains under public ownership, with some type of delegated management to a private firm. Competition exists for contracts, with competition for the market (not in the market) serving as a substitute for public sector regulation apart from contractual provisions and local monitoring and enforcement.

The contractual model offers professional expertise. Private contractors provide expertise typically obtained from operating numerous other facilities and systems together with their knowledge of advanced technologies. Firms also offer technical resources, such as off-site laboratories and more highly trained personnel. Agreements must extend long enough to permit the privatizer to produce the hoped for efficiencies. With long-term contracts, private firms may provide capital for infrastructure repairs, maintenance, and even improvements. The contract approach also offers the perception of local control and the possibility of enhanced operating efficiencies. Disadvantages include the decoupling of ownership and operations, the potential for a lack of accountability, and a possible abuse of monopoly power by the private operator. The conceptual advantages and disadvantages of privatization are considered in detail in Chapter 6.

Outsourcing Arrangements

The most limited type of contractual arrangement involves the outsourcing of ancillary, non-core functions. The public sector may contract with private firms to provide various services, such as billing, vehicle maintenance, meter reading, or public relations. Many use private firms to perform laboratory services. With a service contract, usually a short-term agreement, the private firm takes responsibility for specific tasks, allowing the public sector owner-operator to focus on its core areas, while hiring specialists to handle ancillary work.

Firms performing these services, particularly those operating on a regional or national basis, take advantage of economies of scale and better use of the latest technology. The contract regulates the quality and performance of the service provided.

Operations and Maintenance Agreements

Other types of contracts involve the delegation of more responsibilities to a private firm. The manner in which the public agency performs its role changes from program management to contract management. Under an operations and maintenance agreement, which usually last five to ten years, the contractor assumes responsibility for day-to-day operations of a facility or system. It supervises the public sector's personnel or, in some cases, employs the facility or system's workforce. It may provide additional services, such as billing and collections. Under the contract, rates continue to be set by the municipality, which typically collects revenues, retaining the benefits and sustaining any losses. The contract-operator receives a fixed fee as its remuneration. Possibilities for incentive arrangements exist.

A short-term operations and maintenance contract lasting less than ten years does not involve any financial risk for the contractor or, usually, any responsibility for capital investments. However, the private operator bears compliance risks.

A private firm will only invest funds via a contract operation if it can receive a reasonable return on its investment. With a short-term (five- to ten-year) contract, private firms will focus on achieving cost efficiencies. These savings help provide the needed return on capital. Firms typically want a contract of at least five, if not ten, years, to spread their front-end costs over several years and establish a track record and prove their effectiveness.

Under a longer-term agreement, usually lasting twelve to twenty years, a private firm operates and manages the facility or system. The contractor typically provides the working capital needed to carry out routine operations as well as corrective and preventive maintenance, and possibly, depending on the contract, some asset replacements and certain capital improvements. The contract sets, or the locality regulates, the rates charged customers. The operator bills and collects all the revenues. It keeps whatever it receives after paying operations and maintenance costs and a specified fee to the public sector related, in part, to capital investments, which may remain the government's responsibility.

Long-term Lease Arrangements

A contractor may acquire the long-term lease, twenty to thirty years or less, because of tax considerations discussed later in this chapter, to use infrastructure assets. It assumes responsibility not only for operations and maintenance but also typically for providing capital to maintain (and upgrade) the faculty or system. The assets are returned to the public sector at the end of the contract term.

In a long-term lease, the lessee pays to the public sector owner for the right to operate the assets for a specified time period. The payment may consist of one upfront payment or periodic payments over the life of the lease. The long time period allows the lessee time to recoup its investment, including the payments made to the owner.

Under a direct lease, an operating agreement between a locality (the lessor) and a private firm (the lessee), the lessee takes responsibility for the operation and maintenance of assets already in existence. The public authority, which owns the facility or system, makes no guarantees to the lessee with respect to revenues or operating expenses. Rates are set as part of the lease. The lessee bills and collects revenues, with part returned to the public authority to pay for the assets it owns and has financed.

A lease arrangement must undergo formal review by the U.S. Environmental Protection Agency to determine compliance with the specific requirements and the overall intent of Executive Order 12803, discussed later in this chapter. However, as is true with respect to contractual arrangements generally, less regulatory oversight generally exists with respect to a lease as compared with an asset acquisition.

By the altering the capital recovery pattern for invested funds, leasing also helps deal with customer rate shock. Lease financing permits expense treatment rather than rate-based treatment given purchased infrastructure. With the rate-based approach, investments in capital assets begin with high initial costs that decline over time with depreciation. The typical result: significant, initial rate increases. With leasing, the lessee generally makes level payments to the lessor over the term of the lease, thereby reducing its initial costs and resulting in lower initial rates to customers. However, with a lease, over the long-term, customers generally pay higher rates.

Additional disadvantages to lease arrangements exist. For example, because the lessor will require the lessee to be fully insured, the insurance costs can be substantial.

In sum, public-private partnerships can involve a variety of contractual arrangements. These agreements vary in terms of the scope of the private firm's role. Generally speaking, the greater the private firm's involvement in operating a facility or system and the more capital it will invest, and the longer the term of the agreement desired.

In the United States, contract operations are especially common for small and/or rural communities. These small or remote localities often hire contractors to oversee water and/or wastewater operations for several communities. Most of these contract operators remain small, local businesses that cannot take advantage of economies of scale. They typically lack access to specialized technical expertise.

Design-Build-Operate-Transfer Agreements

Worldwide, governments hire private firms to design-build-operate-transfer water supply and wastewater treatment facilities. As noted in Chapter 2, in the United States, public sector water and wastewater systems have long hired private engineering firms to design, prepare bid specifications, and manage the construction of new facilities, while the public sector owns the facility at the end of the contract term.

Today, design-build-operate-transfer agreements have evolved from design-build agreements. With a conventional municipal procurement arrangement, a qualified engineering firm, selected by a locality typically in a non-competitive process in the United States, designs a facility under a professional services contract. Through a public bid process, the locality then awards the construction contract to the lowest cost private sector bidder, usually not the design-engineering firm, with the municipality owning and operating the facility or system.

With a design-build contract, one firm performs both functions. This approach to procurement represents a lower cost alternative than the traditional separation of the design and construction contracts.

Modern arrangements include design-build-operate-transfer contracts. Under this type of arrangement, the private sector, often a consortium of firms, takes responsibility for designing a facility or system, then builds and operates it under a contract, typically lasting twenty years. To offset the incentive of the design-build contractor to cut corners, because designer-builder does not operate the facility and may make decisions inconsistent with efficient long-term operations, the private sector group can anticipate any operational problems. Under these modern agreements, an incentive exists for the design to achieve the best overall performance during the contract term. As a result of generally shorter construction periods, design-build-operate-transfer contracts also save money on interest costs.

Although the public sector gains ownership of the asset, the contractor typically assumes financial responsibility for the project, including all design and construction liabilities. The private contractor usually provides investment capital for the facility or system as well as working capital, using project financing. Under this type of financing arrangement, lenders look to cash flow a project will generate for the payment of interest and the repayment of the principal.

Serving as the construction manager, the contractor delivers the completed infrastructure to the public agency on a specified date, and at a guaranteed cost. After the asset passes an independent acceptance test of its performance, it is placed in service. The contractor then operates the facility or system for the duration of the contract. The asset is returned to the public sector owner at the end of the contract term. Rates are set as part of the contract, with the municipality continuing to regulate user fees. Similar to a lease arrangement, the operator bills and collects revenues, receiving the revenues as its remuneration.

The design-build-operate-transfer model has several advantages. It streamlines the project schedule and reduces costs by eliminating separate selection processes for engineering, construction, procurement, and operating services. The contractor provides the public sector with cost, schedule, and performance guarantees assuring that the project will perform as required, and the equipment will be maintained, repaired, and replaced, according to specified standards.

Privatization of existing water infrastructure in the United States has generally taken the form of public-private arrangements, as opposed to the full privatization under the British model. The construction of new infrastructure may use design-build-operate-transfer agreements. In pursuing the privatization of existing or new infrastructure, many public entities in the United States looking to unburden themselves of various responsibilities have followed the French model.

Contractual Arrangements: The French Model

Contract arrangements worldwide build on the long-standing French model. France has had a long familiarity with various types of public sector delegation, with private firms providing services to infrastructure owned by local governmental units.[14] Privatization in France, through various contractual arrangements and bidding (more technically, competition for the market), has a long and, generally, successful history. The water industry in France today typifies large-scale private sector operations and management by giant multinational corporations in the context of a fragmented pattern of local, public sector water and wastewater infrastructure ownership.

France took the lead in awarding franchises for water supply to the bidder promising to charge customers the lowest price. The first franchise contract for water distribution in France dates back to 1782 when a private firm was given exclusive distribution rights for fifteen years to supply water to Paris. During the French Revolution, the city of Paris took over the firm and two others. Although many areas of France built and operated their own systems, which they owned, beginning in the mid-nineteenth century, in other areas, such as Avignon, Cannes, and Le Havre, private water franchises became commonplace. Eventually, many localities, including Paris, turned to private entities to operate their systems. The communes contracted out management functions to for-profit companies.

In France, the national government grants localities the autonomy to assume responsibility for providing water and sewage services. On the assumption that local officials and staff, not technicians in Paris, can better handle problems, each mayor and municipal council has the responsibility for drinking water and wastewater management. They have the option of delegating part, all, or none of their responsibilities to private firms.

In contrast to present-day Britain, localities in France own their water-related infrastructure, with water resource management the responsibility of various governmental levels. In terms of geography, the ownership of the water and wastewater infrastructure was (and remains) localized. The French model is based on the maintenance of local control, through asset ownership. Using public-private partnerships, this model allows private firms to tap a profitable investment area.

French private water companies date back to Compagnie Générale des Eaux (now Veolia Environnement SA (Veolia)), established in 1853, to aid municipalities in meeting their water supply needs. Another firm, Société Lyonnaise des Eaux and de l'Eclairage (now Suez Environnement SA (Suez)) was founded in 1880 to assist localities in meeting their gas, water and power needs. The French contractual model contributed to the emergence of these two firms that today demonstrate technological and business expertise worldwide, as they have come to dominate the global water market.

Although the two giant French water companies, Veolia and Suez, today operate on a global scale, in France they operate within a local context. Veolia and Suez historically developed by providing water and wastewater services under contract in France.[15] The two firms learned their trade, prospered, and grew immensely.

Localities make their own decisions about whether water supply and sewage should be publicly run or provided by the private sector under various types of contractual arrangements. Because the responsibilities of localities in France have expanded since the 1950s, many governmental units sought to divest themselves of management responsibilities in the water and wastewater sector, without giving up asset ownership. Eager for the technical expertise of the firms' specialists, wanting to benefit from the economies of scale enjoyed by private companies, and in need of private capital, localities in France turned to the private sector for assistance. Veolia and Suez happily met these needs.

Communes sought professional expertise to implement modern techniques. Technological advance led to a reliance on private firms with expertise in the water and wastewater fields. The public sector also sought to improve the quality of services provided customers, through greater efficiency and higher productivity offered by for-profit companies. Localities found it advantageous to tap specialized expertise, for example, to take preventive measures in treating drinking water and to ensure quality service to customers.

Since the 1980s, with the decay of old systems and the need for capital investments, localities in France turned even more readily to private capital to finance infrastructure maintenance and modernization. With infrastructure requiring repair or renewal, but because of budget constraints, communes were forced to seek private financing. For example, Paris entered into an operations and maintenance contract in 1985 for the management of its water supply system. The Paris water system required major renovations and replacement. The city split the contract into two, with one firm given responsibility on the Left Bank of the Seine River and another for the Right Bank. The two companies buy water wholesale from the city, which retains water treatment, storage, and monitoring responsibilities.[16]

The need to meet EU environmental and health directives played a part in the continued (and growing) reliance on the private sector. These directives strained many localities financial and technical resources. Additionally, leaks from ill-maintained water supply pipes, along with poor metering, led to high levels of unaccounted-for-water that communes also sought to reduce.

In France, the trend toward privatization is ongoing. Contractual arrangements for water supply services now cover 80 percent of the population. Wastewater coverage is much lower at just 35 percent.[17]

A multitude of options has led to the growth of privatization through delegated management by contacts with private providers for various services. There are three major types of contractual arrangements in France: management, leasing, and concession.

Management Arrangements. There are two types of management contracts. Under a services arrangement (les prestations de service), a locality contracts out specific operations and management functions, such as billing. The private firm receives an annual, flat fee for its services, during the duration of the contract, typically up to ten years. Localities requiring technical and administrative expertise and assistance use this type of arrangement. The scope of a service contract can vary from limited to a more extensive range of services.

Under a management (gérance) arrangement, the public sector hires a private firm to provide a greater array of specific services, such as day-to-day operations, but retains responsibility for all other services not contracted out. The duration of this contract varies, but it is normally twelve years. The municipality pays an agreed upon fee for the services rendered regardless of the revenues collected from customers.

Affermage Arrangements. In a leasing (affermage) arrangement, the locality bears financial responsibility for a facility or system, which it owns. This approach is popular where localities can obtain debt financing at preferential interest rates or through subsidies and grants from the public sector for capital investments and infrastructure improvements. The commune then enters into a detailed contract regarding the operation and maintenance (or upgrading) of an existing facility or system, usually for twelve years, with the private firm only providing working capital.

Typically, the private operator assumes responsibility for maintenance of equipment; the facility's or system's expansion remains the locality's responsibility. A contract may provide that either party take responsibility for pipe renewal. Agreements contain provisions dealing with the quality of services, the minimum quantity of water to be supplied to each user, the return of facilities in good working order, and procedures for contractual renewal. The private operator collects user fees, which reflect its costs plus a profit figure. A surcharge, paid to the local public owner, is added to the user fees to finance the cost of fixed assets and capital investments for infrastructure improvements.

Concession Arrangements. In a concession (turnkey) arrangement, a private firm assumes responsibility for constructing (or modernizing), managing, operating, and maintaining a facility or system, which the public sector owns. For localities lacking funding for major capital projects, such wastewater treatment plants, this approach is advantageous. The concessionaire provides or borrows the capital for construction, as well as all needed working and investment capital. Under this type of agreement, consumers pay the concessionaire.

The parties enter into a long-term contract, typically for twenty years, to enable the concessionaire to amortize its capital outlays. The private firm bears all the financial risks. The contract specifies the level of service the concessionaire will provide. The specifics include water quality, supply, and connection of customers to the system, as well as quantity of water to be supplied without charge to the locality for public purposes, such as fire hydrants.

In France, through leasing and concession arrangements, water and sewer rates are set contractually, not by centralized or decentralized economic regulators. A formula contained in a contract fixes rates, with the initial price for water (or sewage service) set by contract with an escalation formula, using an agreed upon price index. Agreements also include provisions for periodic reviews and a cost passthrough mechanism.

The French Model: Competition, Local Control, and Rates

Although a detailed analysis of the French model is beyond the scope of this book, some comments on competition, local controls, and rates are helpful. Competition in France takes place for the right to operate and provide water and wastewater services, not among providers. Competitive bidding for contacts in a locale occurs among operators, especially in the more lucrative metropolitan areas. Bidding enables a commune to select the provider, with the lowest cost bidder typically winning the contract. Once a private firm receives a contract, rarely are water and sewage services returned to the local authority. Over time, the professional competence possessed by a locale, in terms of experienced staff, disappears.

Even after services are contracted away, localities strive to exercise a high degree of control over the activities of private firms. Consumer awareness has increased. More local authorities have engaged consultants to assist them; some employ full-time staff to monitor their water contractors. In short, communes monitor private firms and strive to ensure that operations run smoothly.

In France, because water rates and sewage charges generally do not cover operating and capital costs, public sector subsidies are required.[18] Water and wastewater systems continue to be heavily subsidized, receiving financial assistance from several levels of government, national, regional, and departmental. Taxes paid to the one of the nation's six water finance and planning agencies (Agences de l'Eau), its river basin management authorities, established in 1964 provide technical and financial assistance for a variety projects aimed at improving water quality and controlling pollution. To raise funds, these agencies levy taxes on all water and sewage users. The French National Water Infrastructure Fund (Fonds National pour le Développement des Adductions d'Eau) subsidizes water projects in rural communities.

The Two Leading French Water Firms: Veolia and Suez

Privatization in France has flourished in the context of local, public ownership because major firms could group water systems. These for-profit companies developed both technical expertise and the financial ability to meet capital needs.

Over the years, the leading French water service companies expanded horizontally, acquiring other contractors via mergers and takeovers. Today, three firms, the two leaders, Veolia and Suez, and a third firm, SAUR (Société d'Aménagement Urbain et Rural), subsidiary of a French conglomerate, Bouygues Group, dominate the French water services market. Veolia handles nearly 50 percent of the waterworks in France, with Suez and SAUR servicing about 25 and 10 percent, respectively.[19]

Veolia and Suez grew, prospered, and have become the world's leading multinational water companies. Veolia Environnement, the number one water company in the world, provides more than 80 million people with water and 53 million people with wastewater treatment services. Operating in 64 countries, the company manages in excess of 4,400 contracts. It water division generated more than nearly €12.5 billion in revenues in 2008.[20] Its subsidiary, Veolia Water North America, the largest private contractor of the U.S. municipal water and wastewater systems, operates the Indianapolis water system, analyzed in Chapter 8.

Suez Environnement supplies 68 million people with drinking water and operates more than 10,000 wastewater treatment plants in 70 countries. In 2008, the firm, including its waste management services operations, reported revenues of €12.0 billion.[21] Its U.S. subsidiary, United Water Resources, the second largest private operator of U.S. municipal water and wastewater systems, ran the Atlanta water system from 1999 to 2003 under contract, as examined in Chapter 8.

Federal Incentives for Privatization

The federal government in the United States has implemented both tax and non-tax incentives to facilitate privatization. This section considers both types of incentives, beginning with non-tax ones, focusing on how each impact on the form privatization may take.

Non-Tax Incentives

Executive Order 12803[22] abolished the requirement that public sector must repay the federal government in full for any federal investments in publicly-owned infrastructure sold or leased to a private firm. The executive order significantly modified the federal construction grant recoupment and property disposition process, resulting in a lower repayment of federal grants than under the then existing federal construction grant requirements. Previously, a project had to reimburse the U.S. Treasury for an amount equal to the undepreciated portion of the federal construction grant received if a publicly-owned facility were sold to a private purchaser or took a private partner as a lessee. In some cases, the undepreciated grant amount exceeded the fair market value of an asset, thereby preventing privatization by means of an asset sale or long-term lease. In other situations, a sale, for example, might have generated funds to pay back the undepreciated portion of the grant, but the public sector would have received little of the sale proceeds because the federal government had first claim on the proceeds in repayment of a construction grant. As a result, public officials had a little incentive to pursue an asset sale.

In 1992, President George H.W. Bush signed Executive Order 12803 on Infrastructure Privatization to initiate regulatory and policy changes to facilitate asset sales (or leases) and to increase investments in environmental facilities. The purpose and scope of the order was four-fold: first, to assist local privatization initiatives; second, to remove federal regulatory impediments to private sector involvement;

third, to increase state and local governments' proceeds from privatization arrangements by relaxing federal repayment requirements; and finally to protect the public interest by ensuring that privatized assets continue to be used for their original purposes and that user charges remain consistent with federal requirements designed to protect customers and the public. No specific plan for implementation, however, followed the order.

The executive order defined the term "privatization" as "the disposition or transfer of an infrastructure asset, such as by sale or by long-term lease, from a State or local government to a private party."[23] It clarified the terms under which the federal government is repaid for its investment via a construction grant on the sale or lease of a federally financed asset, in whole or in part, to the private sector. Under the executive order, state and local governments first receive the proceeds from an asset sale or the payment of lease fees, representing their portion of the total project costs. If the transfer price or the leasing fee for a facility is higher than the state and local government investment, the construction grant is repaid at its depreciated value up to the transfer price or leasing fee. Depreciation of federal construction grant facilities is calculated under the Internal Revenue Service accelerated depreciation schedule for the asset in question. With a fully depreciated asset, there is no federal construction grant recoupment.

If a local government has received EPA construction grant funds for a project, such as a wastewater treatment facility, the agency imposes its own requirements before approving certain types of privatization transactions. When an EPA construction grantee pursues an asset sale or a lease, a so-called disposition agreement, under the executive order, it must submit a request for approval of the proposed privatization agreement to the agency and obtain a deviation from federal grant regulations that protect the federal interest in the asset. The grantee must agree to use the proceeds received only for investment in additional infrastructure assets or for debt or tax reduction. The EPA also reviews a sale or a lease privatization proposal for compliance with the Clean Water Act. It further examines the proposal with respect to the current and proposed structure rate and arrangements for future rate increases. To ensure compliance with Executive Order 12803, the EPA reviews the contractual guarantees for assurance that the privatized facility will be used for its original purposes if the private purchaser (or lessee) becomes insolvent.

These requirements pertain to privatization via asset disposition agreements or leases, not contract operation agreements that include both operation and maintenance as well as service arrangements. In other words, contract operations agreements are subject to neither EPA review and approval nor federal construction grant regulations.

Then, in 1994, President William Jefferson (Bill) Clinton signed Executive Order 12893 on Principles for Federal Infrastructure Investments.[24] The executive order applies to federal spending for infrastructure programs in the areas of water resources and environmental protection, among others. The executive order set forth several specific principles: systematic analysis of expected benefits and costs; efficient management; private sector participation; and encouragement of more effective state and local programs. Regarding private sector participation, the order reads:

> Agencies shall seek private-sector participation in infrastructure investment and management. Innovative public-private initiatives can bring about greater private-sector participation in the ownership, financing, construction, and operation of … [water resources and environmental protection] infrastructure programs…. Consistent with public interest, agencies should work with State and local entities to minimize legal and regulatory barriers to private sector participation in the provision of infrastructure facilities and services.[25]

In addition to these non-tax efforts to facilitate privatization transactions, tax changes significantly stimulated the growth of public-private partnerships.

Federal Tax Incentives to Encourage Privatization

Federal income tax incentives focus on tax-exempt bonds as an infrastructure funding mechanism. Federal rules limit the time period for contracts entered into by public entities using tax-exempt financing.

The 1986 Tax Reform Act removed or limited many federal income tax incentives for private investments in infrastructure. It eliminated the then existing 10 percent investment tax credit, basically equal to 10 percent of property costs that could be taken during the first year of operation, scaled back accelerated depreciation, and limited the use of tax-exempt debt financing. As a result, the 1986 Act imposed a tax penalty for privatization transactions, particularly asset sales, thereby reducing the incentives for private capital involvement in water supply and wastewater treatment infrastructure.[26] One estimate placed the post-1986 tax cost of privatization at 30 percent of the capital cost of a purchased facility.[27]

The 1986 act also changed the private activity bond rules. The evolution of private activity bonds has followed a somewhat convoluted route. In brief, until 1968, all interest payments received by investors from state or local bonds were tax exempt. The Revenue Adjustment Act of 1968[28] eliminated the interest exemption for most bonds if: 1) more than 25 percent of the bond proceeds were used in a business by a nongovernmental entity (the private business use of proceeds test) and 2) the repayment for more than 25 percent of the principal or interest on the bonds was derived from or secured by money or property used in a business (the private security interest or payment test). Interest on bonds used to finance projects failing either test continued to be exempt. Interest on bonds passing both tests were taxable industrial development bonds (IDBs), subject to numerous exemptions.

The Tax Reform Act of 1986[29] redefined IDBs as private activity bonds and reduced the percentages for the use of proceeds and security interest (or payment) tests to 10 percent. The Internal Revenue Code now classifies a bond as a private activity bond if: 1) more than 10 percent of the bond proceeds are used by for any private business use and more than 10 percent of the bonds repayments are payable from or secured by payments or property used by any private business; or 2) if it meets a private loan financing test. As a practical matter, bonds issued by municipalities on behalf of private sponsors are private activity bonds, thereby reducing the income tax benefits enjoyed by bondholders. Specifically, interest paid on private activity bonds, except for private activity bonds issued in 2009 and 2010 and certain refunding bonds, represents a preference item for purposes of calculating the alternative minimum tax.

Private business use can arise from asset ownership or the use of property pursuant to a lease or management contract. Thus, if a private entity purchases or enters into a contract to operate (or lease) a water supply or wastewater treatment facility funded by tax-exempt bonds, the private businesses use test is met and the IRS classifies the bonds as private activity bonds, resulting in their adverse federal income tax consequences. In sum, classification of a tax-exempt debt obligation as a private activity bond serves as a barrier to privatization transactions.

If a local government uses tax-exempt debt to finance any portion of a facility or system and then enters into a privatization arrangement, the term of the contract (or lease) is subject to Internal Revenue Service regulations. However, if a local government has no outstanding tax-exempt debt on the facility, the term of the contract (or lease) is not subject to IRS requirements.

The post-1986 IRS regulations contained an exception from the private business use of proceeds test for five-year operation and maintenance contracts, provided the agreement included a termination clause allowing cancellation after three years. Typically, at that time, contracts provided for no-penalty, public sector terminations after three years. By assuring a contractor of only a three-year involvement in a project; this approach sought to maintain continuous pressure on contractors, for example, operations and maintenance firms, to reduce costs. However, the narrow time frame limited operators' ability to invest in infrastructure improvements. It discouraged private contractual involvement in facilities for which efficiency improvements may have taken more than three years to materialize. Because they found it difficult to recover their costs, private firms resisted expending their capital and being involved in public-private partnerships.

For a decade, the private sector focused on short-term operations and maintenance contracts, placing little or no capital at risk. Then, in 1997, the IRS transformed landscape for contract operations. In issuing Revenue Procedure 97-13,[30] which allows operators to enter into contracts for up to twenty years, without resulting in private business use for tax-exempt debt obligations, the IRS made possible long-term contracts with respect to publicly-owned assets. The new tax rule opened opportunities for building mutually beneficial partnerships over an extended term. It also afforded new possibilities for enhanced efficiencies and accompanying cost reductions. The new rule also made it economically feasible for private firm to operate at a loss for several years provided it could recover that loss and make a profit in the later years of the contract.

A long-term contract provides numerous benefits. It allows for investments by a private contractor. A private partner is more willing to invest its own capital if the contract sufficiently long for it to earn a return on its funds. It allows contractors to offer localities an upfront (concession) fee for contractual rights. The longer amortization period lowers the fees that a private partner must charge to ensure an adequate rate of return on its investment over the contract's life.

For the public partner, a long-term contract offers access to the private partner's capital. Other benefits for the public partner include better knowledge of the long-term cost savings, thereby permitting better planning and budgeting as well as spending the savings on other items. Also, more frequent public procurements and possible operating disruptions, with their attendant costs and risks are avoided. As discussed in Chapter 8, a well-drafted contract provides ample incentives for the private partner to perform properly and gives the public partner the opportunity to enforce performance standards or terminate the contract. Detailed performance, default, and termination provisions contained in a contact reduce the risk to the public partner. Carefully structured provisions give the public partner a powerful monitoring and enforcement tool to ensure high levels of compliance throughout a contract's life.

Long-term contracts enable local officials to concentrate their energies on other programs and functions. Local officials face multitude of responsibilities from fixing streets, to running schools, and providing police. The day-to-day management of water and wastewater facilities together with the required environmental compliance has become a burden in many communities, draining managerial and personnel resources better focused on meeting other needs.

On the downside, however, long-term contracts offer less frequent competition by private entities. When locked into a long-term contract, a community cannot benefit from better offers prior termination. With a short-term contract, a municipality can renew or renegotiate an existing contract, solicit new bids, or more quickly return a system to public operation. Periodic rebidding creates competition for (not in) the market, helping solve the natural monopoly problem. However, in my opinion, the benefits of long-term contracts generally outweigh the disadvantages.

The 1997 IRS rule change imposes certain constraints designed to prevent the abuse of tax-exempt financing. In brief, no portion of the private partner's compensation can be based on net profits. This provision removes, however, one of the major incentive localities have to enhance a contractor's productivity. A contractor may share in either cost savings or revenue enhancements, but not both. Furthermore, under the contract at least 80 percent of the compensation provided to the private partner must take the form of a periodic, fixed amount. Thus, a private contractor can have up to 20 percent of its remuneration in the form of variable payments from cost reductions (for example, through operational changes) or revenue sharing formulas (for example, derived from meter replacement programs).

The contract term and contractor compensation under IRS rules are tied together in a concept called the periodic fixed fee (PFF). The PFF equals a stated dollar amount plus annual inflation adjustments for services rendered over a specified period. The greater the amount of compensation based on a fixed fee, the longer the allowable contract term. Provided the contract meets the PFF guidelines, because water or wastewater infrastructure are "public utility property," the contract can provide for up to a twenty-year term. However, under a PFF arrangement, private operators take the risk that their profits will decline (or that they may lose money) if their costs rise more than the sum of the inflation adjustment together with cost reductions achieved by greater efficiencies.

The 1997 regulatory change that extended to contractual time limit to twenty years spurred cities, large and small, to enter into long-term contracts, including Atlanta and Indianapolis, discussed in Chapter 8. By opening a huge, new market to privatization through long-term contracts, publicly-owned facilities (or systems) entered into a flurry of long-term contracts. Between 1997 and 2002, for instance, the number of contracts for the operation of publicly-owned water and wastewater assets nearly tripled.[31]

As public entities struggled with the financial and environmental obligations that arise from the provision of water supply and wastewater treatment services, localities in the United States are turned toward various forms of privatization. Private companies not only obtained ownership of water and wastewater facilities outright through asset purchases, but also entered into a variety of contractual arrangements to provide their expertise, ranging from designing, building, and operating infrastructure, to contracts to provide various services. A number of factors, including state economic regulation and various federal incentives, impact on the form privatization takes in the United States, with public-private partnerships predominating.

The next chapter analyzes the rationale for privatization transactions along with some of the potential disadvantages of these arrangements.

Notes

1. In my analysis of the three privatization modes, I have drawn on National Research Council (NRC), *Privatization of Water Services in the United States: An Assessment of Issues and Experience* (Washington DC: National Academy Press, 2002), 20, 62-77 and Janice A. Beecher, G. Richard Dreese, and John D. Stanford, *Regulatory Implications of Water and Wastewater Utility Privatization*, National Regulatory Research Institute, 1995, NRRI 95-09, 43-57.

2. Peter H. Gleick et al., *The New Economy of Water: The Risks and Benefits of Globalization and Privatization of Fresh Water* (Oakland, CA: Pacific Institute for Studies in Development, Environment and Security, 2001), 1.

3. NRC, *Privatization*, 75-77.

4. Adrian Moore, "Long-term partnerships in Water and Sewer Utilities: Economic, Political, and Policy Implications," Universities Council on Water Resources 117 (October 2000): 24.

5. The British water industry in the nineteenth century is traced in J.A. Hassan, "The Growth and Impact of the British Water industry in the Nineteenth Century," *Economic History Review* 38:4 (November 1985): 531-547 and Robert Millward, "Privatisation in Historical Perspective: The UK Water Industry," in *Money, trade and payments: Essays in honour of D.J. Coppack*, eds. David Cobham, Richard Harrington, George Zis (Manchester UK: Manchester University, 1989), 193-206 and in the first half of the twentieth century in John A. Hassan, "The Water Industry 1900-51: a failure of public policy?" in *The Political Economy of Nationalisation in Britain 1920-1950*, ed. Robert Millward and John Singleton (Cambridge, UK: Cambridge University 1995). For background on the British water industry see John Hassan, *A History of Water in Modern England and Wales* (Manchester UK: Manchester University, 1998), 10-71 and Karen J. Bakker, *An Uncooperative Commodity: Privatizing Water in England and Wales* (New York: Oxford University, 2003), 45-54.

6. Hassan, *History*, 126-142 and Bakker, *Uncooperative Commodity*, 54-62.

7. Hassan, *History*, 142-161 and Bakker, *Uncooperative Commodity*, 62-67.

8. Hassan, *History*, 167-173 and Bakker, *Uncooperative Commodity*, 67-68.

9. Hassan, *History*, 167 and Bakker, *Uncooperative Commodity*, 68.

10. Hassan, *History*, 172.

11. Elizabeth Brubaker, *Liquid Assets: Privatizing and Regulating Canada's Water Utilities* (Toronto: University of Toronto, 2002, 44. See also NRC, *Privatization*, 126 and Mohammed H.I. Dore, Joseph Kushner, Klemen Zumer, "Privatization of water in the UK and France—What can we learn?," *Utilities Policy* 12:1 (March 2004): 41-50, at 43. For a critical assessment of the new firms' capital expenditures and investments see Emanuele Lobina and David Hall, UK Water privatization—a briefing, February 2001, Public Services International Research Unit.

12. Hassan, *History*, 173-179 and Bakker, *Uncooperative Commodity*, 68-72.

13. I have drawn on Beecher, Dreese, Stanford, *Regulatory Implications*, 121-145. See also Janice A. Beecher, "The Role of Economic Regulation in Water and Wastewater Utility Privatization" in *America's Water and*

Wastewater Industries: Competition and Privatization, eds. Paul Seidenstat, Michael Nadol, Simon Hakim (Vienna, VA: Public Utilities Reports, 2000) and Leonard S. Hyman et al., *The Water Supply and Wastewater Industry* (Vienna, VA: Public Utility Reports, 1998), 175-215.

14. I have drawn on Steve H. Hanke and Stephen J.K. Walters, "H$_2$O Ownership: Privatizing Waterworks in Theory and Practice," in *America's Water and Wastewater Industries*, 288-289; Frederico Neto, "Water privatization and regulation in England and France: a tale of two models," *Natural Resources Forum* 22:2 (May 1998): 107-117, at 112-115; Henry Buller, "Privatization and Europeanization: The Changing Context of Water Supply in Britain and France," *Journal of Environmental Planning and Management* 39:4 (December 1996): 461-482, at 463-466; *Water Engineering and Management*, "The Organization of Water Supply and Drainage Services in France" 141:12 (December 1994): 25-28; Liana Maurer-de Loë and Bruce Mitchell, "Public-Private Partnerships: Water and Wastewater Service in France," *Water International* 18:3 (September 1993): 137-146; Jean-Dominique Decamps, "Privatization of Water Systems in France," *Journal of America Water Works Association* 78:2 (February 1986): 34-40.

15. For a brief history of the predecessors of the two water companies see Loë and Mitchell, "Public-Private Partnerships," 142-144. See also Shawn Tully, "Water, Water Everywhere," *Fortune* 141:10 (May 15, 2000): 342-350.

16. *Water Engineering and Management*, "Organization," 28.

17. Xavier Leflaive et al., "Pricing Water: Comparative features in water service organisation in France and Europe," BIPE, March 2001, 33 and Loë and Mitchell, "Public-Private Partnerships," 140-141. Loë and Mitchell estimate that 50 percent of France's population is provided sewage service by private companies.

18. Brubaker, *Liquid Assets*, 56-57.

19. Center for Public Integrity, The Water Barons: Defending the Internal Water Empire, February 4, 2003 <http://projects.publicintegrity.org/water/report.aspx?aid=48> (June 24, 2009).

20. Veolia Environnement, Annual and Sustainability Report 2007, 84. For a critical assessment of the company see Public Citizen, Veolia Environnement: A Corporate Profile, February 2005.

21. Suez Environnement, Sustainable Development Annual Report 2007-2008, Key Figures. For a critical assessment of Suez, prior to its merger with Gaz de France and the spin off of Suez Environnement, see Public Citizen, Suez: A Corporate Profile, February 2005.

22. Executive Order 12803, April 30, 1992, *Federal Register* 57:88 (May 4, 1992): 19063-19065.

23. *Ibid.*, Section 1(a).

24. Executive Order 12893, January 26, 1994, *Federal Register* 69:20 (January 31, 1994): 4233-4235.

25. *Ibid.*, Section 2(c).

26. John G. Heilman and Gerald W. Johnson, *The Politics and Economics of Privatization: The Case of Wastewater Treatment* (Tuscaloosa, AL: University of Alabama, 1992), 129, 130.

27. Randall G. Holcombe, "The Tax Cost of Privatization," *Southern Economic Journal* 56:3 (January 1990): 732-742.
28. Public Law, 90-364.
29. Public Law, 99-514.
30. Internal Revenue Service, 1997-1 Cumulative Bulletin 632.
31. Gary Wolf and Eric Hallstein, Beyond Privatization: Restructuring Water Systems to Improve Performance, Pacific Institute, December 2005, 14.

6

Privatization of Water Supply and Wastewater Treatment Infrastructure: A Conceptual Analysis

Providing safe, affordable drinking water as well as wastewater treatment services represents a necessary but costly endeavor, as these services often represent a key factor in a locality's economic and public health. For its proponents, privatization offers a financial tool and a management technique. Although it offers great potential, it is not a panacea. Privatization may be a sound policy choice for public officials seeking to promote economic growth and community development. However, localities must evaluate the various options and make an informed decision of what is best for their community.

As analyzed in this chapter, America's water and wastewater infrastructure is aging. Massive investments will be needed to repair, replace and/or upgrade existing water and wastewater infrastructure in the United States, as well as meet future demands for increased capacity and comply with new environment and security requirements. Pipeline repairs and replacements represent a significant portion of the projected infrastructure needs. The funds needed for infrastructure renewal in a capital-intensive field will be enormous. The public sector may be unable or unwilling to make substantial infrastructure investments. Facing enormous funding shortfalls, the need for capital may lead local governments to turn to privatization.

Beyond providing funds for upgrading and expanding a facility or system, privatization, either through the purchase of assets or public-private partnerships, according to its proponents also offers cost savings, improved performance, increased efficiency, and the overcoming of a lack of a local, public sector expertise in complying with environmental requirements and meeting water security measures. However, many U.S. communities resist privatizing to maintain and upgrade their water supply and wastewater treatment infrastructure. This chapter presents the potential disadvantages of privatization offered by its opponents, including workforce reductions, rate increases and service declines, loss of public control, contractor bankruptcy, xenophobia, transaction costs, and ideology.[1] Although concerns abound whether privatization will achieve the hoped-for benefits, carefully drafted, monitored, and enforced contracts will meet nearly all the objections, except for transaction costs.

Privatization as a Financial Tool to Meet Capital Needs

Water and wastewater infrastructure in the United States is aging. Many U.S. water and wastewater systems include infrastructure dating back to the early twentieth century. Federal funds built the most recent wastewater systems during 1960s and 1970s, and even these more recent assets need upgrading or replacing. Public sector facilities and systems face a capital-funding crisis, as the upgrading requires a massive capital infusion.

A need exists for sustained investment in water and wastewater infrastructure to prevent a funding gap from which it will be difficult to recover. However, all governmental levels of the American public sector face competing demands for funding. Visible, tangible, immediate public benefits count more for elected officials and the public than the long-term, expensive renewal process of buried, long-lived water and wastewater assets.

The Condition of America's Water and Wastewater Infrastructure

Agreement exists that the U.S. water and wastewater infrastructure is in bad shape and getting worse. Both anecdotal evidence and expert reports support this conclusion.

Anecdotal evidence abounds regarding America's aging water and wastewater industry.[2] Deteriorating facilities sometimes even make national television news. In December 2008, a water main break in suburban Bethesda, Maryland, just outside of Washington, D.C., trapped nine motorists inside their cars in up to two feet of water and shut down streets. At the rupture's peak, some 150,000 gallons of water a minute gushed into a commuter road. The dramatic flood and rescue efforts of stranded motorists were carried live on national television.[3]

There are other examples from America's leading cities. A tunnel bringing half of New York City's water supply from reservoirs in the

Catskill Mountains sprang a leak in the late 1980s. For most of the last two decades, it has leaked about 20 million gallons a day, sometimes losing up to 36 million gallons a day.[4]

Philadelphia has been flooded with sewage on several occasions. The combined sewer-storm water lines in many parts of the city have become overwhelmed by millions of gallons of rain runoff, sending wastewater and urban flotsam into residents' basements.[5]

Beyond these incidents, the 2009 infrastructure "report card" by the American Society of Civil Engineers graded both the nation's drinking water and wastewater systems at D-.[6] In particular, the report card noted the "poor" condition of the country's 16,000 wastewater treatment systems, many of which "have reached the end of their useful design lives. Older systems are plagued by chronic overflows during major rain storms and heavy snowmelt and, intentionally or not, are bringing about the discharge of raw sewage into U.S. surface water."[7]

The Environmental Protection Agency (EPA) estimated the volume of combined sewer-rain runoff overflows discharged nationwide at 850 billion gallons annually. Between 23,000 and 75,000 sanitary sewer overflow occur each year, resulting from blocked or broken pipes. These events release as much as ten billion gallons of untreated sewage yearly into America's surface waters, poisoning these waters.[8]

Our current water system grew with the nation's population increases and urbanization. Periods of growth included the late nineteenth century, during and after World War I, and the post-World War II era. Much of our water distribution system infrastructure comes from the last period, although many cities have underground pipes dating back to the late 1800s.

Five decades after the last massive investment, a significant portion of the U.S. water infrastructure currently in use is reaching the end of its estimated useful life. As a result, the United States faces the need to replace water pipes installed from the late 1800s to the 1950s. The cast-iron pipes from the late nineteenth century have an estimated useful life of 120 years. The cast-iron pipes installed in the 1920s have an average useful life of one hundred years, but the post-World War II pipes only have an average useful life of about 75 years.[9] In the United States there are some 1.2 million miles of water pipes, much of it old and in need of replacing.[10] The replacement needs and are large will come about in a short time period. As a 2001 report by the American Water Works Association concluded, "the pipes laid down at different times in our history have different life expectancies, and thousands of miles of pipes that were buried over 100 or more years ago will need to be replaced in the next 30 years."[11] Without a sufficient, ongoing replacement effort, according to the EPA, by 2020 the percentage of water pipes in the United States that will be classified as poor or worse (very poor or life elapsed) will equal 45 percent.[12]

The cost of future replacement expenses far exceeds contemporary replacement, let alone original installation, costs. By 2030, the average utility in the American Water Works Association's twenty entity sample will spend three and one half times as much on the replacement of worn-out pipes as it did in 2000. Also, as the pipes get older and more prone to breakage, the average utility in this survey will spend about three and a half times as much on repairs in 2030 as it did in 2000.[13] Also, many water treatment plants built or overhauled to meet EPA standards post-1972 will be due for renewal.

Replacement of America's water and wastewater infrastructure represents a major public policy issue. Significant funding challenges exist. Numerous studies document the huge future capital needs facing America's water and wastewater systems.

Future Capital Needs and the Investment Gap

Reports from various groups and the federal government agencies highlight the investment needs and shortfall America faces to: (1) replace deteriorating facilities and comply with federal safe drinking water regulations and (2) replace aging wastewater systems and comply with federal clean water rules. This section surveys these reports dealing with the future capital needs and the investment gap.

Capital Needs. In 2000, the Water Infrastructure Network, a consortium of industry, municipal, state, and nonprofit associations, projected the capital needs to replace old water and wastewater facilities or invest in new ones at roughly $1 trillion dollars over twenty years (2000-2019) or about $47 billion each year, based on certain financing assumptions. Of this annual total, building new and replacing old drinking water infrastructure would require an estimated $24 billion in annual expenditures. Comparable investments for wastewater were projected to require spending $23 billion a year.[14] The Network estimated an investment gap of $23 billion per year to build, replace, and rehabilitate existing and new systems to meet the nation's water supply and wastewater treatment needs. Of this annual gap, $11 billion would be for water systems and $12 billion for wastewater systems.[15]

In 2001, the Environmental Protection Agency released a survey of the nation's drinking water infrastructure needs. The survey concluded that about $151 billion would be needed over twenty years (1999-2018) to repair, replace, and upgrade the nation's 55,000 community drinking water systems (and its nonprofit, noncommunity water systems) in order to protect public health.[16] A community water system regularly serves at least twenty-five year round residents.

A subsequent 2003 EPA study called for the investment of $276.8 billion (in 2003 dollars), an increase of more than $125 billion over its 2001 study, for a twenty-year period (2003-2022) to install, upgrade and replace U.S. drinking water infrastructure, with the bulk of the expenditures going towards the distribution and transmission ($183.6 billion) and treatment ($53.1 billion) areas. One hundred sixty-five billion dollars was designated to meet current needs, improvements, or upgrades to older, deteriorating systems to ensure the continuity of water supply and maintenance of minimum water quality standards, with $111.8 billion allocated to needs that will gradually develop in the future as currently satisfactory systems age, deteriorate, as new systems are built to satisfy a growing and shifting U.S. population, and as improvements to existing systems are required to comply with new water quality and security regulations.[17]

In this 2003 survey, the EPA also estimated current and future needs of drinking water systems based on system size and type. Large community water systems (serving over 50,000 people), numbering 1,041 systems nationwide, would require $122.9 billion over a twenty-year period (2003-2022). Medium community water systems (serving 3,301 to 50,000 people), numbering 7,638 systems nationwide, would require $103.0 billion over the same twenty-year period. Finally, small community water systems (serving 3,300 and fewer people), numbering 43,039 systems nationwide, would require $34.2 billion over the same period.[18]

In a 2004 survey, the EPA placed the capital needs over twenty years (2004-2023) for the nation's wastewater treatment works at $202.5 billion (in 2004 dollars). The national needs were as follows: wastewater treatment systems ($69.1 billion); wastewater collection and conveyance ($65.3 billion); combined sewer overflow correction ($54.8 billion); storm water management programs ($9.0 billion); and recycled water distribution ($4.3 billion).[19]

In its 2007 survey, the EPA concluded that the nation's water system needs would equal $334.8 billion over 20 years (2007-2026).[20] It broke out the national needs by system type as follows: large community water systems, $116.3 billion; medium community water systems, $145.1 billion; small community water systems, $59.4; billion nonprofit non-community water systems, $4.1 billion; American Indian and Alaskan Native Village Water Systems, $2.9 billion; and costs associated with proposed and recently promulgated federal environmental regulations, $7.0 billion.[21]

Funding Gap. Beyond these huge capital investment needs, other EPA reports focused on the projected funding gap between what experts estimated the United States should spend and the amount we are spending (and are likely to spend) to correct these problems. The Environmental Protection Agency issued a 2002 report that identified potential funding gaps between projected needs and spending from 2000 through 2019 for water and wastewater systems.[22] The report considered capital as well as operations and maintenance needs.

With respect to the capital needs funding gap, the EPA's analysis estimated the potential 20-year funding gap for drinking water systems' capital needs at between $0 billion and $267 billion (an average estimate of $102 billion or about $5 billion annually), with a no revenue growth scenario (i.e., at existing spending levels) and between $0 billion to $205 (an average estimate $45 billion or some $2.2 billion a year) in the revenue growth scenario at 3 percent above the rate of inflation.[23] The EPA estimated the potential total 20-year funding gap for wastewater treatment systems' capital spending at between $73 billion to $177 billion (an average of $122 billion or roughly $6.0 billion annually), with a no revenue growth scenario, and between $0 billion to $94 billion (an average of $21 billion or about $1.0 billion annually) in the revenue growth scenario.[24]

With respect to the operations and maintenance funding gap, the EPA's analysis projected the twenty years' drinking water systems' operation and maintenance gap at between $0 billion and $495 billion (with an average of $161 billion) with a no revenue growth scenario and between $0 billion and $267 billion (with an average of $0 billion) for the revenue growth scenario.[25] It estimated the wastewater operations and maintenance gap for the twenty-year period at between $0 billion to $80 billion (an average of $10 billion), for the revenue growth scenario.[26]

Studies by the Congressional Budget Office (CBO) also indicated massive, future investment needs and a huge funding gap. In 2002, the CBO estimated that nation's needed annual infrastructure investments for drinking water systems at between $11.6 and $20.1 billion for the twenty-year period (2000-2019) and between $13.0 and $20.9 billion for wastewater systems during this period. It projected the average annual costs for operations and maintenance at between $25.7 billion and $31.8 billion for drinking water systems during this twenty-year period and between $21.4 billion and $25.2 billion for wastewater systems. It placed drinking water and wastewater infrastructure investments over the twenty years at $492 billion ($24.6 billion annually) under a low-cost scenario and $820 billion ($41 billion annually) under a high-cost scenario.[27]

In another report, the CBO estimated the annual gap between future investment costs and current spending (as of 1999). Its estimated of the annual capital investment gap for drinking water over the twenty-year period (2000-2019) ranged from -$0.2 to $8.3 billion, depending on various financial and accounting variables. For wastewater, the annual capital investment gap ranged from $3.2 billion to $11.1 billion, again depending on various variables. Thus, the CBO estimated the total annual drinking annual water and wastewater capital investment gap at between $3.0 and $19.4 billion during the twenty-year period.[28]

Finally, most recently, the American Society of Civil Engineers projected the nation's total drinking water and wastewater investment needs at $255.0 billion over a five-year period (2009-2013), with estimated spending at $146.4 billion, leaving a total shortage of $108.6 billion during this period.[29] It further estimated an $11 billion shortfall annually to replace aging drinking water facilities that are near the end of their useful lives and to comply with federal safe drinking water regulations. This shortfall projection did not take into consideration any growth in demand for clean drinking water.[30]

The bottom line: there is a funding gap with respect to water and wastewater infrastructure. The public sector faces tremendous challenges in financing the replacement (and expansion) of mains, pipes, and treatment plants. Current levels of public sector funding cannot meet the nation's future water supply and wastewater treatment infrastructure needs. This is a problem that will likely only worsen as state and local governments face a growing fiscal crisis.

The Fiscal Crisis Facing State and Local Governments

For years, even in economic boom times, state and local governments were less than eager to pay for water and wastewater infrastructure development. They often deferred maintenance and capital expenditures. A U.S. General Accounting Office study found that "public drinking water utilities were more likely than their privately-owned counterparts to defer maintenance and major capital projects."[31] The publicly-owned water and wastewater industry now faces the need for maintenance, replacement, and, in some cases, expansion expenditures because of the low priority assigned to water systems in prior budgets. Years of infrastructure under-investment, especially in underground pipes and sewers, have led to a massive need for capital.

In the past decades, the public sector sought to justify underinvestment in water supply and wastewater treatment infrastructure because of lack of funds. With respect to this type of infrastructure, underinvestment takes much longer to be evident to consumers. Underground assets have long lives, typically more than 50 years and sometimes as long as 100 years. Maintenance can be deferred before mains and pipes break, collapse, or create other problems that cannot be ignored. Gradually, underinvestment has led to a decline in services. The range and quality of services provided increasingly are inadequate. Water taste, color and odor have become important issues. Wastewater systems may overflow during or after storms, with raw sewage spilling into streets. These service declines undermine, in part, the public sector's legitimacy as a service provider, thereby providing a rationale for privatization. Although localities want to control the cash flow from services instead of giving any part of the revenues to the private sector, they increasingly must face the harsh funding realities encountered by the public sector's water and wastewater systems.

Drinking water supply and wastewater treatment utilities are capital intensive. These systems require a significant investment in infrastructure having a relatively long service life. For example, water delivery systems involve four elements: first, the capture of the resources; second, the treatment to provide adequate quality for use; third, the transportation through the primary network, such as water mains; and fourth, the delivery to users through the secondary network, such as pipes. Each of these components, namely, sources-of-water-supply, treatment facilities, transmission and distribution systems, and pumping equipment, necessitates fixed capital investments in long-lived, often underground, assets.

Water-related services are more capital intensive compared to electric, natural gas, and telecommunications utilities in the United

States. As measured by the rates of net utility plant capital costs to operating revenues, water utilities are more than twice as capital intensive as electric utilities, the next most capital intensive utility sector, and nearly three times as capital intensive as natural gas utilities, the least-capital intensive of the four utilities.[32] As a result of these capital cost factors and the related capital intensity, communities cannot afford to upgrade their systems, many of which are decades old, some of which are a century old.

Furthermore, because of the water delivery systems' capital intensity, fixed costs associated with supply, treatment, and distribution represent a key element of the industry's cost structure. It is difficult for any water utility, regardless of its ownership or management, to reduce its capital costs. It is important to note that reducing operating costs through increased efficiency, as discussed later in this chapter, among other variable costs, can only offset high capital costs to a limited degree. America's public sector faces the need to rehabilitate and rebuild its expensive infrastructure, consisting aging of pipes and treatment plants, but the state, local and federal levels are now strapped for cash.

State and Local Aspects. As a result of the severe 2007-2009 economic downturn, numerous states face huge revenues shortfalls on multiple fronts, including declines in revenues from personal and corporate income and sales taxes.[33] To balance their budgets, states closed the revenue gap and balanced their budgets by slashing expenditures including laying off or furloughing employees, seeking early retirements, reducing salaries, making across-the-board or targeted cuts in spending, reducing aid to cities and towns, reorganizing agencies, and tapping rainy day funds. States are turning to tax and user fee increases to help budgetary shortfalls. Some states, clustered in the midwest and west, even faced "fiscal peril," as the result of widespread foreclosures, rising unemployment, and poor financial planning and management. Cities across the nation also faced grim fiscal conditions, at least in the near-term, as revenues fell.[34]

The 2009 $787 billion federal economic stimulus package included roughly $250 billion in aid to states and localities. However, this assistance has not been enough to fill the massive funding gap.

Cash-strapped states and localities are thus evermore limited in their ability to finance water delivery and wastewater treatment infrastructure updates. Many face debt ceilings on the amount of tax-exempt general obligation bonds, backed by the guarantee that the issuer will use its taxing power for repayment, they can issue established by law, poor credit ratings, or delays experienced by localities in obtaining funds from state revolving loan programs. Also, general obligation bonds financed by tax increases usually require voter approval, which may not be forthcoming. These bonds dilute an issuer's debt capacity that it may desire to retain for other public purposes. States and localities may be further constrained in their ability to issue tax-exempt debt by a desire to maintain strong credit ratings (and thereby keep future borrowing costs lower) and by the debt service coverage requirements, imposed by bond rating agencies and/or covenants in existing bond issues. Public officials also face numerous other competing demands, such as education, for their limited financial resources.

Apart from user rate increases, a topic discussed in Chapter 9, the public sector could float revenue bonds to finance infrastructure expansions as opposed to maintenance and repair expenditures. With this type of bond, revenues from the operation of the infrastructure project being financed are pledged to pay interest costs and repay the principal. However, investors generally require higher interest yields with revenue bonds than with general obligation instruments, but revenue bonds do not require voter approval and do not impact the issuer's debt capacity. However, rating agencies take the amount of revenue bonds outstanding into account in financial capability analyses for a specific public sector, whether governmental authority, commission, or special district. In short, the fiscal crisis encountered by the public sector has resulted in state and local governments becoming less capable of paying for water and wastewater treatment infrastructure replacements and upgrades.

The American Recovery and Reinvestment Act of 2009[35] provided a program in 2009 and 2010 to expand financing alternatives for state and local governments, especially in early 2009 when they faced a difficult market for selling traditional tax-exempt bonds. The act created a new category of taxable bonds designed to facilitate the financing of state and local capital expenditures. Issuers could elect to treat obligations that would otherwise qualify as tax-exempt for federal income tax purposes (except private activity bonds), including water and wastewater systems, as Build America Bonds (BABs). Interest on BABs was taxable for federal income tax purposes.

Because BABs carried higher yields, the federal government reduced the issuer's financing costs through either a tax credit or a direct subsidy. Under tax credit BABs, investors claimed a tax credit equal to 35 percent of the interest they received on a BAB. To generate the same yield as a taxable bond, the tax credit BABs earned interest at about 74 percent of the coupon on a comparable taxable bond. Although the after-tax yield was the same as on a comparable taxable bond, the interest payable by the issuer was substantially less.

For certain qualified bonds, direct subsidy BABs, the issuer could elect to receive a direct subsidy payment from the federal government in lieu of giving a tax credit to investors. The payment equaled 35 percent of the interest payable on the bond. The federal subsidy ensured that the issuer did not bear the additional cost of the higher yield. These bonds were attractive to states and localities, which ended up with a lower cost of capital than on traditional tax-free bonds. Direct subsidy BABs drew interest from investors, such tax-exempt organizations and foreign investors, that traditionally have not needed to purchase tax-exempt obligations. New investors came forward and tens of billions of dollars of BABs were issued.

Federal Aspects. At present, huge trillion dollar federal deficits as far as the eye can see,[36] a growing debt burden, and a variety of competing concerns, such as healthcare, place limits on what the federal government can do with respect to water and wastewater infrastructure, leading to proposals for a deficit neutral water trust fund, briefly noted in Chapter 9. Also, federal borrowing to stimulate the economy may saturate the market for U.S.-based debt, possibly crowding out states and municipalities. Potentially lower global (i.e., Chinese) demand in an oversaturated U.S. public sector capital market, plus the future risk of inflation, will likely push up U.S. Treasury borrowing costs, also leading to higher rates for non-federal governmental borrowers.[37]

The bottom line: in the capital-intensive water sector, the cash strapped public sector cannot keep up with basic maintenance and repairs much less upgrade costly infrastructure.

Privatization as a Financing Tool

Privatization provides a method of financing water supply and wastewater treatment infrastructure. By converting physical capital into financial capital, privatization though the sale of assets or contractual arrangements may provide new sources of capital and free up public sector resources and debt capacity for other uses, such as education, healthcare, and worker retraining. Private owners (or operators) of water systems can tap capital markets to finance the upgrade of facilities or systems.

As examined in Chapter 5, funding obtained through the various privatization modes, including sale proceeds, payment of a one time, upfront fee, stream of annual payments, or lease rents, could pay for major capital improvements for a publicly-owned system or other municipal projects (the latter, in a contractual arrangement, if permitted by state and local law). A contract may provide for an upfront payment, for instance, that a municipality can use to retire existing debt on a plant, fund other capital improvements, or help balance its budget. If a contractor finances facility (or system) improvements or expansions, communities need not burden their general obligation balance sheets.

Less reliance on tax-exempt financing would increase tax revenues thereby benefiting federal, state, and local governments. The tax-exempt status of the debt traditionally issued by states and localities hurts three levels of government. The federal, state, and local governments collect fewer corporate tax revenues and lose the taxes they would have collected if the bond interest were not tax-exempt. Cities, counties, and school districts realize less property tax revenues because public entities do not pay real estate taxes. However, if a locality can finance infrastructure improvement at below market rates using tax-exempt financing, it incurs fewer costs and may likely charge its customers less than if a system were privately-owned, other things being equal. Because they have access to tax-exempt financing, do not pay income and property taxes, and generally do not cover their non-operating costs, publicly-owned water agencies generally may offer lower water rates to customers.

In sum, the current financial crisis may drive more public sector entities to outsource the management of or lease (or sell) their water and/or wastewater utilities. In theory, privatization can help public agencies deal with operating and capital costs. However, because of the resistance privatization encounters from union leaders and public interest groups, it is unclear whether the public sector will explore options that use private capital, not federal funds or tax-exempt debt, and turn their aging utility infrastructure into financial assets.

While advantages exist to privatization as a financial tool, in addition to the potential disadvantages discussed later in this chapter, other negatives include the loss of grant money as well as access to low-interest loans or tax-exempt financing for capital improvements.

Also, in the future, customers may pay higher rates that they might otherwise have, as a result of municipality's desire for unencumbered dollars to spend as it wants.

Special Capital Funding Needs

Because of population growth in some regions and aging urban infrastructure in other areas, various localities in the United States face special capital needs. Population growth will exacerbate water and wastewater infrastructure needs in certain areas, such as Arizona, Colorado, Nevada, and Texas. By 2050, as noted in Chapter 3, the U.S. Census Bureau estimates the nation's population will reach some 400 million, up from the current 304 million. In addition to the expenditures associated with essential infrastructure replacement and expansion, the availability of future water supplies represents another cost consideration. In many areas, low-cost sources have been tapped. The expense of developing new supply sources has increased. Additionally, environmental constraints make it difficult to develop new sources.[38] To meet the growing demand, many utilities incur high marginal costs to add new water supplies to their supply mix by acquiring expensive water rights.

Some large metropolitan centers in the United States, such as Philadelphia, Cleveland, and Detroit, have the oldest, most run-down infrastructure with some of the greatest capital needs, but face a shrinking center-city population. These areas with decreasing populations encounter the challenge of both a diminishing customer base and a declining tax base, resulting in an even more limited financial capacity to replace their deteriorating water infrastructure. Also, smaller publicly-owned systems lack the financial capacity and operational scale to make required investments, for example, to meet increasingly stringent federal requirements for drinking water and clean water, without drastic rate increases.

Privatization as Managerial Tool to Increase Efficiency and Reduce Costs

Private operations are said to correlate with greater efficiency and effectiveness. It is assumed that private firms will operate more efficiently than public entities because of the profit motive and greater responsiveness to market needs. Because of the incentive structure created by the profit motive, it is assumed that private firms will use fewer resources and be more efficient than public enterprises in supplying the same services.

Private providers have incentives to cut costs through improved efficiency, staff reduction, better use of advanced technology, more flexible management practices, streamlined procurement, and improved information services designed to facilitate better decision-making. They may more readily respond to consumer needs through enhanced services and experimentation with new programs. The profit motive may lead a firm to keep profit margins low on contract so as to expand its market share, thereby boosting it overall profits. In contrast to the public sector, which may have no incentive to cut costs, the private sector is flexible and economical. Additionally, removal of politics from decision-making may result in better management. As private firms grow in size, they can achieve economies of scale and scope. Economies of scale connotes a decline in the unit cost of providing a service as one provider delivers more services. Economies of scope means that the unit costs of providing two services will decline if one provider supplies both services.

Conversely, the public sector may be bound by bureaucratic inertia, lack incentives to innovate, and fail to have a consumer orientation. It is often an inefficient monopoly provider that lacks incentives for efficiency. Public systems generally err on the side of spending more, not less. They are punished if service is unsatisfactory, but may not be rewarded for controlling costs. Public operations may suffer from excessive staffing, or staff with incorrect skills, as a result of political interference from local elected officials and civil service rules, among other factors. Public enterprises generally are less capable of offering the "right" salaries and other incentives to attract and retain good managers. Publicly-owned utilities may also defer maintenance and postpone needed infrastructure improvements, exhibit higher production and operating costs, be less efficient in their procurement practices, adopt cost-saving devices and innovation more slowly, if at all, and set rates further from actual costs.

The private sector is free from many of the institutional barriers to efficient operations encountered by the public sector. These include procurement rules, prohibitions on incentive compensation, bureaucratic requirements that hamper the least-cost options, entrenched work practices, and lack of in-house expertise.

Private firms strive to deal with the labor, chemical, and energy cost elements in operating water and wastewater assets. They achieve cost savings through more efficient work practices, cross-training of staff, reduced chemical use, more efficient energy use, bulk purchasing, and preventive maintenance. Overall, private firms use their hand-on, practical experience gained over time, often at numerous facilities and systems, to run increasingly more efficient operations, thereby achieving economies of scale and scope.

A private operator can achieve cost savings by maximizing a firm's core competencies. These include greater technical acumen and operational competence, better staff training together with more training hours per employee, and enhanced management systems and maintenance programming. Private entities focus on training staff to work more efficiently, particularly though preventive maintenance to head off costly repairs. Because emergency repairs are more expensive than preventive maintenance, firms have a financial incentive to prevent equipment failure.

Private firms may offer bonuses and opportunities for promotions to increase worker productivity. They strive to reduce chemical costs. Municipal systems may overtreat water with various chemicals, such as chlorine. Private companies reduce chemical costs by carefully examining chemical use so that only the proper amounts are used. They may also rely on their national purchasing power to buy chemicals more cheaply in large quantities.

A private contractor will also take a close look at energy use. It may run some equipment during off-peak hours and may cut the vehicle fleet.

Private firms operating numerous facilities can use economies of scale to achieve better prices for equipment, chemicals, and supplies. Private companies provide a higher level of customer service at a lower cost by integrating customer service functions, such as call-in centers, billing, and collections, into a single system. A public-private partnership allows a municipality to benefit from knowledge gained through a for-profit firm's operation of numerous facilities. Private firms can also spread the costs of experts in information technology, energy efficiency, optimal chemical usage, and preventive maintenance across all of the infrastructure they operate (or own). A firm's ability to tap into greater pool knowledge is especially attractive to smaller localities, lacking high caliber personnel or cutting-edge technologies.

Because of an inherent ability to innovate, generally speaking, the market is more efficient than the public sector in providing services. However, there exists only limited scope to introduce competition in the supply of water. Local networks of mains and pipes remain natural monopolies. Typically, there is only one water system in a locality making the issue of choice, and thus competition, irrelevant. It is difficult to unbundle the supply of water because an increase competition in the supply will likely provide few benefits. The costs of producing water, a potentially competitive activity, are low relative to the value added at the transportation and particularly the distribution stages, where a natural monopoly prevails.

When we speak about technological innovation, a word of caution is in order. Water utilities are not as technologically dynamic as electric utilities, for example. Thus, water utilities have fewer opportunities to reduce costs significantly. Raising productivity is difficult because the infrastructure, the system's physical capital, contains much of the technology requisite to productivity gains.

Privatization as Technique to Assist in Complying with Environmental Standards and Implementing Water Security Measures

In addition to aging infrastructure, localities face even stricter drinking water quality regulations, such as the Long Term 2 Enhanced Surface Water Treatment Rule and the Stage 2 Disinfectants and Disinfection Byproducts Rule,[39] and tougher enforcement of drinking water safety laws.[40] On the wastewater side, the EPA seeks to correct combined sewer and sanitary sewer overflows and more strictly enforce the federal Clean Water Act, including focusing on municipal wastewater treatment plants.[41] The steady rise of replacement costs and tighter environmental standards and enforcement increase the complexity and cost of operating both water and wastewater systems, in part, by forcing the use of more advanced technologies.

Water systems also face increases terrorism-related security concerns, including physical and cyber infrastructure protection, containment identification, decontamination, contingency planning, and risk assessment. Implementation of the EPA's 2004 Water Security Research and Technical Support Action Plan[42] will impact nearly every system, almost certainly without full federal funding. The plan, based on a collaborative effort among the agency, various federal partners, the water industry, public sector organizations, and the emergency response community provides a methodology and a set of tools, among other items, to enhance the security of U.S. drinking water supply and wastewater treatment systems.

Because of daunting compliance problems that can overwhelm both their budgets and personnel, localities may choose to enter into various types of contractual arrangements. Beyond providing capital, public-private partnerships can help localities tap the knowledge and experience of skilled partners to comply with environmental regulations and water security measures. Staying apprised of the latest science and governmental regulations takes resources. Implementing needed changes to provide quality drinking water and treated wastewater requires a significant investment not only in capital but also in personnel, knowledgeable and skilled in using modern technologies. Private firms employ technical experts who can be available as needed, especially to smaller communities that lack highly trained, full-time personnel. In sum, privatizing water and wastewater services may improve compliance with environmental standards and water security measures.

The Public Sector Responds

Although critics of privatization assert that efficiency is not the public sector's only (or its main) priority, after several decades of living under the possibility of some type of privatization, some public sector entities have made considerable progress in undertaking the necessary productivity improvements and expense reductions. Municipalities strive to optimize as an alternative to privatization. Optimization involves cost cutting and improved efficiency.[43]

The threat of privatization has led to improvements in municipal efficiency though personnel reductions, cross-training, improved productivity, bulk purchases of materials, upgrading plant equipment, streamlining the procurement of goods and services, and enhanced information and analysis to facilitate better decision-making. In short, some public sector water and wastewater agencies have become more efficient because of pressure from private firms and the existence of private alternatives.[44]

Numerous small, local players comprise the public sector's side of the water supply business. More than 94 percent of the nation's 156,000 public water systems, that is, those regularly serving an average of at least twenty-five individuals daily at least sixty days each year, are classified as "small" by the EPA and serve fewer than 3,300 people.[45] These systems are the most challenged financially and technologically.

Small public providers have limited access to capital markets and constricted managerial resources. They experience difficulties in maintaining (and improving) their infrastructure as well as meeting environmental standards and security measures. Lacking access to specialized technicians, these systems often contract out operations to small, local businesses that cannot take advantage of economies of scale in the manner that larger utilities can. Often, small, local private contractors may not be highly qualified; but unfortunately, many facilities are often too small to warrant a large, more competent contractor's interest.

As a result, need exits for regionalization of the American public sector water industry.[46] Numerous tiny utilities struggle separately to raise capital to maintain their infrastructure, be more efficient, and keep up with increasingly complex regulatory and technological environment. Regionalization involves the consolidation of contiguous or nearby systems in a given area. One or more communities turn over their assets to a regional public authority, not constrained by geopolitical boundaries or local political agendas, and accept little or no control over decisions. Bigger operations achieved through regionalization allow for greater economies of scale and scope.

Regionalization of public systems can help lower capital and operating costs. From a financial perspective, it can assist in raising capital by both improving access to capital markets and lowering the cost of capital required to replace and improve infrastructure. From an engineering perspective, it can improve operational efficiencies and spur technological improvement. From a managerial perspective, it can help reduce costs and assist a system comply with more stringent environmental requirements, at a lower cost. Larger systems, with a broader customer base, in terms of demand levels and patterns, offer possibilities for optimizing operations and achieving cost savings through the better application of personnel, technology, and equipment. Regionalization enables systems to spread fixed costs for accounting, billing, water quality teams, engineering, information technology, purchasing, and water testing, among other functions, over additional customers and often eliminate redundant expenses by reducing administrative and overhead costs.

Despite these advantages, it is difficult, both politically and institutionally, to regionalize publicly-owned systems, even if these transactions would make financial and managerial sense. Regionalization evokes a concern for loss of control over growth and development; municipalities are reluctant to give up local function with a proud history.[47] Water supply traditionally represents a local enterprise in the United States; the identity of a public water system is often tied to a community that resists surrendering control to a regional authority.

Stated differently, independence assures local control. Furthermore, acquiring a nonviable system may strain an acquirer's financial resources and its managerial capabilities.

Potential Disadvantages of Privatization

Potential disadvantages of privatization include: workforce reductions, rate increases, service declines, loss of public control, contractor bankruptcy, xenophobia, and transaction costs. There are also ideological objections. Particular attention is focused in this section on structuring contracts to meet these potential drawbacks, an analysis continued in Chapter 8. When water, a natural monopoly, is privatized, claims of superior efficiency and performance are often realized through contractual provisions and vigilant public authorities who monitor agreements and hold firms accountable. Through a carefully negotiated, structured, and monitored contract, the public sector can ensure that the efficiency gains translate into lower rates or an investment in the long-term maintenance (and updating) of infrastructure by the private sector.

Workforce Reductions

To achieve the expected efficiency gains and cost savings, critics maintain that private operators will reduce the size of a system's workforce by eliminating well-paying public sector jobs, unfairly treating employees, reducing pension benefits, increasing the number of part-time employees, and generally forcing concessions from unionized employees in terms of working hours as well as work practices. Unions favor the retention of water supply and wastewater treatment services in a public domain and generally oppose any type of privatization.

Despite these concerns, private operators typically retain almost all existing employees because of the benefits of having an experienced workforce with valuable knowledge and expertise obtained from serving a community. If a private operator must reduce the number of employees to increase efficiency and decrease costs, staff reductions generally are handled by attrition.

Strategies used by public-private partnerships lessen the impact of privatization on public employees now represent the rule, not the exception. To provide safeguards, contracts can be structured so that existing employees are not harmed. For example, operations and maintenance contracts may require the private firms to retain all existing employees who meet minimal criteria, such as passing a drug test, and not to eliminate jobs for a specified time period, except for financial exigency. Typically, contracts also require the private operator to maintain salary and benefit levels for employees who move from the public to the private sector. The other words, contracts protect employees' existing compensation levels by precluding reductions in salaries and benefits or by requiring equivalent total compensation. The latter approach may, however, lead to a change in the provision of specific benefits. To guard against this type of modification, a contract may provide that employees hired by the private partner may continue to participate in a public employee (defined benefit) pension plan, for example. Where permitted by state law, a private partner can make contributions to the public employee pension system instead of to a new (defined contribution) plan. Or, employees may be given the option to choose the pension arrangement, public or private, they prefer. In short, contracts cover how the operator will handle benefits, particularly if public employees currently enjoy a set of good benefits.

Agreements universally preserve union rights. Under a management (service) contract, the workforce remains as public employees, thereby overcoming potential employee and union opposition to privatization. Techniques also exist to invest some of the savings derived from privatization to transition programs for employees who do not continue to work for a private contractor.

Stepping back from the contractual details, for employees, the private sector generally offers better employee training and merit-based advancement than the public sector. As workers transition from the public to the private sector, greater opportunities often exist for education, training, and career advancement, including ongoing field training, tuition-reimbursed college education, and advancement from the field to other operations the private partner manages, even into corporate positions. Incentive pay arrangements typically exist at private firms, with bonuses tied to performance.

The bottom line is that the fears expressed by unions generally are not warranted. However, because labor costs are a small proportion of total expenses in water or wastewater operations, the efficiency gains are likely small.

Rate Increases and Service Declines

Critics raise contractor accountability issues, focusing on the likelihood of rate increases and services declines as major concerns when a public service is turned over to a private firm. A fear exists regarding future rate increases. Concern about water prices rising immediately post-privatization and over the long-term drives these rate shock worries. Currently, municipalities often hesitate to raise water rates, although water bills nationwide comprise a tiny part of an average family's monthly expenditures, about $20 a month, as noted in Chapter 1.

With an operations and maintenance contract, discussed in Chapter 5, a municipality retains control over rate setting. Privatization agreements generally contain provisions dealing with future rate increases. Contracts typically provide for fixed rate guarantees for the contract period with annual increases often limited to changes in the Consumer Price Index. Private-public partnerships either specify the standards for increasing rates, provide rate schedules under different scenarios, require the public entity to set rates, or bar the private contractor from increasing rates without the public partner's consent.

Critics also fear that the quality of services may suffer under private operations, as a result of a lack of accountability. To increase profits, a private operator may cut costs and reduce service quality or safeguards, at least the argument runs. Additionally, critics maintain a private entity may not be as responsive to public complaints as a publicly-owned system.

These concerns can be met in the bidding, contracting, and monitoring processes, as examined in more detail in Chapter 8. In brief, in considering bids, a governmental entity must obtain detailed information about each bidder's (and its parent's) qualifications, its financial and operational capacity, and its performance and environmental compliance history in other communities. The contracts typically establish objective performance standards and incentives for exceeding standards. If a failure to meet any standard constitutes a material breach, contracts provide for termination. Termination clauses motivate private contractors to at least meet their contractual and other legally mandated obligations.

Contracts contain various performance metrics as to quality, compliance, and customer service designed spell out the desired ends but leave the manner of performing the work to the contractor's discretion. In other words, contractors receive freedom to find the best ways to meet a specified performance objective. Performance standards are, of course, subject to various limitations, such as the physical capabilities of the system, the occurrence of a disabling event beyond the operator's reasonable control, or changes in the law or applicable environmental, health, or safety regulations.

Agreements also include monitoring and continued oversight by the public sector to ensure that the private firm delivers the services contemplated by the agreement. Operators must provide localities with sufficiently detailed monthly and annual operating and financial reports to enable the evaluation of performance. Local governments also receive the right to inspect facilities and audit records at any time, upon reasonable notice.

Loss of Public Control

With public-private partnerships, concern exists about loss of public control over daily operations of a facility or system, such as maintenance tasks. Large private firms generally use out-of-town call centers and non-local procurement to reduce costs.

Despite these fears, local officials need not worry about day-to-day operating and maintenance issues. Control over a facility or system is embodied in the contract with private operator. As discussed in the prior section, through contractual performance standards, broader objectives, such as meeting water quality objectives, are attained. To obtain these goals, a need exists for effective, ongoing monitoring of contractor performance. Agreements typically impose disincentives on a contractor for nonperformance, such as penalties, and contain termination provisions.

A possible problem also exists with respect to lost capacity and expertise. If a municipality terminates a contract and reinstitutes public operations and management, it likely will need to rebuild its capacity in terms of personnel and expertise. However, unless it is a small system, the municipality will likely be able to contract with another private firm to take over a terminated agreement.

A wastewater treatment facility or system presents its own unique set of public control issues. In addition to the operation of a wastewater treatment plant, a publicly-owned entity may provide other community services, including technical assistance on wastewater treatment to industrial customers, septic tank retrofitting, public education and outreach programs, and provision for reclaimed water supplies. A municipality must decide whether to continue these roles itself, include them in the contract for their assumption by the private firm, or these services may be lost.

Contractor Bankruptcy

The possibility exists that a private contractor may go bankrupt. To guard against this possibility, localities must ask for qualifications and references, including existing customers, funding sources and suppliers, in the bidding process and spend time assessing this information. Also, termination provisions outline the conditions under which a contract may be ended. These include termination for cause, for example, in the event of bankruptcy.

Xenophobia

Concern and suspicion exist about contract operators (or lessees) being foreign-owned companies. However, the same federal environmental regulations apply regardless of the identity of a contractor or lessee.

The bottom line: municipalities will closely scrutinize and carefully monitor a private contractor, whether foreign or domestic, through the bidding process, stringent contractual provisions, and ongoing evaluations. In particular, localities need to evaluate each bidder's performance on other contracts and check references before selecting a winner.

Transaction Costs

Privatization involves extensive transaction costs. These expenses accrue from the time and effort expanded in planning, decision-making, negotiating, contract drafting and enforcement, and resolving disputes.

Communities must develop (or retain) expertise to evaluate their options before embarking on any form of privatization. If a municipality goes forward with privatization, it will likely need to engage experts. The process of preparing and overseeing a bid, including the requests for qualifications and for proposals, can be daunting.

Localities will likely engage experts in the area of contract negotiation and design to protect the public interest. The public sector will want to impose strict requirements on a private firm regarding outputs, for example, the quantity and quality of water supplied, as well as information reporting requirements. The level of contract completeness is important. These details become part of complex contracts and end up raising the cost of producing the desired services.

Beyond an agreement spelling out the rights and responsibilities of the private firm and the public sector, contractual enforcement requires effective monitoring of what the firm will deliver. Thus, a need exists for a long-term commitment by the public sector to the oversight process. There is a cost to managing the agreement and monitoring contractual performance, including inspections, reviewing reports and complaints, and compliance with performance metrics. In particular, communities need to retain expert consultants to oversee complex, long-term contracts, such as design-build-operate-transfer arrangements, discussed in Chapter 5, that give a contractor a large degree of autonomy.

Given the high transaction costs of contracting, including various consultants and attorneys, each locality must weigh these (and other) costs against its capital needs as well as the expected benefits of a private firm in providing capital, reducing operating costs, and meeting environmental and other requirements.

Ideological

Some continue to regard water as a public good, part of the nation's natural heritage. For critics of privatization, water services should not be entrusted to a private company to operate and manage. In other words, the public sector ought to own, operate, and maintain its water supply and wastewater treatment infrastructure.

Concern exists about the motives of private, for-profit firms, with some viewing profit-motivated businesses as inherently suspect, if not corrupt. For some critics of privatization, who disdain the private sector, the profit motive may provide an incentive to cut corners on long-term capital improvements, decrease efforts to monitor water quality, and avoid conservation measures because profits depend on the amount of water sold.[48] Also, a mixing of public and private responsibilities may lead to a blurring of accountability and may result in corruption.[49]

Because profit seeking is said to have no place in supplying water, powerful political forces, such as unions and certain public interest groups, oppose any type of privatization.[50] These privatization opponents want to maintain public control over essential services, including water supply and wastewater treatment infrastructure. Simply put privatization critics assert that infrastructure built with pubic funds ought to remain with public entities, and more specifically, the totality of water and wastewater operations ought to continue under direct governmental control.

The predominant mode of privatization in the United States involves a public-private partnership, not the sale of assets. As noted in Chapter 2, public-private partnerships now operate more than

2,000 drinking water and wastewater facilities in the United States. Considerable experience and best practices exist. There are consultants who specialize in helping communities negotiate with private operators. Profits derived from a public-private partnership are not at the public's expense.

These critics fail to see the reasons for entering into public-private partnerships for water supply and wastewater treatment systems including a new funding source to meet capital needs, increased efficiency and cost savings, achieving improved compliance with environmental standards, and overcoming a lack of local, public sector expertise. Most importantly, they fail to see the spending gap between the current levels of water and wastewater infrastructure spending and levels required to maintain and expand infrastructure in the future. Simply put, massive capital expenditures are required to comply with environmental regulations, improve water security measures, and to maintain and expand water and wastewater infrastructure. The funds needed to meet the required capital expenditures will not magically appear. The profits generated by private firms serve as incentives for investment, innovation, and efficiency. Also, although concerns abound about whether privatization will yield the hoped-for community benefits, carefully drafted, monitored, and enforced contracts will meet nearly all objections, except for transaction costs.

As America faces water and wastewater infrastructure funding issues, privatization may become an increasingly attractive option for localities looking to relieve themselves of the financial burdens of providing these services. In theory, privatization offers many benefits, including access to capital, increased operating efficiencies and reduced costs, assistance in meeting stringent environmental standards and security requirements. Localities can surmount the fears that accompany privatization by entering into carefully negotiated, well-written contracts that reserve oversight and ultimate control over these services to public officials.

Using empirical data and case studies, Chapters 7 and 8, respectively, examine the conceptual advantages and disadvantages of privatization, in practice.

Notes

1. I have drawn on Water Partnership Council, *Establishing Public-Private Partnerships for Water and Wastewater Systems: A Blueprint for Success*, 2003, 13-14, 18-13, 26-31, 34-41; Geoffrey F. Segal and Adrian T. Moore,

"Frequently Asked Questions About Water/Wastewater Privatization," September 2003, Reason Public Policy Institute, Policy Brief 26; National Research Council (NRC), *Privatization of Water Services in the United States: An Assessment of Issues and Experience* (Washington, DC: National Academy Press, 2002), 3-9, 18-19, 23-28, 47-55, 101-109; Robin A. Johnson, John McCormally, Adrian T. Moore, "Long-Term Contracting For Water and Wastewater Services," May 2002, Reason Public Policy Institute, How-To Guide 19; Michael Nadol, Paul Seidenstat, Simon Hakin, "Introduction," in *America's Water and Wastewater Industries: Competition and Privatization*, eds. Paul Setidenstat, Michael Nadol, Simon Hakim (Vienna, VA: Public Utilities Reports, 2000), 7-10; David Haarmeyer, "Environmental Infrastructure: An Evolving Public-Private Partnership," in *American's Water and Wastewater Industries*, 32-36; Stephen P. Morgan and Jeffery I. Chapman, "Issues Surrounding the Privatization of Public Water Services," A Report Prepared for the Association of California Water Agencies, September 17, 1996, 13-15, 22-29, 33-38, 44-50; Janice A. Beecher, G. Richard Dreese, John D. Stanford, Regulatory Implications of Water and Wastewater Privatization, National Regulatory Research Institute, July 1995, NRRI 95-09, 3-11, 25-32, 93-96, 101-105; David Haarmeyer, "Privatizating Infrastructure: Options for Municipal Systems," *Journal of the American Water Works Association* 86:3 (March 1994): 42-55, at 43-46; John G. Heilmand and Gerald W. Johnson, *The Politics and Economics of Privatization: The Case of Wastewater Treatment* (Tuscaloosa, AL: University of Alabama, 1992), 18-29, 48-50; Scott Edwards, "The Road Less Traveled, Until Now," Veolia Water North America, n.d. See generally, Meriem Aït Ouyahia, Public-Private Partnerships for Funding Municipal Drinking Water Infrastructure: What Are the Challenges?, Discussion Paper, Policy Research Initiative Project: Sustainable Development, Government of Canada, May 2006.

2. See, e.g., Robert Barkin, "At the breaking point," *American City & County* 124:1 (January 2009): 24-29.

3. Katherine Shaver, "Incorrect Installation Caused Md. Pipe Break," *Washington Post*, May 21, 2009, B1; Katherine Shaver, "As Inspections Dwindled, Water Main Breaks Rose," *Washington Post*, May 7, 2009, A1; Dan Morse and Katherine Shaver, "Water Main Break Forces Dramatic Rescue of Nine," *Washington Post*, December 24, 2008, A1; Rosalind S. Heldenman and Nelson Hernandez, "Breach Renew Fears About Aging Pipe System," *Washington Post*, December 24, 2008, A6.

4. Ken Belson, "Under 700 Feet of Earth, Divers Clear the Way to Repair the City's Drinking Straw," *New York Times*, November 23, 2008, A39.

5. Jennifer Lin, "More rain, old sewers make for nasty story," *Philadelphia Inquirer*, June 4, 2007, A1 and Cynthia Burton, "Pennsport frustrated by backed-up sewage," *Philadelphia Inquirer*, October 15, 2006, B3.

6. American Society of Civil Engineers (ASCE), 2009 Report Card for America's Infrastructure, March 25, 2009, 25, 57. See also Michael Cooper, "U.S. Infrastructure is in Dire Straits, Report Says," *New York Times*, January 28, 2009, A16.

7. ASCE, 2009 Report Card, 58.

8. The statistics in their paragraph are from U.S. Environmental Protection Agency (EPA), Report to Congress: Impacts and Control of CSOs and SSOs, EPA-833-R-04-001, August 2004, ES-5, ES-7, 4-17 to 4-18, 4-25 to 4-26. See also Charles Duhigg, "Sewers at Capacity, Waste Poisons Waterways," *New York Times*, November 23, 2009, A1 and Larry Wheeler and Grant Smith, "Aging Systems releasing sewage into rivers, streams," *USA Today*, May 8, 2008, A5.

9. Michael Cooper, "In Aging Water Systems, Bigger Threats Are Seen," *New York Times*, April, 2009, A14 and Mark Kemp-Rye, "Out of Sight, Out of Mind," *On Tap* 8:2 (Summer 2008): 16-18, 30-31, at 18.

10. Shelly Sigo, "EPA: New Approaches Needed," *Bond Buyer* 359: 32594 (March 22, 2007): 1.

11. American Water Works Association (AWWA), Dawn of the Replacement Era: Reinvesting in Drinking Water Infrastructure: An Analysis of Twenty Utilities' Needs for Repair and Replacement of Drinking Water Infrastructure, May 2001, 5.

12. EPA, The Clean Water and Drinking Water Infrastructure Gap Analysis, September 2002 (2002 Analysis) EPA-816-R-02-020, 15 (Figure 2-8: Shift in the Likely Condition Associated with the Aging Miles of Pipe in the Network (percentage of pipe by classification)).

13. AWWA, Dawn, 6, 13.

14. Water Infrastructure Network, Clean and Safe Water for the 21st Century: A Renewed National Commitment to Water and Wastewater Infrastructure, April 2000, 3-1.

15. *Ibid.*, 3-3.

16. EPA, Drinking Water Infrastructure Needs Survey: Second Report to Congress, February 2001, EPA 816-R-01-004, 11, 12 (Exhibit ES-1: Total 20-year Need). For a critical assessment of this 2001 EPA survey, see Testimony of David G. Wood, Director, Natural Resources and Environment, U.S. General Accounting Office, Subcommittee on Environment and Hazardous Materials, Committee on Energy and Commerce, House of Representatives, April 11, 2002, GAO-02-592T, 6-9.

17. EPA, Drinking Water Infrastructure Needs Survey and Assessment: Third Report to Congress, June 2005, EPA 816-R-05-001, 23-29.

18. *Ibid.*, 24 (Exhibit 1: Overview of Needs by System Size and Type).

19. EPA, Clean Watersheds Needs Survey 2004: Report to Congress, January 2008, ix, 2-1 to 2-2.

20. EPA, Drinking Water Infrastructure Needs Survey Assessment: Fourth Report to Congress, February 2009, EPA 816-R-09-001, 1.

21. *Ibid.*, 1 (Exhibit 1.1: Total National 20-Year Need (in billions of January 2007 dollars)).

22. EPA, 2002 Analysis.

23. *Ibid.*, 6, 38-39.

24. *Ibid.*, 6, 25.

25. *Ibid.*, 5-6, 41.

26. *Ibid.*, 5, 26.

27. U.S. Congressional Budget Office (CBO), Future Investment in Drinking Water and Wastewater Infrastructure, May 2002, 2, 8 (Table 2, Estimates

of Average Annual Water-System Costs, Capital Plus Financing, 2000-2019).

28. CBO, Future Investment in Drinking Water and Wastewater Infrastructure, November 2002, 26 (Table 2-7, Estimates of the Difference Between 1999 Spending and Future Costs for Investments in Water Systems). The CBO subsequently issued a report highlighting the key similarities and the important differences between its estimates and those of the EPA. CBO, Future Spending on Water Infrastructure: A Comparison of Estimates from the Congressional Budget Office and the Environmental Protection Agency, January 2003.

29. ASCE, 2009 Report Card, 25, 57.

30. *Ibid.*, 1.

31. U.S. General Accounting Office, Water Infrastructure: Information on Financing, Capital Planning, and Privatization, August 2002, GAO-02-764, 7.

32. NRC, *Privatization*, 82 (Table 5-1 Capital Intensity for Major Utilities) and Gary Wolff and Eric Hallstein, Beyond Privatization: Restructuring Water Systems to Improve Performance, Pacific Institute, December 2005, 34. See also Janice A. Beecher, Patrick C. Mann, John D. Stanford, Meeting Water Utility Revenue Requirements: Financing and Ratemaking Alternatives, National Regulatory Research Institute, November 1993, NRRI 93-13, 5-9.

33. Pew Center on the States, Beyond California: States in Fiscal Peril, November 2009 and National Governors Association and National Association of State Budget Officers, The Fiscal Survey of States, June 2009. See also Michael Cooper, "Recession Tightens Grip On State Tax Revenues," *New York Times*, February 23, 2010, A14; Jennifer Steinhauer, "New Year but No Relief For Strapped States," *New York Times*, January 6, 2010, A15; Amy Merrick, "States Draw Up Plans for Year of Even Bigger Budget Cuts," *Wall Street Journal*, November 12, 2009, A7; Peter Slevin, "States Straining to Repair Budgets," *Washington Post*, July 7, 2009, A4; Abby Goodnough, "States Turning to Last Resorts In Budget Crisis," *New York Times*, June 22, 2009, A1; Erica Alini, "State Income-Tax Revenues Sink," *Wall Street Journal*, June 18, 2009, A4; Kirk Johnson, "State Revenues Buffeted by Downturn," *New York Times*, June 5, 2009, A12.

34. Christopher W. Hoene and Michael A. Pagano, City Fiscal Conditions in 2009, National League of Cities, Research Brief on American's Cities, September 2009, Issue 2009-2. See also Leslie Eaton, "Cities Brace for a Prolonged Bout of Declining Tax Revenues," *Wall Street Journal*, September 1, 2009, A5.

35. Public Law 111-5.

36. See, e.g., Edmund L. Andrews, "Federal Government Faces Balloon in Debt Payments," *New York Times*, November 23, 2009, A1; Jackie Calmes, "U.S. Deficit Rises to $1.4 Trillion; Biggest Since '45," *New York Times*, October 17, 2009, A1; Jackie Calmes, "In Revision, a 10-Year Deficit of $9 Trillion is Forecast," *New York Times*, August 26, 2009, A4; Lori Montgomery, "Deficit Projected To Soar With New Programs," *Washington Post*, August 26, 2009, A1; Jonathan Weisman and Deborah Solomon," Decade of Debt: $9 Trillion," *Wall Street Journal*, August 26, 2009, A1.

37. Nicole Gelinas, "The Coming Local Government Credit Crunch," *Wall Street Journal*, March 11, 2009, A15.

38. NRC, *Privatization*, 85.

39. Long Term 2 Enhanced Federal Surface Water Treatment Rule, *Federal Register* 71:3 (January 5, 2006): 654-786 and Stage 2 Disinfectants and Disinfection Byproducts Requirements, 40 *Code of Federal Regulations* §§141.620-141.629. See also, EPA, Fact Sheet: Long Term 2 Enhanced Surface Water Treatment Rule, n.d. and EPA, Fact Sheet: Stage 2 Disinfectants and Disinfection Byproducts Rule, December 2005.

40. See, e.g., Charles Duhigg, "Millions in U.S. Drink Dirty Water, Records Say," *New York Times*, December 8, 2009, A1 and Charles Duhigg, "U.S. Bolsters Chemical Restrictions For Water," *New York Times*, March 23, 2020, B1.

41. Charles Duhigg, "E.P.A. Vows Better Effort on Water," *New York Times*, October 16, 2009, B1 and Charles Duhigg, "Clean Water Laws Neglected, at a Cost," *New York Times*, September 13, 2009, 1. See also Steve Hoffman, *Planet Water: Investing in the World's Most Valuable Resource* (Hoboken, NJ: Wiley, 2009), 164-166.

42. EPA, The Water Security Research and Technical Support Action Plan, March 2004, EPA/600/R-04/063.

43. Steve Maxwell, "Where Are We Headed? Ten Key Trends and Developments in the Water Industry," *Journal of the American Water Works Association* 93:4 (April 2001): 114-118.

44. *Water Engineering & Management*, "Privatization Drives Municipal Utilities to be More Efficient, Survey Says," 147:4 (April 2000):11; James A. Parrott and Sharma L. Young, "Current Trends in Public Utility Management and Inventive Strategies for Major Challenges" in *Management Innovation in U.S. Public Water and Wastewater Systems*, eds. Paul Seidenstat et al. (Hoboken, NJ: John Wiley, 2005), 16-18; Wolff and Hallstein, Beyond Privatization, 39-50, 52-56; NRC, *Privatization*, 7, 8-9, 58-62. See also Don Renner, "Privatize Without a Contract," *Water Engineering & Management* 148:2 (February 2001) 34-36; James A. Parrott, "Think Private, Stay Public," *Journal of American Water Works Association* 94:4 (April 2002): 64-65; Alan W. Manning, *Thinking, Getting and Staying Competitive: A Public Sector Handbook* (Washington, DC: Association of Metropolitan Sewerage Agencies and Association of Metropolitan Water Agencies, 1998), 20-30, 67-77. For a case study of a restructured public water utility, see Matthew Gallagher, "CitiState: Bringing A New Level of Efficiency and Effectiveness to Baltimore City's Water Utility," in *Management Innovation*, 287-297.

45. EPA, Small Public Water System Capacity and Development: Basic Information www.epa/gov/ogwdw000/smallsystems/basicinformation.html (July 10, 2009).

46. NRC, *Privatization*, 8-9, 50-51, 88-91. See also Janice A. Beecher, The Regionalization of Water Utilities: Perspectives, Literature Review, and Annotated Bibliography, National Regulatory Research Institute, NRRI 96-21, July 1996.

47. NRC, *Privatization*, 90.

48. *Ibid.*, 87.
49. See, e.g., Mike Hudson, "Misconduct Taints the Water in Some Privatized Systems," *Los Angeles Times*, May 29, 2006, A1.
50. See e.g. Public Citizen, Waves of Regret, June 2005 and Food and Water Watch, Faculty Pipes: Why Public Funding-Not Privatization-Is the Answer for the U.S. Water Systems (September 2008).

7

Privatization in Practice: Evidence from Empirical Studies

Beyond the conceptual arguments presented in Chapter 6, this and the next chapter consider privatization in practice. This chapter examines general and specific empirical studies dealing with the impact of privatization. It begins by summarizing three studies that generally, but not completely, point to the benefits of privatization, including cost savings, increased compliance with environmental regulations, and improved customer and employee satisfaction. The chapter also offers evidence from a report on capital investments by private partners. It then presents more specific empirical studies dealing with cost savings, efficiency, rates, and environmental compliance that present a more mixed picture of the impact of privatization.

The studies in this chapter show that financial considerations and the need to bring operations in compliance with federal water quality standards drive the privatization of water supply and wastewater treatment systems. Although the specific studies are far more mixed than the three general studies, generally speaking, municipalities are content with some form of privatization for their water supply and wastewater treatment infrastructure. These arrangements have led to cost savings, greater compliance with environmental regulations, and increased customer satisfaction. The overwhelming majority of municipalities continue to renew their public-private partnerships and generally retain the same private firms.

Evidence from General Empirical Studies

As noted in Chapter 6, privatization of water and wastewater systems has its critics; those who fear placing the provision of such vital services in the hands of for-profit firms will have an adverse impact on rates charged users and the quality of services provided. These critics largely ignore important issues that these general empirical studies in this section address. First, municipalities do not make the decision to privatize lightly. Localities are often forced to turn over water and wastewater services to private firms because of an inability to meet the capital demands, as well as compliance with federal environmental standards. Second, the three studies largely show that privatization has been widely successful: saving money in both operating costs and the need for future capital investments as well as bringing facilities into compliance with federal water quality standards, improving customer, and employee satisfaction. All of these benefits have been achieved, in most cases, without raising rates. In sum, these three empirical studies present a positive picture of privatization.

A 1995 report, published by the National Regulatory Research Institute, summarized the findings from thirty case studies of privatization, including fourteen for water systems, thirteen for wastewater systems, and three for a combination of water and wastewater systems.[1] The cases involved eleven acquisitions of publicly-owned facilities by private utilities, twelve arrangements to build, own, and operate a facility, and seven operations and maintenance contracts. (Remember, the study occurred prior to the 1997 tax changes, analyzed in Chapter 6). Although the thirty case studies did not constitute a random sample (or a statistically reliable sample), they represented a range of privatization arrangements. Where a water or wastewater system was purchased, the acquired system generally was relatively small in terms of the population served, with two exceptions. The cases spanned sixteen states and included communities of different sizes. Six of the cases involved cities with one hundred thousand or more people; the smallest, had a population of 600. Fourteen of the cases occurred before 1990 with the rest from 1990 to 1995. Seven were still under review as of 1995. In five cases, the privatization arrangements were undone when the localities concluded they could provide services as economically as private contractors.[2]

Before considering the impact of privatization, it is useful to examine why a locality turned to the private sector. Typically, a municipality's decision to privatize involved a combination of reasons, such as a lack of funding and environmental compliance problems. The most citied reasons for privatization were the funds needed for essential capital improvements and environmental compliance issues, both with seventeen mentions. Next on the list were source of supply or system capacity limitations (eleven mentions), a desire to tap specialized management expertise in the water supply and wastewater treatment fields (seven mentions), a potential to lower operating (six mentions) or construction costs (five mentions), and an effort to increase system efficiency (three mentions). A desire to increase cash flows by leveraging public sector utility assets received two mentions.[3] In short, privatization was viewed as an arrangement that would result in an improvement over the existing situation, with the need to preserve local control the leading rationale against privatization.

Although the evaluation of outcomes is subjective, and various parties to the same agreement can have different views of its impact, privatization achieved a number of favorable outcomes. With three exceptions, the capital cost increases were consistent with the anticipated rises. Operating cost increases were greater than expected in three cases, but lower than expected in five cases.[4] Generally, the rate impacts were consistent with expectations. In two cases, rate decreases were promised and achieved; in two cases, the rate increases were higher than promised.[5]

City officials and customers indicated that the level of satisfaction with a privatization arrangement was high in nearly every instance. Municipal officials indicated that promises made by private firms had been fulfilled. Almost no customer complaints were reported. Only one contractor was viewed negatively.[6]

In several cases, disputes arose. Some disagreements occurred over costs that the localities expected their contractors to absorb, but for which the contract language was ambiguous (a problem in the Atlanta case study, discussed in Chapter 8). These disputes typically went to arbitration for resolution. In a few situations the disputes could not be resolved, contributing to the decision by five cities to cancel operations contracts or to repurchase systems, but the deprivatization decisions were not made because of customer dissatisfaction. Although unique circumstances may have played a role in each of these five cases, local officials reestablished control over their systems because they believed that they could operate their facilities less expensively than a private entity.[7]

The study found that city officials generally indicated that they would engage again in privatization transactions. With one exception, they would recommend that a locality privatize its water supply or wastewater treatment infrastructure, or at least consider privatization as an option.[8] The generally positive relationship between municipalities and private firms indicated, as of 1995, a continued interest in water and wastewater privatization across the United States.

A 1999 survey for the National Association of Water Companies, by the Hudson Institute, a pro-privatization organization, reported on a geographically diverse mix of twenty-nine projects serving some three million U.S. customers.[9] The projects were selected using various criteria, including, the type of arrangement, size, scope, and geographic location. The study included nine asset transfers, two outsourcing of billing, four leases, three long-term operations and management agreements, and eleven short-term operations and management contracts. The twenty-nine projects, covering all types of privatization arrangements for existing infrastructure, served a total population base of three million people and represented total contract values excess of $3 billion, including asset transfer acquisition costs and operations and management fees. The projects were geographically distributed across eleven states in the west, southwest, midwest, southeast, and northeast.[10]

As background to the decision to privatize, the study identified common challenges faced by municipalities in providing water supply and wastewater treatment services. First and foremost, municipalities experienced an inability to meet their capital needs. Sixty-two percent (18 of 29) of the projects studied indicated financial issues constituted the primary reason for privatization. Thirty-one percent (9 out of 29) of the projects indicated the growing backlog of required capital investments as the primary reason for privatization.[11] A number of facilities were antiquated, not properly maintained, and/or in need of significant upgrades. In short, privatization, it was hoped, would provide access to capital markets to repair and replace aging facilities, build new facilities, and upgrade infrastructure to ensure compliance with environmental regulations.

Operating inefficiencies and their negative financial impact, including ongoing operating losses, led to privatization. Nine projects (31 percent of the total number) indicated cash flow problems (three projects) or excessive operating costs (six projects) as the primary reason for turning to the private sector. Cash flow issues included both operating losses caused by inefficient operations and/or a desire to affect cost savings. Privatization offered the expectation of delivering services less expensively.[12]

Environmental compliance problems also played a role in the decision to privatize. Municipalities experiencing actual and potential problems in meeting water quality standards turned to the private sector for operating expertise, a proven track record, and the financial ability to address compliance issues. Prior to privatization, 41 percent

(12 of 29) of the projects surveyed were not in full compliance with water quality standards, typically facing excessive iron, lead, and copper concentrations as well as turbidity problems. These compliance concerns represented the primary or secondary driver for privatization in 41 percent (12 out of 29) of the projects studied. They represented the primary driver in 35 percent (10) of these projects. Forty-two percent (5 out of 12) of projects studied that were out of compliance were privatized primarily to deal with these violations. Fifty-eight percent (7 of 12) of projects with compliance issues were privatized because the municipality felt that the private sector had the ability and resources to better manage the compliance and regulatory functions, even if the facilities were not necessarily out-of-compliance.[13] Even public facilities built only a few years prior to the survey outsourced functions to shift responsibility for regulatory compliance to the private sector.

Another type of financial concern surfaced. About 25 percent of municipalities surveyed faced significant rate increases to finance capital investment backlogs.[14] In short, financial issues and the need for compliance with water quality standards represented the primary privatization drivers in 96 percent (28 out of 29) of the projects surveyed.[15]

The study then looked to whether privatization produced the hoped for solutions and/or benefits in the capital formation and management areas. The study evidenced the private sector's ability to commit financial resources to upgrade existing and/or construct new infrastructure. Asset transfers and leasing arrangements facilitated the upgrading of existing facilities and the building of new facilities to accommodate growth as well as ensuring compliance with environmental standards. In these situations, purchasers and lessees funded capital improvements. Asset transfers met the backlog of required capital investments; leases led to funds to satisfy capital issues, compliance standards, and operating capabilities. However, operations and maintenance contracts failed to show a significant level of private sector capital expenditures. Municipalities entering into these arrangements seemingly had sufficient capital to make any investments to upgrade existing infrastructure or build new facilities. Additionally, private firms did not make any capital expenditures in the two outsourcing contracts, with the exception of equipment infrastructure.[16]

Privatization agreements produced improved operating efficiencies. In contrast to the studies summarized in an academic review article, set forth in the next section of this chapter, 17 percent (5 of 29) of the projects generated major cost savings following privatization, with reductions ranging from 10 to 40 percent, thereby avoiding large rates increases. Operating costs were reduced through various processes and improvements, including the installation of computerized management systems, economies of scale in purchasing equipment and supplies, and process control expertise enabling improved facilities' utilization. The private firms' technical expertise also played a role in reducing operating expenditures. As a result of improved operating efficiencies and cost savings, projected, substantial rate increases of between five and fifty percent were avoided. On projects where rates did not decrease, capital investment needs caused rates to rise.[17]

Publicly-owned utilities continued to maintain control over rates by contract through provisions in leases as well as operations and maintenance arrangements. Public utility commissions assured reasonable rates following asset transfers. Thus, through privatization, rate increases were controlled. In some cases rates were reduced after privatization. Faced with significant capital investment requirements, if functions were not privatized, in 24 percent (seven) of the projects studied, publicly-owned utilities would have had to increase rates significantly to finance these expenditures. After privatization, the private firms controlled, and in some cases eliminated, the anticipated rate increases by lowering operating costs and implementing capital expenditure programs. Generally, the operating cost savings covered the cost of capital improvements and avoided projected rate increases.[18]

Privatization also facilitated regulatory compliance with water quality standards. Of the 12 projects (41 percent) that were out of compliance prior to privatization, seven required private firms to make capital investments totaling $23.8 million in these facilities to achieve compliance. Improvements were made with respect to treatment facilities, distribution systems, and meters. After privatization, in four out the twelve cases, the private firms instituted operating procedures and treatment programs to improve water quality, including flushing and chemical dosing programs. By upgrading aging infrastructure, identifying systems improvements, and applying advanced operating techniques, the private companies brought all systems into compliance within one year after privatization.[19]

Private firms made significant upfront payments to the public sector for the acquired assets and leasing fees. With a total acquisition cost of $536.6 million for nine facilities purchased, these privatizations generated significant amounts of capital for municipalities. In six out of twenty nine projects, including all the lease agreements and two of the operations and management agreements, private firms made upfront payments to localities totaling $34.6 million. Municipalities used these payments by purchasers, lessees, and contractors for other infrastructure expenditures, to retire debt, or for general tax relief. The private firms also met infrastructure financing needs by investing $55.3 million in new capital facilities.[20]

Finally, the study reported that the involvement of private firms improved customer service. The firms generally assumed responsibility for customer service operations. By integrating these services into their existing telephone support centers, the companies extended hours of operation and reduced call waiting times. In a large number of the projects surveyed, private companies undertook responsibility for billing and collections functions as well. Integrating telephone centers as well as billing and collection operations into national systems had a positive impact on consumers.[21]

In 2004-2005, the staff of the Water Partnership Council, a non-profit organization of leading providers of operational services for U.S. water and wastewater systems, conducted telephone interviews with representatives from thirty one public entities that contracted the day-to-day management, operations, and maintenance of their water and/or wastewater facilities to a private partner, in whole or in part.[22] While not a representative sample, the facilities surveyed served populations ranging from 4,000 to 1.2 million. The U.S. population covered by the surveyed partnerships totaled 4.7 million people.

The survey reported high satisfaction with the public-private partnerships and the private partners. Fifty percent of the respondents rated overall satisfaction with their partnership as "extremely satisfied"; 47 percent, "very satisfied." No respondent rated overall satisfaction as anything less than "satisfied." Fifty percent of the respondents rated the technical competence of their private partner as "outstanding"; 43 percent, "good." Fifty-seven percent of the respondents rated the quality of communication with their private partner as "outstanding"; 33 percent, "good". No respondent rated the quality of communication as anything less than "satisfactory."[23]

The survey showed that the partnerships had a positive impact on the environment, customers, and municipalities. Seventy four percent of the respondents rated regulatory compliance as better under a public-private partnership than prior to the partnership, 22 percent as equal, and only 4 percent as worse. Ninety three percent of the respondents noted that customer complaints decreased or remained the same under a partnership. Forty-six percent of the surveyed municipalities projected cost savings before entering into a partnership. Ninety-two percent of those respondents noted that the projected cost savings were achieved, with the savings ranging from 5 to 25 percent. The other 8 percent were too early in the contract term to know whether the cost savings would be achieved.[24]

The employees were generally satisfied with privatization arrangements, with 21 percent of the respondents rating employees as "extremely satisfied," 58 percent "very satisfied," and 21 percent "satisfied." None of the respondents reported an increase in employee grievances under a partnership, with 64 percent reporting a decrease in employee grievances. Ninety-three percent of the respondents stated that employees had more educational and training opportunities and more professional growth opportunities with their private partners than they did with the various municipalities. Eighty-seven percent of the respondents reported that employee salaries increased or remained the same under a public-private partnership.[25]

Also, most of the municipalities planned to continue with a partnership when the current contract expired, with only one definitely planning to deprivatize. Seventy-six percent of the respondents rated their likelihood of partnering again as "likely," and twenty one percent as "possibly" (or higher). Localities were also satisfied with their current private partners. In 86 percent of the cases where a privatization arrangement preceded the current partnership, the public partner awarded the contract to the incumbent partner through negotiation or competitive building.[26]

These studies generally show the success of privatization in the overwhelming number of situations. The expectations of localities were met. Private firms reduced operating costs, met increasingly stringent environmental standards, and limited potential rate hikes. Privatization also left customers happy, as private firms more efficiently handled customer service operations. Perhaps most importantly for customers, private firms implemented a wide range of improvements without, in most cases, raising rates.

Evidence of the Impact of Privatization on Capital Investment

Given the huge capital needs and the massive investment gap with respect to water supply and wastewater treatment infrastructure detailed in Chapter 6, evidence of the impact of privatization on capital investment is key. In addition to positive results on capital funding by asset purchasers and lessees contained in the Hudson Institute study, a report by the Water Partnership Council, a pro-privatization industry group, indicated that private partners in public-private partnerships surveyed invested in capital improvements in about one-third of operation and maintenance contracts with a five-year life and close to 100 percent in longer-term contracts.[27] In other words, the longer the contract term, the more likely the private partner will undertake certain capital improvements. The private partner is likely to invest its own funds in capital improvements if the operating cost reductions it achieves offset its cost of capital over a contract's life. However, this report concluded that the public partner in an operations and maintenance contract often retained responsibility for funding major capital improvements. The public partner floated tax-exempt bonds or borrowed from state revolving loan program, either of which usually carried lower interest rates than private debt.

Personnel, energy, and chemicals comprise the three largest cost elements in operating water supply or wastewater treatment facilities, regardless of ownership. Private operators in the report achieved cost savings by implementing a variety of measures including more efficient work practices, cross-training of staff, more efficient energy use, reduced use of chemicals, bulk purchasing to obtain discounts, and preventive maintenance.[28] Often, the operating cost savings realized by private firms covered the cost of some capital improvements. Sometimes, a private partner eliminated the need for capital expenditures by using advanced technology. A private partner also reduced the magnitude of a required capital investment by more effective procurement and construction practices.[29] In the area of environmental compliance, private contractors have the expertise to identify and resolve the root causes of non-compliance. As a result, private firms were often able to attain compliance without the need for major capital expenditures.[30] In sum, greater expertise, improved efficiencies, and heightened accountability for spending decisions lowered capital requirements. Some place the savings enjoyed by public-private partnerships at between 10 to 20 percent for capital works expenditures.[31]

A private partner may also provide its public partner with financial assistance. Assistance may be required if: the local government cannot exceed its debt ceiling or it desires to retain debt capacity for other public services; it encounters delays in obtaining approval for a bond issue or a loan from the state revolving loan fund; or it has a poor credit rating. If the operating cost reductions do not allow the private partner a positive return over the contract's life, it will seek to recoup its investment through an additional service fee charged the local government. The longer the contract, the more years to amortize the financial investment, and the lower the amount of the annual service fee.[32]

Evidence from Empirical Studies of Cost Savings and Efficiency

One of the primary rationales for privatization centers on the ability of private firms to achieve cost savings. Data from the Hudson Institute study and the Water Partnership Council report point to the cost savings derived from privatization. This section summarizes an academic literature review presenting a mixed picture regarding cost savings and a study supporting the operating efficiency benefits of investor-owned water companies in comparison to publicly-owned water entities.

An academic review of all published econometric studies of U.S. water services from 1976 to 1995 found little support for the link between privatization via asset ownership and cost savings in water delivery.[33] It is helpful to summarize these studies in chronological order.

The earliest of the reviewed econometric studies in the United States used a sample of 188 publicly-owned and 26 privately-owned water distribution firms. The researchers found that the private firms had higher operating costs than the government-owned utilities.[34] However, the next two studies found lower costs with private production than with public production. One study used a sample of 143 water distribution firms in six states and gave more attention to operational costs than to institutional and regulatory variables.[35] Another study, using data from 112 firms, 88 public and 24 private entities in 38 states, found that the private firms had significantly lower operating costs, reflecting lower employee productivity in public agencies.[36] Conversely, the next study, using a similar approach to the last article, but a sample of 86 firms, 77 government-owned and 9 privately-owned, found that the private companies had higher costs in comparison to the private entities.[37] Three studies found no significant cost differences between private and municipal production.[38] Three other studies reaffirmed earlier findings, either showing no cost differences between private firms and the public sector,[39] lower costs with private production,[40] or lower costs with public production on average, but more widely dispersed between the best and worst entities.[41] In analyzing the differences according to firm size, one study concluded that private production was more efficient for small-scale operations, but that public production was more efficient for large-scale operations.[42]

Stepping back from these conflicting studies, a recent literature review regarding the American experience concluded:

> [T]here is no strong evidence that private water utilities are demonstrably more productive than public water utilities. Having said this, it is important to be mindful of the relatively small number of studies available. Furthermore, some authors have argued that past studies have not fully accounted for the differing tax rules and regulations which they argue are biased in favour of public utilities.... A second factor that precludes any clear-cut conclusion is the growing importance of public-private partnerships in the field of municipal water delivery.... It might be argued that these partnerships are a reflection of the parties' understandings of the cost savings available to them. However, there are a myriad of financial, tax and environmental regulations which may distort municipal governments' decision making and, thus, make it difficult to conclude that such arrangements are necessarily better for society.[43]

With respect to cost savings derived from long-term contracts, the Water Partnership Contract scorecard, published by Public Works Financing, showed estimated cost savings in scorecard of from 7 to 50 percent on 14 contracts, with terms of from ten to 25 years.[44] These statistics are in line with those in the Hudson Institute study, discussed earlier in this chapter.

Efficiency represents another way to measure the impact of privatization via infrastructure ownership. A 1996 study by the Reason Foundation, a pro-privatization organization, compared the 1992-1994 operations of the three largest investor-owned water companies in California with large publicly-owned water companies serving Contra Costa and Alameda counties in California.[45] The three investor-owned companies, California Water Service Co., San Jose Water Co., and Southern California Water Co., serviced about 60 percent of all customers served by privately-owned companies in California or about 12 percent of California's total water customers. The government-owned companies selected had approximately the same size as the three investor-owned water utilities. Each of the private companies and the public entities had total revenue streams ranging from $325 to $350 million per year. The study sought to overcome not only the variation in accounting methods between the public and private sectors but also the lack of a universal accounting standard within the governmental sector.[46]

The study found that the investor-owned companies were substantially more efficient in their operation of water services than government-owned water entities. Specifically, the government-owned companies had significantly higher operating costs. They spent $330 per connection versus the $273 per connection spent by investor-owned firms, with no apparent differences in the quality of service provided. Employment levels and salaries as a percent of operating revenues were much higher for the government water agencies. Investor-owned firms hired 1.62 employees for every one thousand connections; government-owned firms hired more than twice as many (or 3.49 workers per one thousand connections). The study noted that because government-owned water companies hired significantly more outside consultants and contractors then investor-owned firms, the number of government employees was probably understated. The bottom line: for government-owned firms salaries comprised 37.13 percent of operating revenues versus 13.40 percent for investor-owned companies. The amount of funds channeled to maintenance also explained the difference. Investor-owned firms spent 5.29 percent of the operating revenues on maintenance, while government-owned water companies spent 9.13 percent of operating revenues on maintaining their water facilities.[47]

Critics of this study note the small sample size and that it was region specific. Furthermore, the privately-owned utilities studied used groundwater as their primary supply source; while the publicly-owned utilities studied mostly depended on surface water, which is more costly to treat and transport.[48]

In sum, studies addressing the issue of whether or not privately-owned water firms can deliver their services at a lower cost have reached divergent conclusions. However, these studies fail to analyze the impact of public-private partnerships on operating costs. The Hudson Institute study and the Water Partnership Council report point to the cost savings and operating efficiency benefits from a range of privatization arrangements.

Evidence from Empirical Studies Dealing with Rates

In contrast to positive results shown by the Hudson Institute study, other empirical studies were mixed with respect to the impact of privatization on water rates. One state specific survey found that private water companies in New Hampshire generally have higher rates than their public counterparts and their rates are increasing faster.[49] One reason: municipalities do not pay property and income taxes as private sector owners must. Also, private companies set rates, subject to state utility regulatory approval, in order to generate a profit.

Other studies reached a different conclusion. A small study of two private and two public water companies operating in the Salt Lake Valley of Utah found that the rates of private firms were lower than those of public entities that served the same classes of consumers in similar geographical locations.[50] A massive analysis of every community water system in the United States from 1997 to 2003 concluded that household expenditures on water at the county level decreased slightly as the share of private infrastructure ownership increased.[51] The study controlled for population, income, urbanization, and the share of a county's households whose payments were included in their rent.

Stepping back from these studies, it is important to note that publicly-owned water suppliers have a built-in cost-of-capital advantage. They can raise capital through the sale of tax-exempt bonds. Experts estimate that the tax-exempt status of municipal debt creates a 20 to 40 percent interest cost advantage in comparison to privately-issued debt.[52] Investors buy tax-exempt bonds with lower interest rates if their marginal federal income tax rate is high enough, the after-tax yield is higher than on a taxable debt instrument. This savings helps produce lower rates for consumers supplied by government-owned systems. The tax subsidy flowing to investors results, however, in a loss of income taxes on the interest paid to the holders of tax-exempt bonds. Also, privately-owned systems pay property and income taxes. The tax subsidies on tax-exempt debt together with property and income taxes not paid by governmental entities likely results in a higher net cost-of-capital for publicly-owned water companies than for privately-owned water firms. In other words, the cost-of-capital edge may fade when the tax subsidy and the lost tax revenues are figured in. Also, a private utility can raise additional capital through the sale of stock; a governmental entity cannot tap the equity market.

The Reason Foundation study of California utilities did not find rates lower for water services provided by private firms. Although the private companies paid property and income taxes, and even though they did not enjoy cost-of-capital subsides, their greater operating efficiencies enabled them to provide comparable services at comparable prices.[53]

Evidence from Empirical Studies of Environmental Compliance

The need to meet increasingly stringent environmental regulations comprises one of the primary drivers of the privatization of water supply and wastewater treatment systems. Evidence from the Hudson Institute study, discussed earlier in this chapter, showed the environmental compliance gains achieved through privatization.

An analysis of every community water system in the United States from 1997 to 2003, found, however, little difference between public and private systems in terms of compliance with the Safe Water Drinking Act, controlling for location, year, and water source. Public systems were somewhat more likely to violate the maximum levels of health-based contaminants; privately-owned systems were somewhat more likely to violate the act's monitoring and reporting regulations. The results were reversed for very large systems serving more than 100,000 people, where the municipally-owned systems had fewer contaminant violations, but more monitoring and reporting violations.[54]

Another study concluded that privatized (that is, various types of public-private partnerships) and privately-owned systems almost always had higher drinking water quality violations, particularly monitoring and reporting violations, than public systems. However, for very large systems, the privatized and private systems had lower violation rates than public ones. Very small systems, regardless of ownership, had much higher violation rates because they had fewer resources than larger systems.[55] Others have also concluded that with respect to violations of federal Safe Drinking Water Act regulations, smaller utilities, whether (privately- or publicly-owned), were more likely to violate these standards.[56]

Evidence of Satisfaction with Public-Private Partnerships

Despite the theoretical objections to privatization, discussed in Chapter 6, and the empirical studies indicating mixed results, at least on some points, the National Regulatory Research Institute and Water Partnership Council studies showed high levels of satisfaction with privatization arrangements. More specific evidence supports this conclusion. Water supply and wastewater treatment contracts with private firms are typically renewed at the end of their term. Repeated studies indicated that more than ninety percent of the communities chose to continue privatization at renewal time.[57]

For example, of all privatization contract renewals for water and wastewater in the United States between 1998 and 2001, 75 percent were renewed by renegotiation without competition, 16 percent were renewed by competition (with 10 percent retained by the incumbent and 6 percent won by another bidder), and 8 percent were deprivatized and return to public control.[58] A later study showed an even higher water industry contractual renewal rate during the 1999-2008 period as follows: 1999 (88 percent renewal rate); 2000 (95 percent); 2001 (87 percent); 2002 (97 percent); 2003 (96 percent); 2004 (97 percent); 2005 (93 percent); 2006 (92 percent); 2007 (98 percent); 2008 (95 percent).[59]

Observers disagree whether the competition for the market motivates bidders to reduce costs. Some see communities as not captive to any one private firm, with 6 percent of communities switching to another private firm when existing water and wastewater contracts expired between 1998-2001.[60] Because of the benefits of incumbency, others conclude that competition for the market may have eroded. According to a subsequent study, only between 1.5 percent and 3 percent of contracts were lost to another private competitor from 2002 through 2008.[61]

Despite conflicting conclusions reached by empirical studies on the impact of privatization, whether through asset ownership or public-private partnerships, generally speaking, privatization achieves successful results. The high levels of satisfaction and the renewal of privatization arrangements show that public-private partnerships meet municipalities' and consumers' needs.

Beyond these general and more specific empirical studies reviewed in this chapter, we turn and examine in detail two case studies of private-public partnerships in Atlanta and Indianapolis.

Notes

1. Janice A. Beecher, G. Richard Dreese, John D. Stanford, Regulatory Implications of Water and Wastewater Utility Privatization, National Regulatory Research Institute, 1995, 67-81, 175-201. The National Association of Regulatory Utility Commissioners established the National Regulatory Research Institute in 1976. The institute serves as the association's official research arm.

2. Ibid., 69-70, 85-88 (Table 4-5 Summary of Selected Water and Wastewater Case Studies).

3. *Ibid.*, 71-76.
4. *Ibid.*, 78.
5. *Ibid.*
6. *Ibid.*
7. *Ibid.*, 79.
8. *Ibid.*, 80.
9. Hudson Institute, The NAWC [National Association of Water Companies] Privatization Study: A Survey of the Use of Public-Private Partnerships in the Drinking Water Utility Sector, June 1999, 25-44.
10. *Ibid.*, 25-26.
11. The statistics in this paragraph are from *Ibid.*, 29,31, 49-50 (Table 3 Privatization Drivers, Table 3-A Summary Primary Privatization Drivers, Table 3-B Summary Secondary Privatization Drivers).
12. The statistics in this paragraph are from *Ibid.* (Table 3 Privatization Drivers, Table 3-A Summary Primary Privatization Drivers, Table 3-B Summary Secondary Privatization Drivers), 52 (Table 4-A Summary Compliance Status, Table 4-B Summary Compliance Problems).
13. The statistics in this paragraph are from *Ibid.*, 29-31, 40, 49-50.
14. *Ibid.*, 27.
15. *Ibid.*, 28.
16. *Ibid.*, 35-36, 44.
17. The statistics in this paragraph are from *Ibid.*, 36, 44. See also Douglas Herbst and David Seader," Providing Public Services through Long-Term Service Agreements," in *Local Government Innovation: Issues and Trends in Privatization and Managed Competition,* eds. Robin A. Johnson and Norman Walzer (Westport, CT: Quorum, 2000), 113-114 for examples of reductions in operations and maintenance costs thru public-private partnerships.
18. The statistics in this paragraph are from Hudson Institute NAWC Privatization Study, 41-43, 44, 53 (Table 5 Water Rate Information).
19. The statistics in this paragraph are from i*bid.*, 39-40, 44, 51 (Table 4 Compliance Solutions), 52 (Table 4-C Summary Compliance Solutions).
20. The statistics in this paragraph are from i*bid.*, 37-38.
21. The statistics in this paragraph are from i*bid.*, 41-44.
22. Water Partnership Council, An Evaluation Public-Private Partnerships for Water Wastewater Systems, June 2005.
23. The statistics in this paragraph are from i*bid.*, 5, 9-11.
24. The statistics in this paragraph are from i*bid.*, 5, 11-12.
25. The statistics in this paragraph are from i*bid.*, 5, 15-16.
26. The statistics in this paragraph are from i*bid.*, 9-10.
27. Water Partnership Council, Establishing Public-Private Partnerships for Water and Wastewater Systems: A Blueprint for Success, 2003, 22-23.
28. *Ibid.*, 20.
29. *Ibid.*, 23.
30. *Ibid.*, 37.
31. Elizabeth Brubaker, *Liquid Assets: Privatizing and Regulating Canada's Water Utilities* (Toronto: University of Toronto, 2002), 26.

32. Water Partnership Council, Establishing Public-Private Partnerships, 23.

33. Germà Bel and Mildred Warner, "Does privatization of solid waste and water services reduce costs? A review of empirical studies," *Resources, Conservation and Recycling* 53:12 (October 2008): 1337-1348. See also Okke Braadbaart, "Private versus public provision of water services: does ownership matter for utility efficiency," *Aqua* 51:7 (November 2002): 375-388.

34. Patrick C. Mann and John L. Mikesell, "Ownership and Water System Operation," *Water Resources Bulletin*, 12:5 (October 1976): 995-1004.

35. W. Douglas Morgan, "Investor Owned vs. Publicly Owned Water Agencies: An Evaluation of Property Rights Theory of the Firm, *Water Resources Bulletin* 13:4 (August 1977): 775-781.

36. W. Mark Crain and Asghar Zardkoohi, "A Test of the Property-Rights Theory of the Firm: Water Utilities in the United States," *Journal of Law and Economics* 21:2 (October 1978): 395-408.

37. Thomas H. Bruggink, "Public Versus Regulated Private Enterprise in the Municipal Water Industry: A Comparison of Operating Costs," *Quarterly Review of Economics and Business* 22:1 (Spring 1982): 111-125.

38. Susan Feigenbaum and Ronald Teeples, "Public Versus Private Water Delivery: A Hedonic Cost Approach," *Review of Economics and Statistics* 65:4 (November 1983): 672-678 (analyzed essentially the same data as Crain and Zardkoohi, note 36, but using a more general mathematical method); William F. Fox and Richard A. Hofler, "Using Homothetic Composed Error Frontiers to Measure Water Utility Efficiency," *Southern Economic Journal* 53:2 (October 1986): 461-477; Ronald Teeples and David Glyer, "Cost of Water Delivery Systems: Specification and Ownership Effects," *Review of Economics and Statistics* 69:3 (August 1987): 399-408.

39. Patricia Byrnes, Shawna Grosskopf, and Kathy Hayes, "Efficiency and Ownership: Further Evidence," *Review of Economics and Statistics* 68:2 (May 1986): 337-341.

40. Kambiz Raffiee et al., "Cost Analysis of Water Utilities: A Goodness-of-Fit Approach," *Atlantic Economic Journal* 21:3 (September 1993): 18-29.

41. Arunava Bhattacharyya, Elliott Parker, and Kambiz Raffiee, "An Examination of the Effect of Ownership on the Relative Efficiency of Public and Private Water Utilities," *Land Economics* 70:2 (May 1994): 197-209. See also David K. Lambert, Dimo Dichev, Kambiz Raffiee, "Ownership and Sources of Inefficiency in the Provision of Water Services," *Water Resources Research* 29:6 (June 1993): 1573-1578.

42. Arunava Bhattacharyya et al., "Specification and estimation of the effect of ownership on the economic efficiency of water utilities," *Regional Science and Urban Economics* 25:6 (December 1995): 759-784.

43. Steven Renzetti and Diane Dupont, "The Performance of Municipal Water Utilities: Evidence of the Role of Ownership," in *Drinking Water Safety: A Total Quality Management Approach*, ed. Steve E. Hrudey (Waterloo, Ontario, Canada: Institute for Risk Research, 2003), 214. See also Steven Renzetti and Diane Dupont, "Ownership and Performance of Water Utilities," *Greener Management International* 42 (Summer 2003): 9-18, at 14.

44. *Public Works Financing*, "PWF's 12th Annual Outsourcing Report," 225 (March 2008), 1-11, at 10 (U.S. Water Partnerships Scorecard: Communities with Long-Term Contracts).

45. Kathy Neal et al., Restructuring America's Water Industry: Comparing Investor-Owned and Government Water Systems, January 1996, Reason Foundation Policy Study No. 200, 12.

46. *Ibid.*, 4.

47. The statistics in this paragraph are from *ibid.*, 5, 12.

48. Isabelle Fauconnier, "The Privatization of Residential Water Supply and Sanitation Services: Social Equity Issue in the California and International Contexts," *Berkeley Planning Journal* 13 (1999): 37-73, at 57 and Sue McClurg, "Privatization of Water: Split Opinions," *Western Water* (July-August 1996): 4-13, at 8.

49. Bob Sanders, "State survey finds higher rates among for-profit companies," *New Hampshire Business Review* 27:9 (April 29-May 12, 2005): 1, 17.

50. B. Delworth Garderner, "The Efficiency of For-Profit Water Companies Versus Public Companies," *Universities Council on Water Resources* 117 (October 2000): 34-39, at 38.

51. Scott Wallsten and Katrina Kosec, Public or Private Drinking Water? The Effects of Ownership and Benchmark Competition on U.S. Water Systems Regulatory Compliance and Household Water Expenditures, AEI-Brookings Joint Center for Regulatory Studies, March 2005, Working Paper 05-05, 23-25.

52. National Research Council, *Privatization of Water Services in the United States: An Assessment of Issues and Experience* (Washington D.C.: National Academy Press, 2002), 51.

53. Neal et al., Restructuring 1, 16-17.

54. Wallsten and Kosec, Public or Private Drinking Water?, 10-21, 25. See also Scott Wallsten and Katrina Kosec, "The effects of ownership and benchmark competition: An empirical analysis of U.S. water systems," *International Journal of Industrial Organization* 26:1 (January 2008): 186-205.

55. Jane A. Parkin, Factors Affecting Water Quality for Water Systems, Master's Thesis, Tufts University, May 2006, 58-59, 61-63, 69-72, 74, 75-76, 87-89.

56. Gary Wolff and Eric Hallstein, Beyond Privatization: Restructuring Water Systems to Improve Performance, Pacific Institute, December 2005, 99, Appendix B: Current Role of the Private Sector.

57. See, e.g. Geoffrey Segal, What Can We Learn from Atlanta's Water Privatization, January 21, 2003 <www.reason.org/ commentaries/segal_20030121. shtml> (January 14, 2009).

58. Adrian T. Moore, "Don't Believe the Hype: Successful Water Privatization Is the Norm," *Privatization Watch* 28:2 (April 2004) 6, 13.

59. Reason Foundation, 2009 Annual Privatization Report, 132, 133 (Table 16: Contract Renewals and Lost Government Contracts 1999-2008). See also, *Public Works Financing*, "PWF's 12th Annual Water Outsourcing Report," 2 (Renewals vs. Lost Gov't Contracts in 1999-2007).

60. Moore, "Don't Believe the Hype," 6.

61. Reason Foundation, 2009 Annual Privatization Report, 133 (Table 16: Contract Renewals and Lost Government Contracts, 1999-2008). See also Public Works Financing, "PWF's 12th Annual Outsourcing Report," 2(Renewals vs. Lost Gov't. Contracts in 1999-2007).

8

Privatization in Practice: Evidence from Two Case Studies

This chapter presents two case studies, Atlanta and Indianapolis, which provide a window on the impact of privatization. These two privatization transactions took place in the context of the rearrangement of the ownership of U.S. water supply and wastewater treatment companies, marked by the consolidation that occurred during the last decade of the twentieth century and the first part of this century's first decade. Led by Vivendi and its French rival, Suez, European water companies charged into the United States. Through vertical integration, they planned to offer one-stop shops for water services.

In the first case study of the Atlanta water system, the city gave a private firm, United Water Services, the task of running its antiquated water system in 1999. By 2003, Atlanta retook control of its water system, after four years of broken promises and complaints about poor service, water quality, and maintenance backlogs. The city did not believe it was getting the performance called for by the contract. In reality, the privatization situation was far more complex. The Atlanta case study points to the importance of a careful procurement process and to contractual negotiations and details.

In the second case study, in 2002, Indianapolis entered into a deal with USFilter, a subsidiary of the French-based firm, Vivendi SA, to manage its water operations. Despite some difficult moments and substantial rate increases, both implemented and projected, this public-private partnership generally achieved positive results. This case study indicates, however, the desirability of greater public participation throughout the privatization process and the importance of maintaining good employee relations. It also points to the need for full-cost pricing, a topic analyzed in Chapter 9, and the obstacles such a rate structure faces.

Atlanta's Water and Wastewater Infrastructure

Atlanta tried numerous options during the ninetieth century before settling on the financing and construction of a public water system in 1870. By the first decade of the twentieth century, the building of water mains and sewer lines failed to match the city's growth. Atlanta's public health conditions, resulting from the absence of sewage treatment facilities, led the city's chamber of commerce to lobby for major water and wastewater improvements. The chamber's efforts led to the passage of a bond issue in February 1910. Thereafter, the new facilities built between 1910 and 1914 dramatically improved the residents' public health.[1]

Fast forward to the late twentieth century. Atlanta and the surrounding area witnessed an explosive population growth. Prior to 1999, Atlanta's water and wastewater systems were in a disastrous condition. Particularly, its wastewater treatment system required a massive investment to meet environmental standards. City officials feared that the federal government would demand that the municipality impose a moratorium on new construction unless the city prevented sewage spills into the Chattahoochee River.[2]

Residents were long familiar with the sewage backups. In addition to the stench, heavy rains each year overwhelmed the municipality's combined sewage-water runoff system, releasing sewage into the city's main creeks, killing fish, and giving the water a green tint.[3]

Even in dry weather, broken pipes leaked raw sewage. The overflows, leaks, and chemical pollutants flowed from Atlanta's creeks into the Chattahoochee River, the main source of drinking water for the residents of metropolitan Atlanta. The polluted river became a problem for people living downstream in Georgia, Alabama, and Florida, who also relied on the river for drinking water.

The federal Clean Water Act required the state and the city to cleanup the river. Atlanta's politicians sought a quick fix in the form of building a new, small sewage treatment plant at a cost of $90 million. Environmental groups wanted one of two larger, comprehensive solutions: either create two separate sewer systems one for sewage and another for rainwater or build two deep tunnels to hold the excess water runoff. The deep tunnels would be less costly than the separate sewer system, but still would cost an estimated $1 billion. Other plans were considered and then dropped.[4]

In 1995, a federal lawsuit was filed against the city for violations of the Clean Water Act. In 1998, pursuant to a federal consent decree, the city paid a $2.5 million settlement. The decree required the city to formulate and implement a plan to treat its sewage and set 2007 as the deadline for correcting the identified wastewater problems.[5] In 1999, the First Amended Consent Decree for correcting the identified sewer problems pushed the deadline back to 2014.[6]

While the case was pending in federal court, in January 1997 the Internal Revenue Services (IRS) issued Revenue Procedure 97-13, discussed in Chapter 5, allowing cities to enter into long-term contracts with private firms to manage public works. The next month, Atlanta's mayor, William (Bill) Campbell announced he had approached three unnamed consulting engineering firms for suggestions on how to privatize city's water and wastewater systems in order to solve the sewage problem without inflicting major rate hikes on residents.[7]

In the fall of 1997, the city's sewer crisis became a central issue in Mayor Campbell's bid for reelection. With both candidates backing privatization, Campbell narrowly won reelection.

After Georgia Governor Zell Miller threatened legislation to force the city to privatize immediately, Campbell accelerated his privatization plan. In March 1998, the Atlanta City Council authorized local officials to seek bids for the private management of the city's water system and its largest wastewater treatment plant. However, the mayor rejected calls for post-privatization oversight by either the council or an independent public authority.

Mayor Campbell, dropping the plan to privatize sewers, sought proposals for the operation and maintenance of Atlanta's water system, including water purification and delivery as well as billing and customer service. To deal with the sewer overflows, Campbell hoped that the savings obtained from water privatization would allow the city to float a bond issue for the needed wastewater system improvements. The city was committed to spend upwards of $1 billion to fix its beleaguered sewer system.

Atlanta and United Water

In the privatization bidding process, cost effectiveness became the key with the 30 out of 100 points awarded for this item in evaluating bidders. Performance capabilities, including a bidder's ability to manage operations in a city as large as Atlanta, ranked last among the priorities in the request for proposals. Only 5 out of 100 points would be awarded in evaluating bidders on performance capabilities.[8]

The bidding and approval process went on a fast track. Bids were due on July 2, 1998, with a contract presented to the city council for approval on August 17, and a private takeover, hopefully on September 4. Suggestions to delay the rushed process went nowhere.

Five firms bid on the contract. The firms were as follows: United Water Services Atlanta, a joint venture of United Water Resources, Inc. and Suez Lyonnaise des Eaux (Suez); Atlanta Water Alliance team consisting of Air and Water Technologies Corp., Compagnie Générale des Eaux, and Philadelphia Suburban Corp.; Atlanta Water Corp. team anchored by the SAUR SA; OMI Atlanta consisting of Thames Water OMI Inc. and CH2M Hill Cos. Ltd.; USFilter team consisting of USFilter Corp. (owned by Vivendi) and Aquarion Co.[9]

Ultimately, United Water Services Atlanta (United Water) won the contract. Suez already owned about 30 percent of the United Water. At that time, United Water, a shareholder-owned water services firm, operated thirty-two water systems in the United States, including one in Jersey City, N.J., that it took over in 1996 and was then the nation's largest water system operated under contract. United Water provided water and wastewater services to more than 7.5 million people in 400 communities in nineteen states.

In its winning bid, United Water agreed to pay the city $21.4 million per year over twenty years to operate and maintain the water system.[10] The annual payment amounted to less than one half of the $49.5 million per year that the city spent running the system. Estimates of cost savings likely dominated the decision to award the contract to United Water.

United Water recognized that the contract was unlikely to be profitable in the short-term—one to three years.[11] In taking over operations, the firm faced a maintenance backlog, especially of broken water meters, a mandate to install valves at each meter to prevent contaminants from entering the system, the need for a major information technology update, construction-related challenges, and more than $30 million in unpaid water bills, some dating back years. In addition, United Water pledged not to lay off employees during the life of the contact but to only reduce the workforce through attrition.

In October 1990, the city council approved the $428 million, 20-year contract with United Water to operate and manage its drinking water system.[12] It represented largest water privatization contract in U.S. history, up to that time. The council also approved an increase in sewer charges that would raise the average bill by 44.5 percent over three years, but water rates within the city would not rise for five years (or until 2003).

United Water took over the system on January 1, 1999. It gained approximately 140,000 customer accounts, 1.5 million customers both inside and outside of Atlanta, and 479 employees. The firm assumed responsibility for operating and maintaining two drinking water treatment plants, twelve water system storage tanks, seven zone transfer pumping stations, 25,000 fire hydrants, and about 2,400 miles of network pipes, half made up of 50-year old cast iron pipes long past their useable lifespan and some more than a century old.[13]

Operational and maintenance problems soon mounted. In July 1999, a water main break interrupted service to 200 homes, forcing the company to deliver cases of bottled water. By late August 1999, the firm faced 4,000 pending work orders and more than 7,000 requests for service, some up to three years old. Ultimately the backlog of work orders grew to more than 13,000.[14] Repairing meter leaks took longer than the 15 days required by the contract. Problems continued into 2000. From December 1999 to February 2000, it took the company on average 79 days to fix a broken water main. In early 2000, a meter installation took two months. Debris floated in drinking water in some areas of the city.

Reflecting the trend to consolidation of the water supply industry worldwide, in 2000, for $1.36 billion Suez acquired the remaining shares of United Water it did not own.[15] United Water, in turn, became a wholly-owned subsidiary of the French firm. Previously in June 1999, Suez had purchased two water treatment companies, Nalco Chemical Co. for $4.1 billion and Calgon Corp. for $420 million.

Complaints continued in 2000 and 2001 about erratic customer service, low water pressure, and discolored tap water. Boil-water advisories were issued when the water supplied was unfit from human consumption. United was less than efficient in collecting unpaid water bills.[16]

At the end of 2001, United Water asked the city to amend the contract.[17] As a result of either its low-ball bid or the failure to assess accurately the system's condition and its limitations, the firm filed a change order seeking to increase its annual contract fee by $4 million. The company sought to backdate the fee three years to the beginning of the agreement in January 1999 and going forward extend it over the contract's remaining life. It also asserted that the city should assume responsibility for the cost of pipe and water main repairs in excess of what had been anticipated in the contract.

In April 2002, feeling the public backlash, Atlanta's new mayor, Shirley Franklin, ordered a review of whether United Water had met the terms of its contract with the city. The report confirmed the complaints about the discolored tap water, failure to repair leaks, tardy meter installation, and insufficient maintenance. United Water fell behind on its administrative duties. The report highlighted United Water's failure to collect millions of dollars in unpaid bills as required by the agreement. In August 2002, the mayor gave the firm a 90-day contract correction period to address non-performance issues or the city would terminate the contract.[18]

In response, United replaced its regional president and sought to improve its quality-of-service. In January 2003, a city audit showed that the firm had failed to collect water bills totaling $57 million, more than twice the amount outstanding ($23.7 million) when United Water took over four years earlier. Furthermore, the firm only delivered just under $10 million in annual savings, about half of the projected savings.[19]

On January 24, 2003, the city and United Water put out a join press release announcing an "amicable dissolution" of the contract. Neither the city nor the firm found the agreement to be realistic or workable. Both agreed that the contract did not provide an "economically viable framework" for either party in the future.[20] Deciding that it could do a better job of running the system, the city resumed control of its water system on April 29, 2003.[21] After the city took back its system, the mayor raised water rates and chose to build underground tunnels to limit sewage overflows.

Atlanta and United Water: An Assessment

The failure of the largest privatization effort in the United States garnered considerable attention. However, it was not an unmitigated disaster. On the plus side, privatization provided the city more direct oversight and imposed more accountability with respect to its water system. Under public management, the city could not have imposed a cure period.

United Water's service was far from perfect. Seemingly, the firm cut costs so it could operate within the parameters of its low bid. It reduced the number of employees and the training they received, further compounding service delivery problems. However, it completed more repairs than were finished under public operation. For instance, United Water completed about 4,000 fire hydrant repairs a year compared with approximately 3,000 before privatization.[22]

In response to consumer complaints and service deficiencies, the company asserted that it did not know about the system's underground main and pipe conditions when it signed the contract. Executives explained that they inspected aboveground facilities, but allegedly were unable to ascertain the condition of the underground pipes. The large amount of the network underground meant the information on the system's operations was not easily observed, creating a challenge for the private firm. According to Troy Henry, United Water's regional president in 2002, "We were never allowed to go out with any crews in the field. And we all took our chances and took their word that the data was accurate. Once we got to running the system, we found that the system was in much greater decay than we had anticipated."[23]

United Water encountered much more repair work than it bargained for. Instead of about 1,200 expected water meter repairs each year, United Water experienced more than 11,000, hardly an underground problem. Water main breaks annually occurred at nearly triple the anticipated rate of about 100.[24]

In the ideal world, United Water should have carefully inspected Atlanta's system so that the problems that eventually surfaced would have been more apparent. For whatever reason, the firm did not scrutinize the city's water system as closely as it should have. Even if it did not know what it was pricing in its bid, the firm should have expected undetected problems in water system as old as Atlanta's and built that contingency into its bid. It had experience in running old water systems, such as the one in Jersey City, N.J. The firm likely thought it could amend the contract if needed, as it sought to do in 2001.

The city was amiss. City officials failed to do the necessary procurement development work before it requested bids. They signed a contract not knowing what the water system needed by way of maintenance work. Lacking the records needed to establish a baseline; they had less than perfect knowledge of the exact location of the system's water mains and pipes and their condition. In short, Atlanta did not know the state of its water infrastructure and cost of operating and maintaining its system.

The contract presented a number of problems. To deal with uncertainties regarding the condition of underground assets, United Water wanted the city to make various representations and warranties regarding the system, but the city held firm and none were made. Mayor Campbell refused to clarify any contractual language, saying the firm agreed to sign an "as is" contract. As a result, United Water and the city had numerous run-ins about who was responsible for what. The city's attorney who helped negotiate the deal, asserted, "To maintain the integrity of the procurement, we did not change the contract." Troy Henry, United Water's regional president, maintained, "The contract had a tremendous amount of gray. It was very subject to interpretation."[25] As a result, relations between the company and city officials became strained.

The vague contractual language presented problems. The contract lacked definitiveness with respect to some of its performance standards and the operator's responsibilities. The ambiguous contract made assessing responsibilities difficult. The contract failed to provide a clear answer as to when a pipe needed to be repaired or replaced at city expense and when the pipe should be repaired or replaced, perhaps repeatedly, at private expense.[26] In other words, the contract created perverse incentives for each party to classify as many costs as possible into the category it was not responsible for. For example, under the contract, United Water was responsible for the first $10,000 of any capital repair or replacement in the system; above that amount the city would pay if it elected to undertake the repair or replacement.[27] In most instances, the city failed to pay for any repairs or replacements.[28]

Apart from ambiguities with respect to repairs and replacements, the contract provided too few details on needed upgrades. The contract also failed to include an arbitration clause to resolve disputes. If an internal mediation mechanism failed to resolve a controversy, either the company or the city could initiate a lawsuit.[29] In short, ambiguous or missing contract terms may have doomed the partnership.

What We Can Learn From Atlanta's Experience:
The Bidding and Selection Process

Most elements of an operations and maintenance contract are open to negotiation, including user rates and contractor guarantees. As is true of any negotiation, the parties ought to aim at achieving a win-win situation, which satisfies both sides' major objectives and achieves a mutually beneficial arrangement. With respect to infrastructure privatization transactions, the public sector must provide a contractor with adequate incentives for efficient, effective performance. Conversely, profits without risk sharing and accountability do not serve a community's interests.

Learning from the defects in Atlanta's privatization process, parties must conduct their due diligence regarding a system's status, backed up by a careful inspection and data. After an accurate assessment of existing conditions and the limitations of facilities, they must agree in writing on a system's status and the state of its infrastructure.

Apart from the due diligence specifics, a locality considering some type of privatization arrangement must analyze and evaluate its water (or wastewater) system needs, review its facilities and current technologies, compare the risks and benefits of various alternatives, evaluate the financing possibilities, and assess the potential interest by private firms. To deal with the poor condition of underground assets that have not been inspected for many years, a locality must first perform a one-time condition assessment. It must know what it has before analyzing what it needs. An asset condition assessment includes both an asset condition and deficiency analysis, as well as a remaining useful life and repair evaluation. This type of assessment allows local officials to anticipate the end of asset lifespans and plan preventive maintenance, repair, and replacement projects.

Today, the June 1999 Governmental Accounting Standards Board Statement No. 34 requires public sector units to inventory, capitalize, and depreciate major, general infrastructure assets. Statement 34 requires states and localities to list long-life infrastructure assets and their value in annual financial statements (or use a modified approach).[30]

A city must carefully design the bidding process, pre-qualifying potential bidders to ensure their financial, managerial, and technical capabilities. In making a bid, a private party must carefully assess a contract's profitability potential. Criteria important to assessing the profitability of proposed privatization agreement include: the potential to improve the efficiency of operations; the proximity to the company's other utility operations; the potential for system growth; the terms of a proposed contract; and the projected need for capital investments.

Because of its impact on a firm's ability to make a profit, the opportunity to improve the efficiency of a system's operations represents a key factor in evaluating a privatization candidate. Operating efficiency can be improved by reworking resources in place, for example, by training workers or correcting practices or by investing in cost-effective improvements, such as information technology. Personnel savings can come about as a result of attrition or retraining. Energy and chemicals represent not significant cost elements. Utilities can

195

achieve savings through the bulk purchases of chemicals. As discussed in Chapter 6, a potential for correcting operational inefficiencies exists because public entities often lack the financial or technical expertise possessed by private firms.

The criteria for selecting the winning bidder is critical. Atlanta selected United Water the lowest cost bidder with a mid-range technical score. The low bid selection model does not always work. Too low a bid may compromise quality. Rather, the public sector ought to award contracts on an overall best value-basis, not on price alone.

A municipality need not, unless required by state law, award a contract on a low-bid basis. It is better to use a best value technique where the public sector selects the winner bidder on the best combination of cost and value, among key selection criteria. A best value approach includes a private partner's successful operating history of other systems, an analysis of the contractor's financial strength and technical expertise as well as the price. Avoiding low bid arrangements, the focus ought to be on having a well-run system, encompassing service quality, efficiency, cost effectiveness, and stability.

In a private-public partnership, the private firm provides professional management, technical expertise, and financial controls. To achieve the maximum benefits, the locality must select a contractor with a proven track record of successful operations. The "best" contractor must meet a community's specific needs. Because of the technical and managerial skills requisite for success, the low bidder may not be the most responsible contractor.

The public sector must scrutinize the bidders' track records. Contractors ought to operate facilities that are similar in size, technical and process complexity, and operating budget. Contractors must have demonstrated financial stability.

What We Can Learn from Atlanta's Experience: Structuring a Long-Term Contract

The public sector and the winning bidder must focus on negotiating and drafting the contract.[31] A detailed contract helps ensure accountability between the partners and lessens conflict. If the details are not specific enough, disagreements can arise as was the situation in Atlanta.

Contracts must clearly state objective performance expectations with respect to quality and reliability, and strive, as much as possible, to eliminate ambiguities. The less subjective the assessment, the less likely disputes will arise. To ensure the accountability, objective, explicit performance criteria are required. A need exists to select a set of indicators (objective variables to be measured) and standards (values of the objective variables that are considered good or poor) that are sufficiently detailed to be meaningful for oversight decisions, yet are available and attainable at a reasonable cost.

The contract must clearly describe the division of responsibilities between the contractor and the public agency. Each of these responsibilities requires specific, objective performance measurements—clear, measurable indicators—with rewards or penalties, as appropriate, on key items. In a water system, some important components of a measurement system for against which to measure a contractor's performance include: economic efficiency, measured by factors such as cost effectiveness and distribution system water loss; environmental quality measured by compliance with water quality standards; and customer satisfaction measured by customer complaint (and resolution) records and service performance. Other standards include: billing accuracy and organizational development, including employee health and safety; training hours per employee; customer accounts per employee; and water delivered per employee.[32]

Standards in a wastewater contract include: sewer overflow rates; collection system integrity; and wastewater treatment effectiveness rates. Organizational development matters include wastewater processed per employee.

The contract must allocate the risks and the responsibilities that accompany the arrangement. The risks include permit risks, day-to-day operational risks, financial risks, and casualty and business interruption risks. The contract must determine which responsibilities will remain within the province of the public sector and which the contract operator must undertake. For example, an operations and maintenance contract must allocate maintenance responsibilities between the private firm and the public agency. The options include the private partner taking all the risks for maintenance, repair and replacement up to a specified annual dollar amount subject to an agreed upon annual increase to the private firm passing on the entire cost of maintenance and repairs to the public sector. Typically, the public sector assigns to its private partner the financial responsibility for non-compliance with regulatory requirements, such as environmental standards. Contracts typically specify which party will bear capital replacement and improvement costs.

A contract may provide an incentive-based compensation arrangement based on the contractor's success in meeting objective performance goals. As discussed in Chapter 5, up to 20 percent of a contractor's fees can be based on performance incentives, in accordance with Internal Revenue Service Revenue Procedure 97-13, for example, for exceeding minimum contract standards and/or minimum environmental standards. Conversely, a contract may provide if the private party violates regulatory standards, for instance, with each violation beyond a specified minimum resulting in a penalty per event. The agreement may impose a penalty below the statutory requirements so as to send a signal that some types of performance failures are unacceptable.

In addition to objective performance expectations, a contract ought to provide a performance review and evaluation process. Penalties for nonperformance and methods for addressing deficiencies in the incentive-penalty structure and/or adjusting performance standards ought to be specified.

Accountability and continual oversight are key. Contracts uniformly contain periodic reporting and monitoring provisions. Various monitoring techniques include inspections, reports, public complaints, and an assessment of meeting performance standards. Consumer involvement, specifically, the customer complaints, provide monitoring information and an oversight mechanism with respect to operator behavior. The public sector must analyze the costs of monitoring and determine who will assume monitoring responsibilities. The greater the future risks and uncertainties, the stronger these requirements ought to be.

In sum, the partners must negotiate and structure a contract with the "right" rewards, risks, benefits, and opportunities. Specifying measurable outputs (costs, quality, and reliability) reduces subjective assessments and diminishes the possibility for conflicts.

Contracts typically provide a mechanism for resolving disputes. It is difficult to write agreements that cover all the contingencies that may arise over time. Even well-designed contracts may require renegotiation and readjustment at some point. Contracts must provide mechanisms for these adjustments.

Indianapolis and Its Water Supply System

In April 2002, after the city of Indianapolis acquired the Indianapolis Water Co., a private firm that had supplied water to the city, it entered into an operations and maintenance contract with USFilter, a subsidiary of the French-based firm Vivendi Universal SA (now Veolia Environnement).[33]

The Indianapolis Water Co. (IWC), a privately-owned water supply utility, had been in existence since 1881. During the late nineteenth century, Indianapolis briefly took the firm over, but then returned it to private ownership. In 1956, the IWC went public. Most of its shareholders were locally-based. In the 1980s and 1990s, the firm acquired other non-water supply businesses to increase its revenues and profits. By the mid-1990s, more than half of its revenues came from non-water supply sources.[34]

In 1997, NiSource Inc., an investor-owned regional power and gas corporation, acquired IWC Resources Corp. and its largest subsidiary, for $288 million. Then, in 2000, NiSource purchased the Columbia Energy Group, a regional natural gas firm. As a result of becoming a holding company subject to the federal Public Utility Holding Company Act of 1936, NiSource was required to divest itself of some its assets. When NiSource sought to sell some of its non-power and gas-related assets, including IWC, the city of Indianapolis discovered it had a right of first refusal to acquire IWC, which it then exercised. NiSouce balked, litigation ensued, and preliminary rulings seemed to favor the city. Thereafter, negotiations for the sale began. The city signed a letter of intent to buy IWC's assets from NiSource for $515 million in July 2001, subsequently raising questions about whether the city overpaid the firm. However, in addition to its initial acquisition costs, NiSource had invested $211 million in plant improvements over four years.

In December 2001, the city set up the Department of Waterworks to own the water company. The new department is governed by a bipartisan seven member Board of Waterworks appointed by the mayor, with three member nominated by the president of the City-County Council (the city of Indianapolis and Marion County), three by the minority leader of the council, and the final one by the mayor, subject to the unanimous approval of the other six members. Rather than running the IWC as a city department or putting it under a local, charitable trust, Citizens Energy Group, that provides natural gas, the Board of Waterworks, acting as IWC's board of directors, decided to contract the system's operation and management to a private firm.

Indianapolis and USFilter

Between December 2001 and April 2002, the waterworks board requested and received proposals for a public-private partnership, evaluated the proposals, chose a set of top bidders, basically, United Water and USFilter, and made recommendations to the City-County Council. On a 100 point scale, USFilter's bid had 77.4 points; United Water's bid tallied 65.2.[35] The City-County Council selected USFilter Operating Services, Inc. a subsidiary of USFilter Corp., as the private partner.[36] After the final negotiations were completed the Department of Waterworks entered into a contract with the USFilter subsidiary.[37]

Previously in 1999, Vivendi Environnement SA, a unit of Vivendi SA, one of the world's two leading water supply and wastewater treatment firms, acquired USFilter Corp. for $6.2 billion to gain a foothold into U.S. water business. It was the largest French acquisition ever of an American company.

As discussed in Chapter 5, Vivendi's origins go back to Compagnie Générale des Eaux, a private water company established in France in the mid-nineteenth century. Over the past century and one half, the firm gained water concessions all over France, becoming that nation's largest private water supplier. In 1998, the company changed its name to Vivendi SA, reflecting its transformation into a multinational conglomerate, including not only Vivendi Environnement, the unit concerned with water and wastewater management but also a number of media, construction and telecommunications businesses. In late 2000, Vivendi became Vivendi Universal, following its merger with Seagram Co. Ltd. and Canal Plus SA.

After gaining the approval of state utility regulators, on April 30, 2002, the city bought the assets of the Indianapolis Water Co. from NiSource for $515 million, floating bonds to finance the purchase. The system consisted of twelve water treatment plants, fifteen storage tanks, nineteen water pumping stations (18 in operation), 30,000 fire hydrants, and 4,000 miles of mains and pipes.[38] On May 1, 2002, the USFilter subsidiary took over the system's operations and management pursuant to a twenty-year contract. As the nation's largest public-private partnership for water services, company agreed to operate the drinking water system for twenty years at a total cost of about $1.5 billion. As a part of the agreement, the public sector would spend about $1.1 billion on operations and maintenance service fees during the contract period. The remaining $400 million reflected capital improvement projects expected to be managed by the firm with funds provided by the Department of Waterworks.

The agreement sets forth performance as well as operations and maintenance standards and incentives for the contractor to alleviate taste and odor problems, among other water quality issues. The performance-based incentives may amount to up to 20 percent of the firm's annual fee. The contract includes forty performance goals, including water quality, operations and management, customer service, which the company must reach to qualify for the incentive payments. If the firm fails to meet any of these performance criteria, it would not receive a portion of its service fee.[39]

Under the contract, the private firm, now renamed Veolia Water Indianapolis LLC (VWI), operates and manages the IWC, subject to oversight by both the Board of Waterworks and two advisory groups. A portion of the incentive arrangement relies on the yearly evaluation by the Citizens Advisory Group (CAG). If VWI fails to obtain at least an 85 percent satisfactory rating from the CAG, subsequently increased to 95 percent in 2006, it loses 1 percent of its total incentive-based payment.[40]

The city decided to buy IWC and manage it through a public-private partnership for three reasons: first, a desire for local ownership and oversight, but not management, with public control through the Board of Waterworks; second, to gain expected financial benefits for the city; and third, to achieve increased operating efficiencies either because of a perception of the public sector's inefficiency or the hoped for efficiency of a private firm.[41] With respect to the 2002 deal, elected officials in the consolidated city-county government, including the City-County Council's president and the chair of its Public Works Committee, as well as the mayor of Indianapolis, supported the public-private partnership decision. A minority of the council members and some IWC employees opposed the decision.[42] It is important to note that Indianapolis has had a history of public-private partnerships.[43] For example, in December 1993, Indianapolis signed a five-year operations contract with the White River Environmental Partnership, a consortium of private firms, including IWC Resources and two Suez subsidiaries, to operate the city's advanced wastewater treatment plant. The city entered into the arrangement because it wanted to give up operational control, but not ownership of the facility. It also sought to leverage the plant's assets to generate new revenue sources for wastewater capital improvements. The city selected the partnership option, which offered substantial potential cost savings through operational efficiencies. The agreement provided for payment of about a $15 million fee to the consortium for the first year of operations, which began in January 1994, and a lower annual fee in the four subsequent years.

Between 1993 and 1994, the facility's operation and maintenance budget decreased from $30 to $17 million. Effluent violations dropped from seven to one. Employee grievances declined from 38 to one. The number of public employees was reduced from 322 to 196. Although rate increases were anticipated, the city held rates constant because of the cost savings associated with the arrangement.[44]

In 1997, after three years of contract performance that exceeded expectations, the city replaced existing five-year contract with a new 10-year arrangement. All of the consortium's promises had been fulfilled. The city had obtained three key benefits from the five-year deal. First, it saved $78 million through privatization, exceeding the expected savings of $65 million. Second, the partnership improved the plant's environmental compliance. Third, employee grievances decreased 99 percent; accident rates dropped 91 percent.[45]

Indianapolis and USFilter (now Veolia Environnement North America): An Assessment

The city derived four benefits from the public-private partnership for its water supply: public ownership but private management; better water quality; a five-year rate freeze with future rate increases subject to the approval of the Board of Waterworks and the Indiana Utility Regulatory Commission; and improved customer service.[46] Indicative of the arrangement's benefits in 2004, the National Council for Public-Private Partnerships, a nonpartisan, nonprofit organization promoting partnerships, awarded Indianapolis and VWI its Public-Private Partnership Award in the service category for delivering cost and quality benefits.[47]

Water Quality. Generally speaking, drinking water quality improved. Taste and odor complaints dropped from more than 500 in 2001 (prior to VWI's management) to 24 in the first ten months of 2004.[48] However, some water quality problems continued. In January 2005, for example, more than one million people were put on a boil-water alert, schools were closed, hospitals and restaurants were forced to use bottled water. VWI subsequently blamed an employee for entering the wrong value into a computer at the system's largest water treatment plan, resulting in an incorrect mix of chemicals used to treat water. Fortunately, the incorrectly treated water was diverted into a creek and no illnesses were reported.[49]

Also, in 2005, tests by the Indiana Department of Environmental Management found the system's drinking water safe, although levels of disinfectant byproducts were elevated at 11 of 19 locations at which the agency tested the water. Disinfectant byproducts consist of substances left over from treating drinking water with chemicals, such as chlorine. Long-term exposure to high levels of byproducts may cause cancer, another health threats. Because the standard for disinfection byproducts is calculated on a rolling one-year average, an elevated level on one test did not constitute a violation of standards.[50] Then, in October 2005, the U.S. Attorney's Office sent subpoenas to four employees of VWI in an apparent investigation of falsified water quality reports,[51] but no prosecutions followed.

Service Problems. Freezing fire hydrants plagued the system. In the winter of 2003, responding to criticism for its fire hydrant maintenance, the company acted to prevent hydrant freezing, including fixing leaky, frozen units.[52] Complaints about frozen hydrants surfaced again in January 2010.

Billing errors contributed to customer dissatisfaction. Those calling about billing problems faced long "hold times" in 2002 and early 2003. In response, VWI hired more temporary and permanent call center workers and formed a quality billing invoice team to catch invoice errors, aimed at curbing the number of daily calls.[53]

More billing problems surfaced again in 2008, when community members sued Veolia, alleging that the company failed to read water meters on schedule, overestimated water usage and overcharged hundreds of thousands of customers.[54] Although a judge dismissed the suit in 2009, because the Veolia subsidiary's contract with the city does not allow customers to sue the utility over service issues,[55] in response to numerous complaints making similar claims as the lawsuit, the Indiana Utility Regulatory Commission in April 2008 began an informal investigation into the firm's meter reading and billing practices.[56]

Problems also surfaced with respect to financial and employee matters as well as oversight and the degree of public participation.

Financial Issues. To reduce VWI's initial losses in the context of its parent's financial difficulties, it is unclear whether the firm skimped on paying for routine maintenance the use of purification chemicals, testing, and repairing infrastructure problems, as it was required to do so.

Similar to the Atlanta situation, the Indianapolis contract was a money-loser, at least initially. Jean-Michel Seillier, the VWI employee who oversaw the contract, noted that firm lost money on the arrangement in 2002-2003, but that it would lose less each year for several years thereafter. He stated: "The first year we are talking about $10 million [in losses], the next year [2003] it was $5-6 million. And this year [2004] is going to be minus two, and the next year [2005] it will be just minus a little thing ... the break even [point] is going to be ... 2009 or 2010 where this will be a profitable project."[57] It is uncertain whether VWI cut corners to minimize these losses.

In 2002, when USFilter's subsidiary entered into the contract with Indianapolis, Vivendi Universal's financial performance had deteriorated significantly. Following its acquisition spree, Vivendi Universal announced a €12.3 billion loss for the first half of 2002. Its shares declined in value weighed down by its mammoth debt burden and allegations regarding its accounting practices. The conglomerate began to sell off parts of its extensive holdings to reduce its indebtedness, its stake in Philadelphia Suburban, another water supply firm and including USFilter's water equipment division.

Then, in December 2002, Vivendi Universal sold half of its remaining stake in Vivendi Environnement to institutional investors, reducing its interest to 20.4 percent. Vivendi Environnement, its water and environmental services subsidiary, was renamed Veolia Environnement SA in April 2003, following the sale of some of USFilter's assets and other internal restructuring. In 2003 and 2004, Veolia sold the water treatment and consumer services businesses it owned to further reduce its debt load and concentrate on its core business of water and wastewater operations and maintenance contracts.

To improve VWI's profitability after the expiration of the five-year rate freeze, in 2007, residential water rates increased by 27 percent.[58] Then in April 2009, VWI requested a 17.6 percent rate hike; the Indiana Utility Regulatory Commission approved a 12.27 percent increase.[59] VWI sought another rate increase in September 2009.[60]

Employee Concerns. As a result of poor communications, employee concerns became manifest. The agreement required a two-year moratorium on layoffs of IWC employees, except for cause. The contractor also committed itself to honoring the existing collective bargaining agreements.[61] The firm adhered to these provisions.

Communications between the city, Veolia, and union and non-union employees were; however, contentious from the outset. In particular, disputes surfaced over employee benefits. When the city purchased IWC, the Indianapolis mayor stated in writing that employee benefits would be unchanged.[62] In soliciting proposals for the private operation of the assets, the city required that the total value of employee benefits be maintained, a different standard than the one stated by the mayor.

The city maintained that generally benefits have improved; while IWC employees claimed they have worsened. A class action lawsuit brought by non-union employees contested the loss of certain benefits. Although the suit was dismissed,[63] a loss of defined benefit pension benefits for non-union employees occurred under the public-private partnership.[64]

Since the partnership began, the union has filed at least seventeen complaints with National Labor Relations Board, prevailing in 14. Reducing the size of the workforce and bringing in employees from outside the area, resulted in loss of institutional memory and expertise. Job dissatisfaction likely increased; employee morale may have declined.[65]

Contractual Oversight. Another problematic area has centered on the city having only one employee responsible for overseeing the contract, along with the part-time members of the Board of Waterworks. VWI serves more than one million people. The partnership has a complex system of intergovernmental contracts with the other cities and counties extending beyond Marion County, Indiana. It also manages four smaller, nearby water companies. Board of Waterworks oversight apparently focuses almost exclusively on financial issues.

Public Participation. Prior to USFilter taking over in May 2002, a lack of transparency and openness characterized the public sector's decision-making process regarding the partnership. There was only minimal public participation in the decision to go the partnership route. One official City-County Council public hearing was held with respect to the decision together with normal public comment periods at council meetings. Basically, the public was informed about decisions already made.

A history of public-private partnerships in Indianapolis likely contributed to the minimal public involvement. As noted earlier, the public sector decision-makers were familiar with these partnerships and how they worked.

After the May 2002 takeover, public participation was mixed to negative. Veolia actively encouraged public input into the partnership, with the private partner seemingly more receptive to citizen input than the public partner. With respect to the public attendees at its meetings, the Board of Waterworks discouraged (or was indifferent to) input.

Two advisory groups provide avenues for public participation and input apart from complaints.[66] A twelve member, volunteer Citizens Advisory Group (CAG), meeting every other month, offers a customer and community perspective and input on issues brought to it. The thirteen member volunteer Technical Advisory Group (TAG) provides a monthly forum for the discussion of programs and activities related water quality and source water protection, among other items. The TAG generates useful input to VWI on technical problems.

At their meetings, which are open to the public, the CAG and the TAG advise VWI, not the Department of Waterworks. As noted earlier, the CAG is responsible for completing an annual evaluation of VWI's performance. Thus, VWI has a stake in the success of the CAG and the involvement of its members, although questions exist about the CAG's ability to assess the firm effectively as well as the selection process and CAG members' lack of experience in water utility or environmental matters. A lack of publicity led to minimal public involvement beyond the members of the two groups. With the CAG having responsibility for a small percentage of Veolia's incentive compensation, this group likely offers the best hope for genuine public participation in the privatization venture.[67]

What We Can Learn from the Indianapolis Experience

In the Indianapolis private-public partnership, operations went from private to private; assets went from private to public ownership. Looking to future public-private partnerships, the Indianapolis experience, to date, points to heightened emphasis on transparency and participation as well as sound employee relations. A need exists for both public access to meetings and contractual processes as well as participation and involvement in the decision-making process and thereafter. These steps will help build community awareness and support for a project. Localities ought to involve consumers from the beginning of the privatization decision-making process. Meaningful citizens groups can help oversee the partnership and monitor the private partner's performance.

By breaking the information monopoly held by local officials and enhancing community participation, citizen involvement will give more credibility to the privatization process and its subsequent outcome. In particular, officials ought to make a contract public before it is signed. Citizen involvement also aids in monitoring post-privatization performance and provides enhanced accountability.

The success of a public-private partnership rests on trust and the support of consumers. If confidence is eroded or there is a lack of disclosure, a partnership and its chances for success are eroded. More generally, during the contractual negotiations and once the parties enter into a contract, open communication is essential.

Good employee relations provide another key foundation for a sound public-private partnership. Beyond a focus on worker retention and job satisfaction, a need exists for clear communication with employees prior to the implementation of a partnership and thereafter. As a result of poor communications with the employees in the Indianapolis partnership, both the contractor and the city suffered damage to their reputations. Better communications with employees may lessen problems, including lawsuits, in future public-private partnerships.

Despite the seeming successes of the public-private partnerships operating the water and sewer systems in Indianapolis, in July 2009, city officials requested expressions of interest by entities to own or operate these assets. City leaders hoped to derive more than $400 million to repair roads, bridges, and sidewalks and make other infrastructure improvements while protecting customers from substantial rate increases.[68]

In March 2010, the Indianapolis City-County Council and the Citizens Energy Group signed a memorandum of understanding pursuant to which citizens will own and manage the two systems on a nonprofit basis for the benefit of the community, hopefully ensuring outstanding service at the lowest possible rates.[69] The City-County Council approved the sale in July 2010, subject to the approval of the Indiana Utility Regulatory Commission that was expected in the spring of 2011.

Privatization in its various forms is a complex issue, with many gray areas. Only by examining the alternatives and the possibilities offered by meaningful contractual negotiations, drafting, and enforcement can we work through and achieve a balance between the public interest and the private sector's role in financing, building, and operating America's water and wastewater infrastructure.

Notes

1.   John Ellis and Stuart Galishoff, "Atlanta's Water Supply, 1865-1918," *Maryland Historian* 8:1 (Spring 1977): 5-22 and Stuart Galishoff, "Triumph and Failure: The American Response to the Urban Water Supply Problem,

1860-1923" in *Pollution and Reform in American Cities, 1870-1930*, ed. Martin V. Melosi (Austin, TX: University of Texas, 1980), 49-51.

2. I have drawn on Alan Snitow, Deborah Kaufman, Michael Fox, *Thirst: Fighting Corporate Theft Of Our Water* (San Francisco: Jossey-Bass, 2007), 65-84; Rick Brooks, "A Deal All Wet," *Wall Street Journal*, January 31, 2003, C4; Douglas Jehl, "As Cities Move to Private Water, Atlanta Steps Back," *New York Times*, February 10, 2003, A14; Public Citizen, Waves of Regret, June 2005, 4-6; Geoffrey Segal, "What Can We Learn From Atlanta's Water Privatization," January 21, 2003 <www.reason.org/commentaries/segal-20031021.shtmsl> (January 14, 2009).

3. Charles Seabrook, "How Atlanta's sewers threaten the Chattahoochee," *Atlanta Journal-Constitution*, July 1, 1997, B8 and Charles Seabrook, "Sewer probe cites a sprawling mess," *Atlanta Journal-Constitution*, October 16, 1997, C4.

4. Darryl Fears, "Mayoral hopefuls bury sewer tunnel saga," *Atlanta Journal-Constitution*, March 23 1997, C8.

5. United States of America and State of Georgia v. City of Atlanta, Consent Decree, September 24, 1998. See also Charles Seabrook, "Atlanta Sewer Deal," *Atlanta Journal-Constitution*, April 14, 1998, A6.

6. United States of America and State of Georgia v. City of Atlanta, First Amended Consent Decree, December 20, 1999.

7. Charmagne Helton, "Mayor: Some jobs will be lost," *Atlanta Journal-Constitution*, February 8, 1997, E2. See also Charmagne Helton, "Atlanta's Sewer Problems," *Atlanta Journal-Constitution*, March 4, 1997, C5.

8. Carlos Campos and Julie B. Hairston, "Wading into private waters," *Atlanta Journal-Constitution*, March 27, 1998, A1.

9. Carlos Campos and Julie B. Hairston, "5 bid to run Atlanta water system," *Atlanta Journal-Constitution*, July 3, 1998, F2 and Julie B. Hairston, "Water Privatization," *Atlanta Journal-Constitution*, August 23, 1998, D6.

10. Twenty-Year Operations and Maintenance Agreement Of Water System Between United Water Services Unlimited Atlanta LLC and The City Of Atlanta, December 24, 1998 (Atlanta Agreement), Section 5.03. See also Carlos Campos and Julie B. Hairston, "Council approval next step for low bidder's contract," *Atlanta Journal-Constitution*, August 28, 1998, D1.

11. Christopher C. Williams, "United Water Sees Profits From Project in 18 Months," Dow Jones Newswires, August 28, 1998.

12. United Water Resources, Press Release, "Atlanta Approves Nation's Largest Public-Private Partnership for Water Operations With United Water," October 15, 1998. See also Julie B. Hairston, "Council OKs Water System Privatization," *Atlanta Journal-Constitution*, October 15, 1998, A1 and United Water Resources, Press Release, "United Water and City of Atlanta Sign Nation's Largest Public-Private Partnership for Water Operations," November 10, 1998.

13. Atlanta Agreement, Schedule 4-System. See also Carlos Campos, "Atlanta water flows to United," *Atlanta Journal-Constitution*, January 1, 1999, D2.

14. See, e.g., Ann Hardie, "Backlog damming water company's tries at timeliness," *Atlanta Journal-Constitution*, August 30, 1999, B1; Ann Hardie, "City, firm

up to their necks in complaints," *Atlanta Journal-Constitution*, September 6, 1999, B1; D. L. Bennertt and Julie B. Hairston, "Atlanta may throw out United Water," *Atlanta Journal-Constitution*, January 19, 2003, C8.

15. United Water Resources, Press Release, "United Water Resources Shareholders Approves Acquisition by Suez Lyonnaise Des Eaux," January 20, 2000.

16. City of Atlanta, Bureau of Water, Annual Performance Audit, n.d.

17. D. L. Bennettt, "City water firm wants $80 million," *Atlanta Journal-Constitution*, December 22, 2001, E1.

18 . Colin Campbell, "Mayor lets criticism flow in water tome," *Atlanta Journal-Constitution*, August 20, 2002, B2; Sarah Rubenstein, "City blasts United Water", *Atlanta Business Chronicle*, August 9-15, 2002, A1; Sarah Rubenstein, "City finds pros, cons for United water," *Atlanta Business Chronicle*, September 27-October 3, 2002, A3. See also D.L. Bennett, "Franklin assails United Water," *Atlanta Journal-Constitution*, June 12, 2002, B1; Tedra DeSue, "Water Sell-Off Woes," *Bond Buyer* 340:31417(June 27, 2002):31; Milo Ippolito, "Dirty tap water stirs flood of complaints," *Atlanta Journal-Constitution*, June 8, 2002, E1.

19. D. L. Bennett, "Water funds audit shows goals unmet," *Atlanta Journal-Constitution*, January 22, 2003, B5; D. L. Bennett and Julie B. Hairston, "Atlanta may throw out United Water," *Atlanta Journal-Constitution*, January 19, 2003, C8; D. L. Bennett, "Firm Fails to Collect $57 million in Atlanta Water Bills," *Atlanta Journal-Constitution*, January 3, 2003, D1; D. L. Bennett, "United Water has leaky finances," *Atlanta Journal-Constitution*, December, 14, 2002, H1.

20. City of Atlanta, Press Release, "City of Atlanta and United Water Announce Amicable Dissolution of Twenty-year Water Contract," January 24, 2003.

21. Milo Ippolito, "Atlanta takes over water system," *Atlanta Journal-Constitution*, April 30, 2003, B5.

22. Geoffrey Segal, "What Can We Learn."

23. Quoted in Martha Carr, "Water woes in Atlanta a cautionary tale for N.O.," *Times-Picayune* (New Orleans), June 29, 2003, 1.

24. Jim Wooten, "Atlanta should keep water deal," *Atlanta Journal-Constitution*, September 24, 2002, A17.

25. The quotations in this paragraph are from Carr, "Water Woes."

26. Atlanta Agreement, Section 4.01 and Schedule 3-Operations and Maintenance Performance Standards. See also Gary Wolff and Eric Hallstein, Beyond Privatization: Restructuring Water Systems To Improve Performance, Pacific Institute, December 2005, 35, 57.

27. Atlanta Agreement, Section 4.02 and Schedule 16-Capital Repair or Replacement Cost Allocation Examples.

28. Remedios del Rosario, David L. Seader, John E. Sale, "Cost Savings for Atlanta's Water Systems Through Contract Operations and Management," in *America's Water and Wastewater Industries: Competition and Privatization*, eds. Paul Seidenstat, Michael Nadol, Simon Hakim (Vienna, VA: Public Utilities Reports, 2000), 173.

29. Atlanta Agreement, Section 9.01.

30. Governmental Accounting Standards Board, Statement No. 34, Basic Financial Statements—and Management's Discussion and Analysis—for State and Local Governments, June 1999, Paragraphs 18-26, 30-37, 116-120, 132-133, 154-166.

31. I have drawn on U.S. Conference of Mayors Urban Water Council, Mayor's Guide to Water and Wastewater Partnership Service Agreements: Terms and Conditions, April 25, 2005 and Dan Elias, Crafting an Agreement for Private Operation and Maintenance of Water or Wastewater Facilities, International City/County Management Association, October 1999.

32. For further details on performance standards see Pat Crotty, Selection and Definition of Performance Indicators for Water and Wastewater Utilities, AWWA Research Foundation, 2004 and American Water Works Association, Benchmarking Performance Indicators for Water and Wastewater Utilities: 2007 Annual Survey Data and Analyses Report, 2008.

33. I have drawn on Kathleen R. Kennedy, The Intersection of Water Privatization and Public Participation In the United States: A Case Study Of The Indianapolis Water Company, Indianapolis, Indiana, Master's Thesis, University of Montana, May 2005; Public Citizen, Waves of Regret, June 2005, 7; Public Citizen; Veiloa Environnement: A Corporate Profile, February 2005, 7; Food & Water Watch, Faulty Pipes: Why Public Funding-Not Privatization-Is the Answer for U.S. Water Systems, September 18, 2008, 18.

34. Kennedy, Intersection, 39-42.

35. Doug Sword, "Move slowly on water deal, city urged," Indianapolis Star, March 2, 2002, C1.

36. USFilter, News Release, "City of Indianapolis Selects USFilter To Manage Waterworks System," March 19, 2002. See also Doug Sword, "City's purchase of water company nears completion," Indianapolis Star, March 19, 2002, B5.

37. Management Agreement By and Between USFilter Operating Services, Inc. and the Consolidated City of Indianapolis, Department of Waterworks, as of March 21, 2002 (Indianapolis Agreement).

38. Ibid., Exhibit 3-Waterworks Overview.

39. Ibid., Sections 4.01(a), 4.05, 4.07(a), 5.03 and Exhibit 12-Incentive Criteria.

40. Ibid., Exhibit 12-Incentive Criteria, Discretionary Measures and Kennedy, Intersection 62-63.

41. Ibid., 81-88.

42. Ibid., 56-59.

43. Former Indianapolis Mayor Stephen Goldsmith described his privatization efforts in the Twenty-First Century City: Resurrecting Urban America (Washington, DC: Regnery, 1997). See also To Market, To Market, To Market: Reinventing Indianapolis, eds. Ingrid Ritchie and Sheila Suess Kennedy (Lanham, MD: University Press of America, 2001).

44. Janice A. Beecher, G. Richard Dreese, John D. Stanford, Regulatory Implications of Water and Wastewater Utility Privatization, National Regulatory Research Institute, July 1995, 191-192, citing Privatization Watch, "Indy Sewage Contract is a Success," 221 (May 1995): 1,4. See also U.S.

Environmental Protection Agency, Response To Congress On Privatization Of Wastewater Facilities, July 1997, EPA 832-R-97-001a, 28-29; Goldsmith, *Twenty-First Century*, 199-211; *To Market*, 288-294; John Holusha, "Cities Enlisting Private Companies for Sewage Treatment," *New York Times*, May 5, 1996, 18.

45. Robin Johnson and Adrian Moore, Opening the Floodgates: Why Water Privatization Will Continue, Reason Public Policy Institute, Policy Brief 17, August 2001.

46. Kennedy, Intersection, 94-98.

47. Veolia Water North America, Press Release, "City of Indianapolis and Veolia Water Partnership [Receive] National Recognition," November 18, 2004.

48. *Ibid.*

49. Kevin O'Neal, "Indy Water issues boil alert to all customers," *Indianapolis Star*, January 7, 2005, A1; Staci Hupp, "No fines likely for water company," *Indianapolis Star*, January 8, 2005, B1; John Fritze, "Typo led to boil advisory," *Indianapolis Star*, January 19, 2005, A1.

50. Tammy Webber, "Drinking water found to be safe," *Indianapolis Star*, October 7, 2005, A9.

51. Tammy Webber, "Water system under state, federal scrutiny," *Indianapolis Star*, October 4, 2005, A1 and Rebecca Neal, "Water test results probed," *Indianapolis Star*, October 3, 2005, B1; Tom Spalding, "...and a hot mess," *Indianapolis Star*, January 5, 2020, A1; Vic Rychaert, "Indy fire chief orders hydrant review," *Indianapolis Star*, January 7, 2010, A1; Jason Thomas, "Utility, IFD plug away at hydrant problem," *Indianapolis Star*, January 8, 2010, A21; Jon Murray, "Hydrant oversight could be lacking," *Indianapolis Star*, January 18, 2010, A1.

52. Terry Horne, "Firm acts to prevent hydrant freezing," *Indianapolis Star*, February 22, 2003, B1.

53. Matthew Tully, "City water company sees complaints rise," *Indianapolis Star*, February 27, 2003, A1.

54. Bond v. Veolia Water North American Operating Services, Inc., Marion Superior Court, Complaint and Jury Demand, April 23, 2008, no. 49D07-0804-CC-018081.

55. Bond v. Veolia Water North American Operating Service, LLC, January 13, 2009, no. 49D07-0804-CC-018081.

56. Jon Murray, "Water users might sue city agency over billing," *Indianapolis Star*, January 15, 2009, A19; Jon Murray, "State begins informal probe of complaints by water users," *Indianapolis Star*, April 27, 2008, B1; John Russell, "Water utility overbills users, lawsuit says," *Indianapolis Star*, April 24, 2008, A1.

57. Quoted in Kennedy, Intersection, 66.

58. Jeff Swiatek, "More of your money will do down the drain," *Indianapolis Star*, April 5, 2007, A1 and Will Higgins, "Water bills may rise sharply," *Indianapolis Star*, February 16, 2007, A1.

59. Dan McFeely, "Water rate hike grudgingly approved," *Indianapolis Star*, July 1, 2009, A19.

60. Francesca Jarosz, "Water pressure," *Indianapolis Star*, October 1, 2009, A1 and *Indianapolis Star*, "Metro on the go," September 24, 2009, A18.
61. Indianapolis Agreement, Section 4.02(a) and (e).
62. John Strauss, "Water utility workers say mayor's vow sprang some leaks," *Indianapolis Star*, December 18, 2002, B1.
63. Plummer v. Consolidated City of Indianapolis, Southern District of Indiana, August 17, 2004, No. 1:03-CV-00567-DFH-WT. See also Fred Kelly, "Judge dismisses workers' suit against water utility operation," *Indianapolis Star*, August 18, 2004, B5; Fred Kelly, "City water workers go to court," *Indianapolis Star*, August 30, 2002, A1; Matthew Tully, "Water workers sue over benefits cuts," *Indianapolis Star*, August 30, 2002, A1.
64. Indianapolis Agreement, Section 4.02(e).
65. Wolff and Hallstein, Beyond Privatization, 44.
66. Kennedy, Intersection, 90-91.
67. *Ibid*, 114-126.
68. Bill Ruthhart, "On the block," *Indianapolis Star*, September 29, 2009, A1.
69. Francesca Jarosz, "Price tag for city's utilities," *Indianapolis Star*, March 10, 2010, A1.

9

Conclusion: The Future Role of Private Enterprise in Meeting America's Water Supply and Wastewater Treatment Crisis

This book has examined America's pressing water supply and wastewater treatment needs in terms of water scarcity and infrastructure financing. This chapter summarizes how the private sector can help meet the scarcity and capital problems. It then examines how rate increases, regardless of ownership or operation; provide a means to meet the capital needs of America's water supply and wastewater treatment industry.

Private Enterprise Can Help Meet the Scarcity Problem

Chapters 3 and 4 analyzed the topic of water scarcity in the United States and role of private firms in meeting this challenge. Barring the abrupt, potential impact of global climate change, existing technologies can help increase water supplies and conserve water. Private firms, as technologies suppliers and service vendors, can serve water supply and wastewater treatment systems and their customers, whatever these systems' ownership and management arrangements. As water scarcities become more prevalent, more rapid technological advances and commercialization may be on the horizon.

Private Enterprise Can Help Meet the Capital Needs

The United States faces enormous water and wastewater infrastructure needs, as discussed in Chapter 6, that will require huge capital expenditures in coming decades. Meeting the capital demands for infrastructure repairs, maintenance, and expansion as well as ever more stringent environmental requirements and enforcement represents a difficult challenge necessitating long-term capital investments. Simply put, water supply and wastewater treatment are capital-intensive businesses.

In the past, the public sector and private firms deployed capital to repair and upgrade systems and bring them into compliance with changing (and heightening) environment requirements, thereby supplying funds to meet the capital demands. Today, however, the public sector faces funding constraints.

State revolving loan programs, funded in large part by federal grants, as discussed in Chapter 2, make inexpensive debt financing available to public wastewater providers and public and private water supply entities. Congress could amend the funding statute allow private utilities access to the Clean Water State Revolving Fund programs. However, both of these programs, as presently funded, only put a slight dent in the current and projected capital needs.

Looking towards the future, the federal government may ultimately provide major funding for upgrading the nation's water and wastewater infrastructure. Industry and public interest groups, among others, have recommended federal funding increases. For example, in 2001, the Water Infrastructure Network, a coalition of local elected officials, drinking water and wastewater service providers, and state environmental and health officials, advocated that the federal government provide state water and wastewater infrastructure financing authorities with an additional $57 billion in grants over five years.[1] The funds would be used to replace aging mains and pipes and upgrade treatment systems. More recently, other groups have proposed a funding increase for existing federal programs, such as the state revolving loan fund programs, designed to assist water and wastewater systems with infrastructure projects.[2] However, apart from an economic stimulus approach focused on jobs creation, it likely will take a public health emergency to force the federal government to provide significantly more funding for water and wastewater infrastructure.

To deal with the federal government's fiscal constraints, others have recommended the creation of a deficit-neutral Clean Water Trust Fund to provide an assured funding source to help the United States meet its water infrastructure needs.[3] The proposed Water Protection and Reinvestment Act of 2009,[4] for example, would authorize the financing of a clean water trust fund at approximately $10 billion a year through a variety of new taxes on businesses, particularly those that benefit from clean water or contribute to water pollution. The bill would impose a 4 percent excise tax on containers of water-based beverages, including soft drinks, but not juice, milk, or alcoholic beverages; a 3 percent excise tax on various items, such as toothpaste, cosmetics, and cooking oil that enter the water supply and necessitate the cleaning of water at sewage treatment plants; a 0.5 percent excise tax on pharmaceutical products that have been found in water systems; and a 0.15 percent surtax on corporate profits.[5]

In a 2009 report,[6] prior to the introduction of the bill, the U.S. General Accounting Office noted that possible funding sources for a clean water trust fund, as a dedicated funding source for water infrastructure projects, include: an excise tax on products that contribute to the wastewater stream, including beverages, fertilizers, and pesticides, flushable products (such as soaps and detergents), water appliances and plumbing fixtures; an additional tax on corporate income; and federal water tax on users. In its report, the GAO noted, "Implementing any of the funding options...poses a variety of challenges, including defining the products or activities to be taxed and establishing a collection and enforcement framework."[7] Also, obtaining stakeholder support for a particular option or mix of options is difficult because they do not always see a strong connection between the products to be taxed and wastewater infrastructure use. Industry groups, of course, are opposed to a tax on their respective product groups. Beyond funding sources, the GAO identified three main design issues for a clean water trust fund: how it should be administered; what type of financial assistance should be provided; and what activities should be eligible for assistance.

In the past, a ready capital market existed in the United States for building, maintaining, and expanding water supply and wastewater treatment infrastructure. Investors lent money to public sector water and wastewater agencies by purchasing tax-exempt bonds.

However, states and municipalities face their own fiscal crises, as examined in Chapter 6. Given the public sector constraints in meeting current and future capital needs, the focus may turn to the privatization of existing systems (or facilities) via asset sales or various types of public-private partnerships. Private firms, whether as asset owners or through contractual arrangements in public-private partnerships, may provide some of the required capital. However, public-private partnerships do not automatically bring capital to meet a publicly-owned utility's financial needs, apart from careful pre-contract signing negotiations on this point.

Privatization through Asset Sales

Prior to the 2008-2009 credit crisis and the 2008 stock market crash, investors stampeded into attractive investment vehicles in the United States. Water-related hedge and index funds proliferated, but most were hampered by the paucity of publicly-traded U.S. water investment vehicles.

The water supply and wastewater treatment industry, characterized by long-term stability and high predictability, remains attractive to the private sector. It represents strong, consistent growth over the long-term. Thus, for existing water and wastewater facilities (or systems) requiring a capital infusion, an asset sale represents on possible financing avenue.

Water supply in the United States represents a relatively fragmented business sector ripe for consolidation. Consolidation offers private equity firms, among others, the opportunity to build larger, stronger, even more valuable entities. The impact of large-scale consolidation and ownership rearrangements on customers, shareholders, and employees is; however, beyond the scope of this book. Prior to September 2008, the huge premiums paid for companies in this sector by certain acquirers served as a negative for other prospective purchasers, particularly private equity firms.

In deploying their capital, private investors as asset acquirers want superior returns on their investments and an ability to exit ventures when they want to. When private companies need funds, they can go to the capital market and sell new shares (equity) to investors. Although diluting existing owners by bringing in new shareholders, the additional funds presumably improve these firms' growth and future profit prospects. Over the long-term, they become a more attractive place for investors to put their capital.

To encourage the allocation of private capital to water infrastructure acquisitions by the private sector, a need exists for state regulatory standards that encourage private investment through "fair" returns on equity and mechanisms to reduce the regulatory lag for expenditures between rate-making proceedings. The regulatory lag generally accompanying the traditional rate setting process increases the financial risk for investor-owned utilities. Regulators could also the lower financial and regulatory risks through expedited rate proceedings and preapproval for capital expenditures. However, states exhibit different policies with respect to the recoupment of infrastructure improvements.

Some require a company to spend funds and then submit a rate request. Because of the time lag in granting a rate increase, this approach is less advantageous than those jurisdictions that grant rate increases in advance of investments.

Private firms seeking to acquire water or wastewater systems diligently assess prospective purchases. As acquisitions typically require large initial and subsequent capital investments in facilities and other assets, generally speaking, as discussed in Chapter 5, under a rate-of-return approach, state regulators tightly control rate increases thereby putting limits on a firm's return on its invested capital. As a result, private companies will identify cities and regions where regulators understand the costs involved in supplying quality water and are willing to let private operators raise rates accordingly. They will invest where a clear path to sufficient returns exists.

It is well known that water utilities in the United States historically have never generated sufficient operating cash to fund their capital expenditure needs. They produce negative net cash flows, year in and year out. As a result, water utilities issue equity and debt to fund part of their capital spending not covered by internally generated funds.

Among other private sector firms, the private equity community offers expertise in acquiring and enhancing assets and running them in a strict, financially-oriented manner. Private equity firms bring money, extensive business operations expertise, distribution and marketing contacts, financial management and control systems experience, and a more stable operating environment by removing the possible conflicts with a large, unrelated corporate owner or the pressures of public ownership.

The 2008-2009 credit crisis and the accompanying deleveraging made it harder for potential acquirers to secure debt and equity financing. In particular, private equity firms were unable to borrow funds needed for infrastructure asset acquisitions. Also, merger activity subsided.

Foreign-based companies, such as the German-based utility giant RWE AG, became eager sellers of U.S. assets. These firms found it difficult to generate a sufficient rate of return in a highly capital-intensive industry with extensive public health and environmental externalities.

In 2005, for example, RWE's international water division generated operating income of $1.75 billion, or about one quarter of the German utility's total income. However, the division's return on capital equaled just 7.4 percent, about one half of the firm's overall rate of return on its capital and slightly below its capital costs. In other words, the division did not make enough money to justify its investments. As a result, RWE refocused on its electricity and gas business and concentrated on Europe, the part of the world it knows best, selling its non-European, non-electric and gas assets.[8]

More generally, potential asset acquirers are reluctant to enter certain markets if regulatory forces constrain their ability to earn a "sufficient" profit. As permitted by regulators, these firms historically tapped equity and debt markets roughly every two years to fund their capital expenditure plans.[9] State utility regulators typically allow a 10-11 percent return on equity[10] with debt carrying costs (interest and repayment of principal) passed through to customers. In other words, the rate-of-return regulatory model allows firms to access capital markets regularly to meet their infrastructure investment needs. The ability to derive an authorized return on equity in excess of a firm's cost of capital allows privately-owned water utilities to invest in infrastructure repairs, maintenance, and expansion.

For state regulators, the balancing interests of consumers and private firms is sometimes difficult. To satisfy investors, regulators must provide assurances of adequate returns on long-lived assets. To protect consumers, regulators must ensure that the water remains safe and affordable. The situation in Felton, California illustrates the difficulties facing state regulators and private asset owners.[11]

American Water Works Co., through a subsidiary California-American Water Co., obtained ownership of the Felton, California water system in 2002, when it acquired the holdings of a Connecticut-based company, Citizens Communications, which had long controlled the asset. Eight months later, when American Water Works was being acquired by the German utility firm RWE AG, specifically, Thames Water Aqua Holdings GmbA, RWE's holding company for its global water business, for $4.6 billion in cash and the assumption of about $3.0 billion in debt, it sought approval from the California Public Utilities Commission to raise rates by 74 percent over three years. It noted that the water rates in Felton, California were unchanged since 1998 and pointed to the cost of infrastructure repairs and the need to invest $1.1 million between 2002 and 2005 to replace old facilities.

In response to the rate increase request, a group called FLOW (Friends of Locally Owned Water) was formed. In addition to fighting the rate hike, residents complained about the response times to broken water mains as calls were routed to RWE's national call center. After more than one year, the state utility regulatory commission decided that American Water could raise rates by 44 percent over what consumers were paying. In 2005, nearly 75 percent of the voters in Felton supported a local ballot initiative, Measure W, which allocated up to $11 million for the issuance of tax-exempt bonds to buy the water system. In 2008, the local public water system, which Felton joined, bought the water system for $10.5 million in cash and the repayment of a $2.9 million Safe Water Drinking Act debt. Earlier in 2008, RWA had spun off American Water Works, which became the nation's largest investor-owned water company.

Privatization through Contractual Arrangements

Because economic regulation applies to facilities owned by nearly all private utilities, but generally not to contractual arrangements, in the United States the privatization of existing assets has taken the form of public-private partnerships. As noted in Chapter 5, in these public-private partnerships, water and wastewater infrastructure remain under public control. A key question exists in these public-private partnerships, which party (or parties) will make the needed major capital investments in repairing, maintaining, and expanding the infrastructure. The various components of a water delivery system, for example, necessitate substantial capital investments in long-lived assets, such as mains and pipes. Because of the water industry's capital intensity, fixed costs represent a key element of the sector's cost structure, with the fixed costs of water supply, treatment, and distribution assets high in comparison to the variable (operating) costs, such as personnel. It is difficult for any water or wastewater utility, regardless of ownership, to reduce its capital costs. Reducing operating costs can only offset the high capital costs to a limited degree.

The extent that companies foresee a need to invest their own funds to repair, replace, or upgrade infrastructure impacts both on the decision to enter into a contractual agreement and the structure of the agreement entered into.[12] Thus, private operating and maintenance firms, but not service companies, can provide capital for both maintenance and expansion. However, to invest significant amounts of capital for network renewal and expansion, private firms require long-term arrangements. Private firms will only invest capital, particularly for improvements and expansion, that will produce positive financial results for them during the contractual period.

The Benefits of Long-Term Contractual Arrangements

As discussed in Chapter 5, long-term contracts offer private firms an incentive to invest capital in existing and new facilities that will provide efficiency benefits and cost savings far into the future. Private companies need a long period during which to reduce costs and recoup their investments. Don Correll, then United Water's Chairman, noted that with a short-term, three to five year contract, "it is almost impossible for us [as a private firm] to assume any kind of maintenance, repair or modest capital investment. But as we're seeing emerging now with a 20-year contract, ... that allows for United Water to invest in the system ... and assume some more of those capital risks ... and we might be able to reduce [the municipality's] costs even more as well.... We can assume ... a higher level of maintenance and repair because we know that we ... have the opportunity to recover and earn a return on those investments."[13]

Examples exist of substantial investments by private partners in long-term operations and maintenance contracts. In the 1997, pursuant to the long-term lease and service agreement for the Cranston, Rhode Island wastewater treatment system, Triton Ocean State LLC, a subsidiary of Poseidon Resources Corp., the winning bidder, made an upfront payment of $48 million to the city and provided $30 million of private financing for federal- and state-mandated capital improvements.[14] Also, in the 1997 agreement between USFilter Operating Services of Wilmington Inc. and the City of Wilmington, Delaware, the company agreed to make a $15 million capital investment in the contract's first two years to increase the efficiency of a water treatment plant.[15]

Pricing Water and Wastewater Services

Rate increases provide another means of meeting the capital needs of America's water supply and wastewater treatment industry. In particular, utilities in areas with burgeoning populations where demand strains supply will need to find the financial resources to fund new infrastructure. The capital programs required to provide facilities to accommodate population growth will likely raise water rates significantly in these areas.

Apart from rate increases, other options, beyond the scope of this book, include capital faculty charges imposed on new users as they connect to a system and developer extension charges under which a developer pays a utility to finance a new facility or the cost of new infrastructure. Also, a utility can impose an infrastructure replacement surcharge on users.[16]

Beyond these details, a more basic question exists. The American public thinks that water, in the form of rainwater, falls out the sky, in abundant amounts. As a human right, it ought to be basically free. However, it costs billions and billions of dollars a year to collect, treat, store, and distribute water and process sewage in the United States. Yet, we do not recognize the true value of water. We do not current pay anywhere what it is really worth to us.

In the future, Americans will likely pay higher rates for water and wastewater services, whether these systems are publicly or privately run. To avert a water scarcity crisis in the United States, it will be necessary to charge more for water to enhance conservation efforts. Market pricing of water would stimulate the widespread adoption of existing conservation technologies, and lead to more investment in research and development, which would further more rapid technological advances and hopefully promote commercialization.

In addition to the price mechanism providing an incentive for more efficient water use, higher rates will generate additional funds needed to pay for the cost of major replacements and upgrades to facilities and systems. Some optimistically advise publicly-owned drinking water and wastewater treatment utilities to raise rates to deal with the large backlog of deferred maintenance and fund needed repairs, replacements, and upgrades. According to one report, "[a]lthough average rate increases of about 3% higher than the rate of inflation for the next 20 years could fund current estimates of needed improvements, some communities would face much higher rate increases to meet their needs, and some communities cannot afford to pay 3% more than inflation."[17] Other estimates indicate that if local utilities themselves financed the investment gap, average water and sewer rates, nationwide, would more than double.[18] However, sharply higher rates would reduce demand, thereby limiting capital funding availability, at least to some degree.

Rate increases will stem from efforts to price water at its "true cost." In the future, we will likely see the transformation of water into a commodity, one that can be bought, sold, and moved around, with users bearing more and more costs. In other words, we will likely move away from the concept that water belongs to everyone as a public good and thus need not be market priced. We will likely view users as customers who access water as an economic good through its purchase, not as citizens having a "right" to water supply as a service. A severe water shortage or a public health disaster will help shake public belief that water is free good.

In the ideal world, full-cost rates will help utilities obtain much of the needed revenues from customers to maintain, replace, modernize, and expand facilities and systems, thereby benefiting consumers. With the public bearing the "true" cost of water, they hopefully will pressure utilities to be more efficient and keep rates under control.

This optimistic scenario encounters three obstacles: political resistance; the current rate structure of federally funded, publicly-owned wastewater treatment systems; and equity considerations. Local officials and water boards often lack the will to practice full cost-based rate making. It is easy to say: let utilities pay for capital investments through full cost-based pricing, factoring in past, current, and future costs, including operations, maintenance, capital for replacement, upgrading, and environmental compliance, into user fees. In the past, many publicly-owned water systems subsidized households with revenues from industrial and commercial users. Agriculture historically benefited from low, below market rates. Elected officials sought to protect residential customers from higher rates because of the adverse political consequences.

Rate increases may be more acceptable in the future when consumers see improved quality and service and when they are better informed as to the scarcity and capital needs issues. However, community support for rate increases may not be forthcoming, thereby negating the goal of publicly-owned systems becoming more economically self-sustaining.

Second, federal funding has had a different impact on drinking water and wastewater treatment systems. With respect to drinking water systems, the adjustment to full-cost pricing may be somewhat easier. Although the Drinking Water State Revolving Fund programs provide loans to systems, most drinking water systems were built without substantial federal funds. Traditionally, publicly-owned drinking water systems considered operations, maintenance, and some infrastructure costs in establishing rates. However, they may not have accounted for the replacement of distribution mains and pipes some of which were installed 100 years ago and currently need (or will require) replacement. In contrast, publicly-owned wastewater treatment systems were substantially federally funded. Wastewater treatment plants built in the 1970s and 1980s had some 87.5 percent of their costs paid for by federal and state grants, thereby allowing artificially low sewer rates for customers throughout the United States.[19] In developing their rates, most wastewater treatment systems have focused on meeting the costs of operations and maintenance. They paid insufficient attention to funding for the eventual rehabilitation, replacement, and upgrading.

Despite the objections of customers, political resistance, and rate practices, as a condition of receiving federal or state financial assistance, publicly-owned water and wastewater utilities may be required to establish user rates meeting certain minimum standards. Although the Safe Drinking Water Act, as amended, does not specifically require drinking water utilities to impose minimum user charges, the Environmental Protection Agency addressed the issue indirectly in its guidance to states. Under the Safe Drinking Water Act Amendments of 1996,[20] states must develop programs to ensure that drinking water systems have the financial, managerial, and technical capacity to comply with federal drinking water regulations. The EPA's guidance with respect to implementing state programs suggests that the criteria for assessing any system's financial capacity include a determination of whether water rates and charges are adequate to cover the cost of water.[21]

With respect to wastewater treatment systems, however, only more general requirements apply to wastewater utilities receiving loans under the Clean Water State Revolving Loan Fund programs. Also, full cost recovery rates are harder because paying for piped sewage is costly and more of the benefits are external to users.

Third, the transformation of water into a commodity must, however, be balanced by equity and fairness concerns. In striving to raise capital and manage demand through new and higher rate structures, equity considerations enter into the pricing picture. Questions exist about the impact on the less affluent of raising the price of an essential, nonsubstitutable commodity. A concern that exists that those who lack the financial wherewithal will be priced out of the market.

Everyone needs water to live. Some cannot afford to pay the higher water rates. As rates rise to meet the infrastructure funding needs and to encourage more efficient water use, localities will look to provide some type of subsidy to low-income households that cannot afford the higher rates. The subsidy offered by assistance programs would cover the portion of each residential customer's water and sewer bill that is unaffordable.

On the federal level, utility bill assistance programs currently exist, including the U.S. Department of Health and Human Services (HHS) Low Income Home Energy Assistance (LIHEAP) Program, authorized by the Omnibus Budget Reconciliation Act of 1981,[22] and the Universal Service Fund programs for Low-Income Customers offered by the Federal Communications Commission (FCC).[23] The HHS funds the LIHEAP program by block grants to the states. In turn, local poverty agencies implement the program by providing financial assistance directly to low-income households that meet specified criteria.[24] The FCC's Lifeline Support program reduces eligible consumers' monthly charges for basic telephone service and its Link Up Support program reduces the cost of initiating new telephone service. These programs are funded by rates paid by telecommunication carriers' customers and are administered by a third party, the Universal Service Administration Co., with contributions assessed against the revenues of telecommunications carriers. In turn, the fund reimburses eligible telecommunication carriers for providing service to eligible low-income customers.[25]

Apart from federal subsidies for low-income water and wastewater customers, several local funding possibilities exist. The public sector could provide a direct subsidy out of local, general tax revenues, if a system is sold or under private management. Cross subsidies by those customers who pay higher rates, perhaps even higher than the actual costs, offer another possibility.

So that low-income customers can afford the full cost of privatized services, public-private partnership contractual provisions could require discounts or financial assistance programs for low-income customers. Municipalities could earmark part of the cost savings from these partnerships to financial assistance programs. Under a voluntary subsidy program, a private entity, as owner or operator, could ask consumers to contribute to a subsidy fund to help low-income households pay their water and wastewater bills.

Notes

1. Water Infrastructure Network, Water Infrastructure Now: Recommendations for Clean and Safe Water in The 21st Century, February 2001, 5. See also Water Infrastructure Network, Clean and Safe Water for the 21st Century: A Renewed National Commitment To Water and Wastewater Infrastructure, April 2000, 4-1 to 4-5.
2. American Water Works Association, Association of Metropolitan Water Agencies, National Association of Water Companies, National Rural

Water Association, A National Agenda for Drinking Water: Prepared for President-elect Barack Obama, n.d.

3. See, e.g. Food & Water Watch, Clean Waters: Why America Needs a Clean Water Trust Fund, October 2007, 9-13.

4. Proposed Water Protection and Reinvestment Act of 2009, 111th Congress, 1st Session.

5. *Ibid.*, Section 101(b) and (c).

6. U.S. General Accounting Office, Clean Water Infrastructure: A Variety of Issues Need to Be Considered When Designing a Clean Water Trust Fund, May 2009, GAO-09-657.

7. *Ibid.*, 17.

8. The statistics in this paragraph are from Mike Esterl, "Great Expectations for Private Water Fail to Pan Out," *Wall Street Journal*, June 26, 2006, A1 and RWE, Annual Report 2005, Letter from the CEO, 4.

9. Wall Street Transcript, Analyst Interview, Heike Doerr, Janney Montgomery Scott LLC, October 6, 2008 and Goldman Sachs Group Inc., American Water Works Co., Inc., June 2, 2008, 9.

10. Nicholas DeBenedictis, Chairman, CEO & President of Aqua America, Inc., Interview, Wall Street Transcript, November 3, 2008. See also Citigroup Global Markets, Equity Research, American Water Works Co., Inc., June 2, 2008, 24.

11. I have drawn on Jim Carlton, "Calls Rise for Public Control of Water Supply," *Wall Street Journal*, June 17, 2008, A6; Mike Esterl, "Great Expectations;" David L. Beck, "Groundswell for Local Control," *San Jose Mercury News* (California), November 3, 2004, A14. See also Public Citizen, RWE/Thames Water: A Corporate Profile, October 2005, 10; Alan Snitow, Deborah Kaufman, Michael Fox, *Thirst: Fighting The Corporate Theft of Our Water* (San Francisco: Jossey-Bass, 2007), 49-61. For a history of American Water Works Co. see Gilbert Cross, *A Dynasty of Water: The Story of American Water Works Company* (Voorhees, NJ: American Water Works Co., 1991).

12. U.S. General Accounting Office, Water Infrastructure: Information on Financing, Capital Planning and Privatization, August 2002, GAO-02-764, 50-53.

13. *Water Environment & Technology*, "Partnership Perspective" 12:8 (August 2000): 59-65, at 61.

14. Wastewater Treatment System and Lease and Service Agreement between The City of Cranston, Rhode Island and Triton Ocean State LLC, March 7, 1997, Sections 3.5, 6.1, and 13.1. See also Michael A. Traficante and Peter Alviti, Jr., "A New Standard for a Long-Term Lease and Service Agreement," in *Reinventing Water and Wastewater Systems: Global Lessons for Improving Water Management*, eds. Paul Seidenstat, David Haarmeyer, Simon Hakin (New York: Wiley, 2002), 304, and Jane Word, "The pros and cons of long-term privatization," *American City & County* 113:5 (May 1998): 54-78, at 54, 56.

15. Professional Services Agreement, Dated as of December 8, 1997, Between The City of Wilmington, Delaware and USFilter Operating Services of Wilmington, Inc., Section 3.8. See also James H. Sills, Jr., "The Challenges

and Benefits of Privatizing Wilmington's Wastewater Treatment Plant," *in Reinventing Water and Wastewater Treatment Systems*, 285-286.

16. See generally Patrick C. Mann, Financing Mechanisms for Capital Improvements for Regulated Water Utilities, National Regulatory Research Institute, November 1999, NRRI 99-16.

17. Gary Wolff and Eric Hallstein, Beyond Privatization: Restructuring Water Systems To Improve Performance, Pacific Institute, December 2005, 13.

18. Water Infrastructure Network, Clean & Safe Water, 3-4.

19. Wolff and Hallstein, Beyond Privatization, 29.

20. Public Law 104-182.

21. U.S. Environmental Protection Agency, Guidance on Implementing the Capacity Development Provisions of the Safe Drinking Water Act Amendments of 1996, July 1998, EPA-816-R-98-006, 12-13.

22. Public Law 97-35.

23. On May 8, 1997, in In the Matter of Federal-State Joint Board on Universal Service, Federal Communications Commission (FCC), Report and Order, FCC 97-157, the FCC established the rules to govern the Universal Service program. On April 29, 2004, In the Matter of Lifeline and Link-Up, Federal Communications Commission, Report and Order and Further Notice of Proposed Rulemaking, FCC 04-87, the FCC expanded the eligibility criteria to include income-based criteria. In the Telecommunications Act of 1996, Public Law 104-104, Congress directed the FCC and the states to take the steps necessary to establish support mechanisms to ensure the delivery of affordable telecommunications service to all Americans, including low-income consumers.

24. U.S. Department of Health & Human Services, Administration for Children & Families, Low Income Home Energy Assistance Program, Fact Sheet, About LIHEAP, Funding, Guidance, Policies and Procedures.

25. Universal Service Administration Co., 2007 Annual Report: 1997-2007 Helping Keep Americans Connected for a Decade. See also Matt Richtel, "Providing Cellphones for the Poor," *New York Times*, June 15, 2009, B1.

Index